Pro Project Management with SharePoint 2010

Mark J. Collins

Pro Project Management with SharePoint 2010

ISBN-13 (pbk): 978-1-4302-2829-5

ISBN-13 (electronic): 978-1-4302-2830-1

Printed and bound in the United States of America 9 8 7 6 5 4 3 2 1

President and Publisher: Paul Manning
Lead Editor: Jonathan Hassell
Technical Reviewer: Jeff Sanders
Editorial Board: Steve Anglin, Mark Beckner, Ewan Buckingham, Gary Cornell, Jonathan Gennick, Jonathan Hassell, Michelle Lowman, Matthew Moodie, Duncan Parkes, Jeffrey Pepper, Frank Pohlmann, Douglas Pundick, Ben Renow-Clarke, Dominic Shakeshaft, Matt Wade, Tom Welsh
Coordinating Editor: Corbin Collins
Copy Editor: Damon Larson
Indexer: BIM Indexing & Proofreading Services
Artist: April Milne
Cover Designer: Anna Ishchenko

Distributed to the book trade worldwide by Springer Science+Business Media, LLC., 233 Spring Street, 6th Floor, New York, NY 10013. Phone 1-800-SPRINGER, fax (201) 348-4505, e-mail orders-ny@springer-sbm.com, or visit www.springeronline.com.

For information on translations, please e-mail rights@apress.com, or visit www.apress.com.

Apress and friends of ED books may be purchased in bulk for academic, corporate, or promotional use. eBook versions and licenses are also available for most titles. For more information, reference our Special Bulk Sales–eBook Licensing web page at www.apress.com/info/bulksales.

The source code for this book is available to readers at www.apress.com.

To Donna, my beautiful wife and my best friend.
Thank you for sharing the adventure with me!

Contents at a Glance

Contents

About the Author

■**Mark Collins** has been developing software and managing software development projects for 30 years in a variety of industries and a wide range of technologies. He wrote his first project plan using Microsoft Project 1.0. Fortunately, the available tools have improved significantly. He is often called upon to provide order and process to the project at hand. With a pragmatic approach, he implements the ideal balance of implementing structure while minimizing overhead.

A second underlying theme in Mark's career has been the improvement of software development methodologies. The process and structure applied in development projects will determine the quality and productivity you can achieve. To that end, Mark has developed several computer-aided software engineering (CASE) tools. His latest application suite is called Omega Tool (see www.thecreativepeople.com).

For questions and comments, you can contact Mark at markc@thecreativepeople.com.

About the Technical Reviewer

■**Jeff Sanders** is a published author and an accomplished technologist. He is currently employed with Avanade Federal Services in the capacity of group manager/senior architect, and is also manager of the Federal Office of Learning and Development.

Jeff has years of professional experience in the field of IT and strategic business consulting, leading both sales and delivery efforts. He regularly contributes to certification and product roadmap development with Microsoft, and speaks publicly on Microsoft enterprise technologies. With his roots in software development, Jeff's areas of expertise include operational intelligence, collaboration and content management solutions, distributed component-based application architectures, object-oriented analysis and design, and enterprise integration patterns and designs.

Jeff is also CTO of DynamicShift, a client-focused organization specializing in Microsoft technologies, specifically SharePoint Server, StreamInsight, Windows Azure, AppFabric, Business Activity Monitoring, BizTalk Server, Commerce Server, and .NET. He is a Microsoft Certified Trainer, and leads DynamicShift in both training and consulting efforts.

He enjoys spending time with his wife and daughter, and wishes he had more of it.

He may be reached at jeff.sanders@dynamicshift.com.

Acknowledgments

First, I want to acknowledge that anything that I have ever done that is of any value or significance was accomplished through the provision of my Lord and Savior, Jesus Christ. This book was well beyond my own ability, and it was nothing short of God's amazing grace that enabled me to complete it. He has once again proven that "I can do all things through His anointing" (Phil 4:13).

Next, I want to say a big thank you to my beautiful wife, Donna. I can honestly say that I would not be who I am if it were not for what you have sown into my life. You are the embodiment of a Proverbs 31 wife. I am truly blessed to be able to share my life with you. Thank you for your loving support and for making life fun!

I am also very thankful for all the people at Apress who made this book possible and for all their hard work that turned it into the finished product you see now. Everyone at Apress has made writing this book a pleasure. Thank you!

Finally, I want to thank Jeff Sanders, Jonathan Hassell, Adam Heath, Corbin Collins, and Damon Larson. Each of you contributed your time and talent to make this book a success. Thank you!

■ ■ ■

CHAPTER 1

Introduction

The primary activity of project managers is to keep track of information. Work items are completed, milestones are achieved, defects are reported, tests are passed . . . and the list goes on. More than simply capturing this information, project managers need to analyze this data and provide meaningful status reports. SharePoint is uniquely suited to this environment. As you'll see throughout this book, SharePoint can be used as a repository for all of these project management artifacts. Using a combination of web and Microsoft Office applications, you can provide easy access to enter, view, and report on your project data.

About This Book

This book is written for individuals who are tasked with providing a Project Management Information System (PMIS). You may be a project manager who realizes the need for a better system than e-mails and spreadsheets. Or you may be an IT/IS staff member asked to support the project management office (PMO). The exercises in this book will show you step by step how to utilize the features in SharePoint to build a custom solution that fits your specific needs. Each chapter will begin with an explanation of a project management activity. This will explain the purpose of the feature that will be implemented in the chapter. This will help the developer to understand the problem that is being solved and set the context for why the feature should be implemented. The rest of the chapter will then provide detailed instructions for creating the described feature. Most of the projects that are presented here can be implemented by someone with minimal experience in SharePoint.

My approach to managing projects is based on practical application. I like ideas that work. Activities that add little value to the overall goal steal time and focus from those that are beneficial. Unfortunately, what works well in one environment may not be that effective in another. So flexibility is another key factor. Having a repertoire of management techniques will help you find the right one for any given situation. This book is intended to give you a few more tools to hang on your tool belt.

My goal in writing this book is to give you the concepts and practical examples from which you can draw upon to create your own PMIS. I recommend that you work through all the projects in this book. When you have finished, you'll have a working site that you can refer back to. Then you can create your own SharePoint site and implement the features that fit your environment, using your initial site as an example. If you're comfortable working with SharePoint, you could also simply read this book and then implement the portions that fit your specific needs.

Prerequisites

This book assumes that you have Microsoft SharePoint Server 2010 installed. It also relies on Microsoft SharePoint Designer 2010, which is a free product that you can download from Microsoft. A couple of the chapters use Visual Studio 2010 to implement some advanced features. If you don't have Visual Studio installed, you can still implement most of the projects in this book.

Some of the chapters assume you also have the Microsoft Office applications installed, including Word, Outlook, and Excel. Again, you can implement most of the features without these, but because the Office applications are so well integrated with SharePoint, they add a lot to the user experience.

Project Management Activities

This book is structured around the typical project management activities. Each chapter covers a specific project management task. The topics included are based primarily on my experience of managing many successful projects. This includes a variety of management styles and disciplines. Rather than attempt to dictate any particular approach, my motivation is to give you practical techniques so you can pick and choose, and then adapt to your specific needs.

This book is *not* intended to tell you how to manage a project. Instead, once you have decided how your projects should be managed, the material in this book will show you how to create a system that will help you do that more effectively. That being said, however, I think you'll find that the examples presented here will give you some good ideas that you may want to try in addition to (or instead of) your existing activities. In each chapter I'll also give you ideas for extending or adapting the implementation. Feel free to be creative. The best solution is one that fits the way you work.

Requirements

A good set of requirements is the starting point for successful projects. Part 1 of this book describes ways to capture and manage requirements. Typically, this task is performed by a business analyst, and there are various approaches to extracting a set of requirements. This book is focused on collecting the end result of this process. The chapters in this part show you how to use SharePoint to store the results of the requirement-gathering process.

Implementation

Part 2 of this book demonstrates techniques for managing the implementation phase of a project. The activities covered are based on the agile methodology. The topics covered include

- Capturing user stories

- Providing a project backlog (stack)

- Scheduling iterations (sprints)

- Tracking work items including tasks, issues, and defects

- Reporting, including burndown charts and key performance indicators (KPI)

While the terminology and some of the techniques are specific to the agile methodology, the sample implementations can be tailored to fit other development methodologies.

Testing

Part 3 of this book deals with the testing activities. It provides for storing specific test cases as well as general testing documentation such as test plans and information about testing tools and configurations. In this part, you'll also provide a mechanism for recording defects and tracking their resolution. Finally, various reporting features will be demonstrated for communicating testing progress and overall quality indicators.

Postproduction Phase

Once the initial implementation is complete, you'll need to handle product support and issue reporting and resolution. In Part 4 of the book, you'll implement a facility for reporting issues and enhancement requests. These will be processed through a workflow that includes tasks for analysts, developers, testers, and customer support, as appropriate. By the end of this part, you will have built a full-featured, tasked-based issue-tracking system.

■ ■ ■

PART 1

Requirements

Requirements are a key part of any project management system. They can feed many other project management activities during the implementation, testing, and even post-production phases. In this section, I'll demonstrate some techniques for collecting and managing requirements.

In Chapter 2, you'll build a simple list for tracking requirements. Requirements can be expressed in various ways, so this list will be somewhat generic and allow attachments to provide details as appropriate. In Chapter 3, I'll show you how you can allow anyone to submit a requirement via e-mail. SharePoint stores these incoming e-mails in a document library. You will also add a simple workflow to review and extract the requirement details.

The project demonstrated in Chapter 4 will enhance the list you implemented in Chapter 2 by providing a mechanism for scoring each requirement. This gives you a way to quickly prioritize the existing requirements. In Chapter 5, you'll enhance this list further by allowing relationships between individual requirements. You will also allow and track communication regarding requirements by using a discussion list.

■ ■ ■

Collecting Requirements

In this chapter, you'll create a simple list that will be used to track requirements. The remaining chapters in this section will add more capabilities to this list.

Defining Requirements

Requirements can be expressed in many forms. For example, use cases are used to effectively communicate processing rules for specific scenarios. Other requirements, such as system or legal constraints, will normally be described in other formats. Deliverables, such as report definitions, are usually best defined with a sample output provided by an image or Excel spreadsheet. Rather than trying to force all requirements into a common format, it will usually work better to design the requirements-tracking system to allow multiple formats.

One approach that is often used is to compile all requirements into a single document. However, this approach makes it difficult to track individual requirements. Each requirement should be as specific as practical and then mapped to implementation and testing plans. To account for this when a single document is used, often the paragraph number is used as the unique identifier for mapping purposes. This works well for the traditional waterfall approach where the requirements are fully documented before the implementation begins. For iterative techniques this quickly becomes unmanageable.

A SharePoint list is the ideal solution. Each item is uniquely identified and can be mapped to subsequent activities. Because a list can contain items of different types, a single requirements list can contain many different types of requirements. The approach used in this chapter is to create a simple list with columns that are common to all types. A single text field is used to store the requirement description. When other formats are needed, such as a diagram or spreadsheet, these are provided as attachments.

Creating a Project Management Site

Start by creating a SharePoint site. This site will be used for all of the projects in this book. Use the Team Site template, as shown in Figure 2-1. This will create some standard lists, such as Tasks, Calendar, and Shared Documents, that will be useful for managing projects.

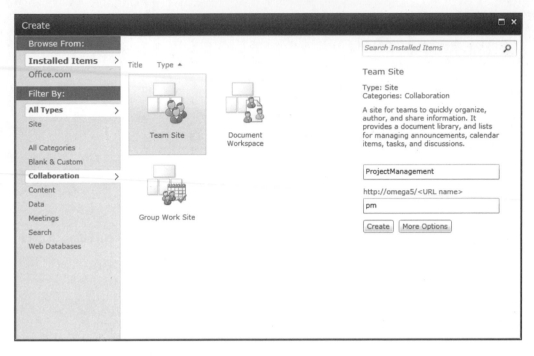

Figure 2-1. *Creating a new ProjectManagement site*

You will create a `Requirements` list that will contain the following pieces of information:

- *Title*: Very brief summary of the requirement

- *Requirement type*: The format of the requirement (use case, deliverable, etc.)

- *Functional area*: The organizational entity requesting or primarily affected by this requirement

- *Priority*: Initial assessment of the criticality of this requirement

- *Description*: Text field that describes the requirement

Defining Functional Areas

To allow for a dynamic list of functional areas, you'll need to create a list that will store the possible values. You will use SharePoint Designer to first define a content type and then create a list based on this content type. To start SharePoint Designer, from the Site Actions menu, select the *Edit in SharePoint Designer* link, as shown in Figure 2-2.

Figure 2-2. *Starting SharePoint Designer*

Defining the Content Type

In SharePoint Designer, select the *Content Types* link from the Navigation pane, as shown in Figure 2-3.

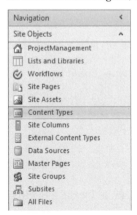

Figure 2-3. *Selecting the Content Types link*

The Content Types page lists all the existing content types. Click the Content Type button in the ribbon to create a new content type. In the Create a Content Type dialog box, enter the name **Functional**

Area. Select Item for the parent content type, which can be found in the List Content Type group. Put the new content type into a new group called Project Management. The completed dialog box should look like Figure 2-4. Click the OK button to create the content type.

Figure 2-4. *Creating a new content type*

The Functional Area content type should now be in the content type list in the Project Management group. Scroll to the bottom of the list and click the *Functional Area* link to display its properties. Then click the *Edit content type columns* link to modify the list of columns. The content type should have a single column, Title, which was inherited from the Item content type.

Add the following columns to this content type (these columns can be found in the existing site column collection):

- Manager's Name

- E-Mail

Save the changes by clicking the Save button in the title bar. The column list should look like Figure 2-5 when you've finished.

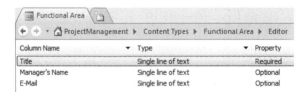

Figure 2-5. *Defining the Functional Area content type*

Creating the Functional Areas List

Now you'll create a `Functional Areas` list that is based on this content type. In SharePoint Designer, select the *Lists and Libraries* link in the Navigation pane, as shown in Figure 2-6.

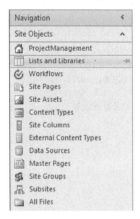

Figure 2-6. *Selecting the Lists and Libraries page*

In the Ribbon, click the Custom List button, as shown in Figure 2-7.

Figure 2-7. *Clicking the Custom List button*

In the dialog box that appears, enter the name **Functional Areas**, as shown in Figure 2-8, and click the OK button.

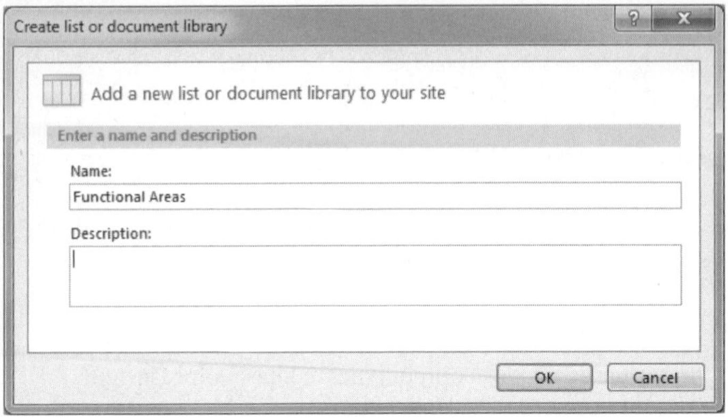

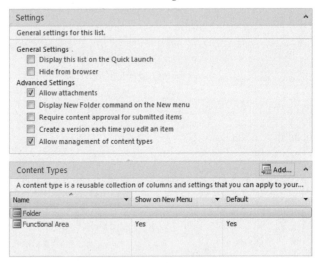

Figure 2-8. *Creating a new list*

This list should now be included in the Lists and Libraries page. Click the *Functional Areas* link to edit this list. In the Settings section, select the check box to "Allow management of content types." Also uncheck the box to "Display this list on the Quick Launch." In the Content Types section, click the Add button and then select the `Functional Area` content type, which should be in the `Project Management` group. Then delete the `Item` content type and make sure `Functional Area` is set as the default type. These two sections should look like Figure 2-9.

Figure 2-9. *The Functional Area settings*

Save the changes to this list definition.

■**Tip** It's a good idea to adopt your naming convention early on. The most important thing to keep in mind is consistency. It doesn't matter so much what conventions you use as long as you use them everywhere. One convention I use is to make the names of lists plural (e.g., Functional Areas). This is consistent with the standard lists such as Tasks and Announcements. Content types, on the other hand, are singular, as they represent a single object. You don't have to follow this convention, however, and you can rename the standard lists to match your naming preferences.

Populating the Functional Areas List

The Functional Areas list is not likely to be viewed or modified frequently so you unchecked the box to remove it from the Quick Launch. To display this list, click the *Lists* link in the Quick Launch menu. From the All Items page, click the *Functional Areas* link.

■**Tip** Notice that the list only displays the Title column. When the list was created, it was based on the Item content type, so the view that was created only included the Title column. This list is now based on the Functional Area content type, which includes two other columns. From the List ribbon, click the Modify View button and add the Manager's Name and E-Mail columns to the view.

Use the *Add new item* link to add several functional areas. When you're done, the list should look like Figure 2-10.

		Title	Manager's Name	E-Mail
		Accounting ⊠ NEW	John Smith	jsmith@somewhere.com
		Marketing ⊠ NEW	Jane Doe	jadoe@somewhere.com
		Operations ⊠ NEW	Stan Operator	stano@ops.somewhere.com
		Human Resources ⊠ NEW	Sally Jones	sjones@somewhere.com
✛ Add new item				

Figure 2-10. *Displaying the Functional Areas list*

Defining the Requirements

Now you're ready to define the Requirements list. Like the previous list, you'll start by defining the content type, but first you will need to define some new site columns. From SharePoint Designer, select the *Site Columns* link in the Navigation pane.

Adding Custom Site Columns

You will need to create the following custom columns:

- Functional Area: A lookup column for the list you just created

- Requirement Type: A choice field to specify the requirement format

- Requirement Description: A multiline text field for entering the requirement

- Submitted By: The user who submitted the requirement

Functional Area

Now that you have created a list to store the dynamic collection of functional areas, you'll create a column that can be used to reference it. Click the New Column button in the ribbon and select the Lookup column type, as shown in Figure 2-11.

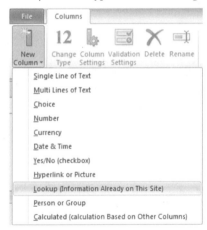

Figure 2-11. *Choosing the column type*

In the Create a Site Column dialog box, enter the name **Functional Area** and create a new group called Project Management, as shown in Figure 2-12.

Figure 2-12. *Creating a site column*

In the Column Editor dialog box, shown in Figure 2-13, select the Functional Area list as the source for this column and choose the Title field as the one to be displayed for the value of this column. You can also select additional columns to be included. These will be automatically added to your list or content type when this column is added. You won't need that for this column, so just leave them all unchecked.

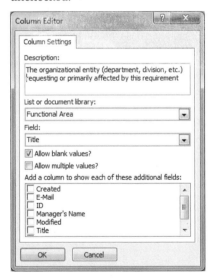

Figure 2-13. *Configuring the lookup column*

■**Tip**   I left the "Allow blank values?" check box selected. That will make this an optional column on the Requirements list. If this is an important piece of information in your requirements process, you might want to make it required by unchecking this box. Also, you can select the "Allow multiple values?" check box, which will allow multiple functional areas to this requirement. This could be useful depending on how you intend to use this data.

Save this column definition by clicking the Save button in the title bar.

Requirement Type

Next, you'll create a column to define the type of requirement (e.g., use case, legal constraint, or deliverable). This will use a Choice column type where the possible values are hard-coded in the column definition.

■**Note**   Unlike functional areas, requirement types are more static, so defining a hard-coded list of allowed values should be acceptable. Arguably, someone could devise new ways of expressing a requirement. However, it is a relatively simple matter for a developer or power user to add a new option using SharePoint Designer. Functional areas are designed so that an end-user can set up new areas themselves. These are the kinds of trade-offs that you will need to make as you design your own system. Perhaps in your organization, though, functional areas are static and a Choice column is sufficient.

Click the New Column button in the ribbon and select the Choice column type. Enter the name **Requirement Type** and select the Project Management group (that you just created), as shown in Figure 2-14.

Figure 2-14. *Creating the Requirement Type column*

In the Column Editor dialog box, enter the possible values for this column. You can use the values shown in Figure 2-15 or enter types that are more suitable for your scenario. I added an Other type, set this as the default value, and made the column required (by leaving the "Allow blank values?" box unchecked). You could remove the default value, which will require the user to choose a type before submitting the requirement. Also, you have the option to allow the users to add other values not defined by this list. To do that, select the "Allow "fill-in" choices" check box.

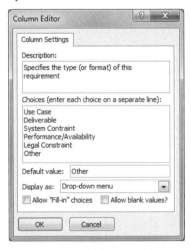

Figure 2-15. *Configuring the Requirement Type column*

Additional Columns

Add the remaining columns as follows:

- Requirement Description: Use the Multi Lines of Text column type.

- Submitted By: Use the Person or Group column type.

For the Submitted By column, there are several ways to configure this in the Column Editor. You can choose to allow blank values and also to allow multiple values. You can limit this to individuals or also allow groups. You can also choose which user field is displayed in the column—such as the Account (login), Name, or Work e-mail. A suggested configuration is shown in Figure 2-16.

Figure 2-16. *Configuring the Submitted By column*

Put these site columns in the same Project Management group to keep all your custom columns together. The list of custom columns should look like Figure 2-17.

Figure 2-17. *The list of new column definitions*

Defining the Content Type

Now you're ready to create a Requirement content type, which is pretty easy once the columns are defined. Click the *Content Type* link in the Navigation pane. Then click the Content Type button in the ribbon. Enter the name **Requirement** and select Item as the parent content type. Put this in the same Project Management group that you created for the Functional Area content type, as shown in Figure 2-18.

Figure 2-18. *Creating the Requirement content type*

Select the Requirement content type, which will display the Content Type Settings page. Click the *Edit content type columns* link. There should be a single column named Title, which was inherited from the Item content type. Add the following columns to this content type:

- Requirement Type
- Functional Area
- Priority
- Submitted By
- Requirement Description
- Date Created

■**Note**   Some of these columns are standard columns shipped with SharePoint. You'll need to find the group that these columns are in. Within each group, the columns are listed in alphabetical order. You can also use the search option provided by the Site Column Picker dialog box. Just start entering the column name in the search box, and the list will show only matching columns.

The completed column list should look like Figure 2-19.

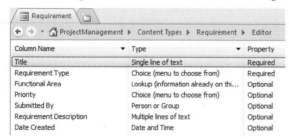

Figure 2-19. *The completed column list*

Creating the Requirements List

The last step is to create a new list based on the Requirement content type. You'll do this the same way that you created the Functional Areas list. Select the *Lists and Libraries* link in the Navigation pane and then click the Custom List button in the ribbon. Enter the name **Requirements**, as shown in Figure 2-20.

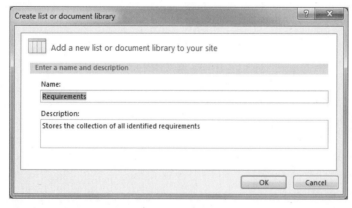

Figure 2-20. *Creating a new Requirements list*

Select the Requirements list to display the List Settings page. Select the "Allow management of content types" check box. Add the Requirement content type to this list, set this as the default content type, and then remove the Item content type.

Testing the Requirements List

Go to the SharePoint site and select the Requirements list. This list will be empty and will only include the Title column.

Defining the All Items View

Just like with the Functional Areas list, you will need to add the desired columns to the view. From the List ribbon, click the Modify View button. Select the columns that you want displayed and specify the order they should appear on the page. The completed section should look like Figure 2-21.

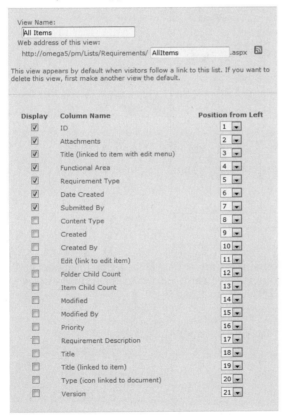

Figure 2-21. *Defining the All Items view*

Adding Requirements

Now your list is ready to use. Click the *Add new item* link to create a new requirement. The New Item form should look like Figure 2-22.

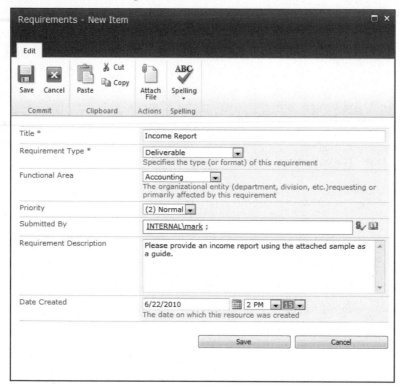

Figure 2-22. *Entering a new requirement*

Notice that the Functional Area drop-down list contains the areas that you added to the associated list. The Requirement Type defaulted to Other, but the other values were available in the drop-down list. After saving this form, the Requirements list should look like Figure 2-23.

Figure 2-23. *The Requirements list with a new entry*

Notice the ID column, which is assigned by the system. This is a unique identifier that can be used when mapping this requirement in future activities.

Summary

In this chapter you created a Requirements list to store and manage requirements as they are identified. In the process, you also used several SharePoint techniques, including

- Defining new site columns using SharePoint Designer
- Creating a Lookup column based on an associated list
- Creating a Choice column using hard-coded values
- Creating new content types using SharePoint Designer
- Creating custom lists based on a content type

In subsequent chapters you will build upon this initial implementation.

CHAPTER 3

■■■

Processing Incoming E-mail

In this chapter you'll provide a facility that allows individuals the ability to contribute to the requirement-gathering process by simply sending an e-mail.

Incoming E-mails

The requirements process often requires input from people outside your organization. They may not have access to your SharePoint site, or they may prefer to send an e-mail with their requirements instead of filling out a form. You may want to empower your end users to submit feedback, which can be helpful in planning a future release. You might need to accept unsolicited enhancement requests from your internal or external customers.

Understanding SharePoint's E-mail Capability

You could allow these to accumulate in an inbox and periodically review them with Outlook talking an appropriate action. However, there is a better way to keep track of these. SharePoint provides a facility for handling incoming e-mails. This provides a convenient way to archive these e-mails and make them available to appropriate individuals.

In addition to lists, which you used in the previous chapter, SharePoint also provides document libraries. A *document library* is used to store documents such as pictures or spreadsheets. Anything that can be saved as a file can be stored in a document library. SharePoint also provides the infrastructure for controlling access to these libraries.

SharePoint allows you to enable a document library to accept incoming e-mails. As part of this configuration, you'll assign an e-mail address to the document library. Once this is set up, the e-mails sent to that address, along with any attachments, are automatically added to the document library.

Another advantage of using a document library to store the e-mail is the ability to create a workflow for the incoming e-mail. You can use SharePoint workflows to notify someone of the new document or assign a task for someone to review the incoming e-mail.

Configuring Incoming E-mail

In this chapter I'll show you how to set up and use incoming e-mail support in SharePoint. The first step is to configure your SharePoint server to support incoming e-mails. There are two ways to do this, and they are referred to as *automatic mode* and *advanced mode*. In automatic mode, you will run the Simple Mail Transfer Protocol (SMTP) server on the SharePoint server. The SharePoint server communicates directly with the SMTP server. In advanced mode, the SMTP server can run at a different location. You must tell the SharePoint server the location of the drop folder in which the incoming e-mails will be placed. SharePoint checks this folder periodically and processes any new items that have been "dropped" there.

■**Note**   The SMTP server provided with Windows Server implements simple file-based e-mail processing. Incoming messages are stored as a file in a drop folder. It has no support for individual mail boxes. In an e-mail address, the text after the @ symbol specifies the server that the message is sent to, and the text to the left of the @ symbol specifies the mailbox on that server. The SMTP server ignores the mailbox information. All messages sent to that server are placed in a single drop folder.

Using Automatic Mode

The easiest way to configure incoming e-mail is to simply install the SMTP server on the SharePoint server and configure SharePoint to use automatic mode.

■**Caution**   The SMTP server can only be used on a server OS. If you are running SharePoint on a desktop OS (Vista or Windows 7) you will need to use advanced mode. Also, if you are using a SharePoint farm, you must install the SMTP server on each of the SharePoint servers in the farm.

Installing the SMTP Server Feature

To install the SMTP server, run the Server Manager application, which can be found in the Administrative Tools Start menu. Right-click the Features node and select Add Features, as shown in Figure 3-1.

Figure 3-1. *Adding new features*

In the Add Features Wizard, select the SMTP Server feature, as shown in Figure 3-2.

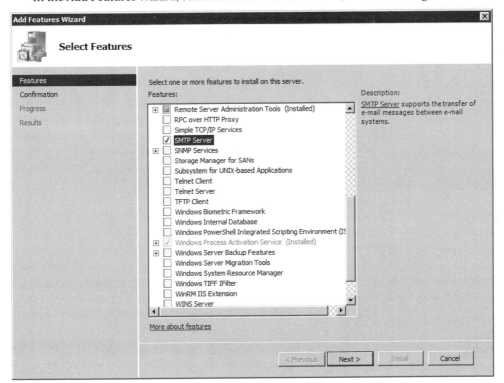

Figure 3-2. *Selecting the SMTP Server feature*

If there are other features that are required by the SMTP server, you'll see a pop-up informing you of the required features. If that happens, click the Add Required Features button, and these features will be added as well. The confirmation page is then displayed. It will list the SMTP server plus any prerequisite features.

Click the Install button to begin the installation. The progress page will be displayed. When the install has finished, the results page shown in Figure 3-3 is displayed.

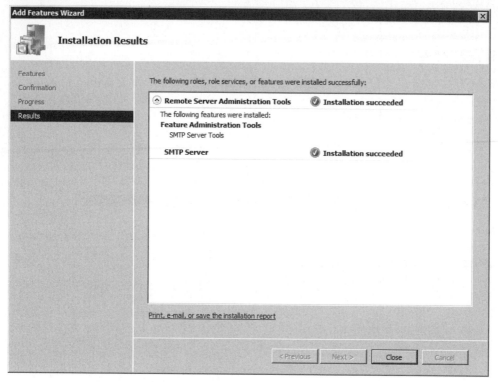

Figure 3-3. *Results page showing a successful installation*

Starting the SMTP Service

The SMTP server is implemented as a Windows service. For some reason, by default, this service is set up to be started manually. You can verify this by selecting the Services application from the Administrative Tools Start menu. Find the Simple Mail Transfer Protocol (SMTP) service and check its startup type. It is normally set to Manual, as shown in Figure 3-4.

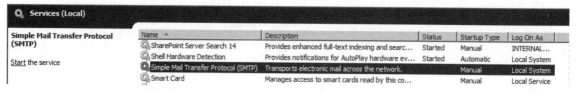

Figure 3-4. *Checking the SMTP service status*

Right-click this service and choose Properties. In the Properties dialog box, change the startup type to Automatic. After you have applied this change, click the Start button to start the service. In the future, the service should start by itself whenever the server is rebooted.

Configuring the SMTP Server

To configure the SMTP server, you'll need to use version 6.0 of IIS Manager. This can be found in the Administrative Tools menu, as shown in Figure 3-5.

Figure 3-5. *Starting IIS Manager (version 6)*

A default domain is created for you based on the fully qualified Active Directory name for this server, as shown in Figure 3-6.

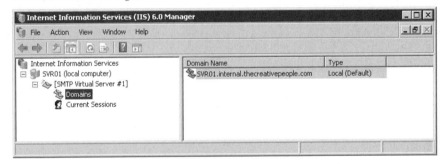

Figure 3-6. *Showing the default e-mail domains*

If you right-click this domain and choose Properties, you can view and edit the drop folder (see Figure 3-7).

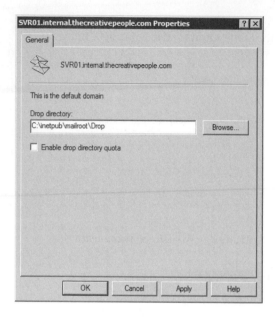

Figure 3-7. *Setting the drop folder*

By default, this will be in the C:\inetpub\mailroot\Drop folder. You can change this to a different location, but it must be on a local disk.

Configuring SharePoint

Launch the SharePoint 2010 Central Administration application, which you can find in the Start menu in the Microsoft SharePoint 2010 Products folder. From the System Settings page, click the *Configure incoming e-mail settings* link, as shown in Figure 3-8.

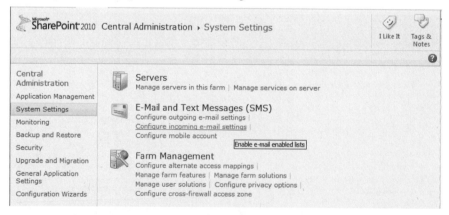

Figure 3-8. *Selecting the incoming e-mail settings*

The Configure Incoming E-Mail Settings page, shown in Figure 3-9, will be displayed.

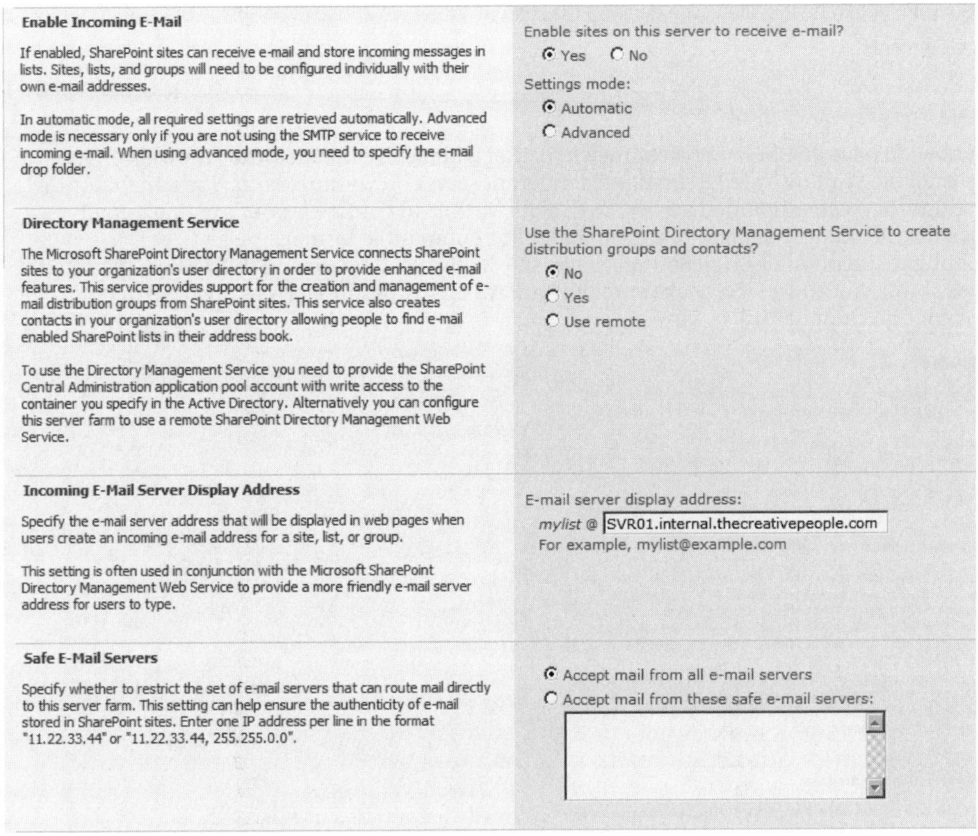

Enable Incoming E-Mail

If enabled, SharePoint sites can receive e-mail and store incoming messages in lists. Sites, lists, and groups will need to be configured individually with their own e-mail addresses.

In automatic mode, all required settings are retrieved automatically. Advanced mode is necessary only if you are not using the SMTP service to receive incoming e-mail. When using advanced mode, you need to specify the e-mail drop folder.

Enable sites on this server to receive e-mail?
- ⦿ Yes ○ No

Settings mode:
- ⦿ Automatic
- ○ Advanced

Directory Management Service

The Microsoft SharePoint Directory Management Service connects SharePoint sites to your organization's user directory in order to provide enhanced e-mail features. This service provides support for the creation and management of e-mail distribution groups from SharePoint sites. This service also creates contacts in your organization's user directory allowing people to find e-mail enabled SharePoint lists in their address book.

To use the Directory Management Service you need to provide the SharePoint Central Administration application pool account with write access to the container you specify in the Active Directory. Alternatively you can configure this server farm to use a remote SharePoint Directory Management Web Service.

Use the SharePoint Directory Management Service to create distribution groups and contacts?
- ⦿ No
- ○ Yes
- ○ Use remote

Incoming E-Mail Server Display Address

Specify the e-mail server address that will be displayed in web pages when users create an incoming e-mail address for a site, list, or group.

This setting is often used in conjunction with the Microsoft SharePoint Directory Management Web Service to provide a more friendly e-mail server address for users to type.

E-mail server display address:

mylist @ [SVR01.internal.thecreativepeople.com]

For example, mylist@example.com

Safe E-Mail Servers

Specify whether to restrict the set of e-mail servers that can route mail directly to this server farm. This setting can help ensure the authenticity of e-mail stored in SharePoint sites. Enter one IP address per line in the format "11.22.33.44" or "11.22.33.44, 255.255.0.0".

- ⦿ Accept mail from all e-mail servers
- ○ Accept mail from these safe e-mail servers:

Figure 3-9. *The Configure Incoming E-Mail Settings page with Automatic mode*

Configuring SharePoint for automatic mode is really easy. Click the Yes radio button for the "Enable sites on this server to receive e-mail?" option. For the settings mode, choose Automatic. You can leave the rest of the values with their default settings.

Using Advanced Mode

While automatic mode is pretty simple to set up, there are situations in which it is not available. Probably the most common is when you install SharePoint on a desktop OS. If the SMTP server is not installed on the local machine, the Configure Incoming E-Mail Settings page, shown in Figure 3-10, will not allow the Automatic option to be selected.

■**Caution**   SharePoint can be installed on a desktop OS such as Windows 7; however, this is not supported for production environments.

You will need to have an SMTP server somewhere that will receive the incoming messages. One option is to install the Windows SMTP server on a different server on your network. You can follow the same instructions that were explained earlier. You might be able to configure your existing e-mail system to save the incoming messages to a drop folder in a compatible format.

In the Configure Incoming E-Mail Settings page, select advanced mode and then enter a path to the drop folder, as shown in Figure 3-10. Make sure that you set up the permissions to the drop folder so the SharePoint service account has full control.

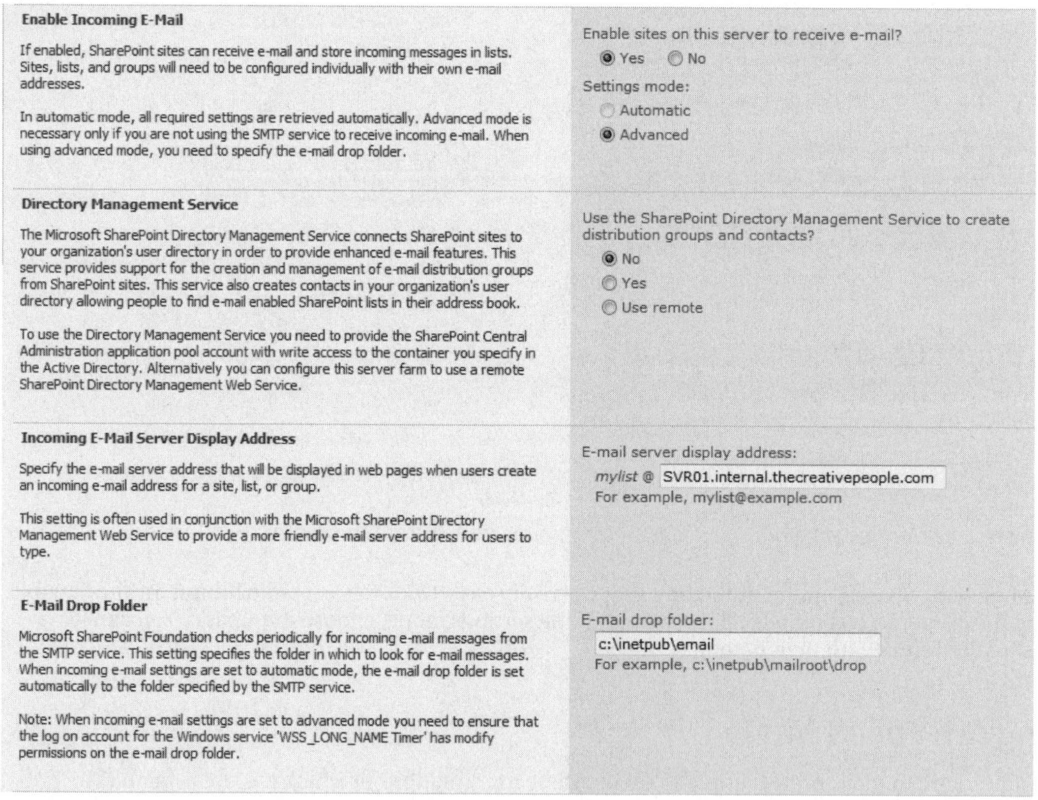

Enable Incoming E-Mail

If enabled, SharePoint sites can receive e-mail and store incoming messages in lists. Sites, lists, and groups will need to be configured individually with their own e-mail addresses.

In automatic mode, all required settings are retrieved automatically. Advanced mode is necessary only if you are not using the SMTP service to receive incoming e-mail. When using advanced mode, you need to specify the e-mail drop folder.

Enable sites on this server to receive e-mail?
◉ Yes   ○ No
Settings mode:
○ Automatic
◉ Advanced

Directory Management Service

The Microsoft SharePoint Directory Management Service connects SharePoint sites to your organization's user directory in order to provide enhanced e-mail features. This service provides support for the creation and management of e-mail distribution groups from SharePoint sites. This service also creates contacts in your organization's user directory allowing people to find e-mail enabled SharePoint lists in their address book.

To use the Directory Management Service you need to provide the SharePoint Central Administration application pool account with write access to the container you specify in the Active Directory. Alternatively you can configure this server farm to use a remote SharePoint Directory Management Web Service.

Use the SharePoint Directory Management Service to create distribution groups and contacts?
◉ No
○ Yes
○ Use remote

Incoming E-Mail Server Display Address

Specify the e-mail server address that will be displayed in web pages when users create an incoming e-mail address for a site, list, or group.

This setting is often used in conjunction with the Microsoft SharePoint Directory Management Web Service to provide a more friendly e-mail server address for users to type.

E-mail server display address:
mylist @ [SVR01.internal.thecreativepeople.com]
For example, mylist@example.com

E-Mail Drop Folder

Microsoft SharePoint Foundation checks periodically for incoming e-mail messages from the SMTP service. This setting specifies the folder in which to look for e-mail messages. When incoming e-mail settings are set to automatic mode, the e-mail drop folder is set automatically to the folder specified by the SMTP service.

Note: When incoming e-mail settings are set to advanced mode you need to ensure that the log on account for the Windows service 'WSS_LONG_NAME Timer' has modify permissions on the e-mail drop folder.

E-mail drop folder:
[c:\inetpub\email]
For example, c:\inetpub\mailroot\drop

Figure 3-10. *The Configure Incoming E-Mail Settings page with advanced mode*

■Tip   To send an e-mail to SharePoint, the e-mail address will be `<list name>@<server name>`. The server name is the domain name specified when configuring the SMTP server. By default this is the fully qualified Active Directory name for the server. In my example this is `SVR01.internal.thecreativepeople.com`. This is probably not an address that is reachable from outside your network. If you are using Microsoft Exchange or a similar enterprise e-mail system, you should consider setting up an address on your e-mail system and configure this to forward the e-mail to the SharePoint server.

Configuring an Incoming List

Now that SharePoint is configured to receive e-mails, you can create a list and set it up to receive incoming e-mails. Launch SharePoint and go to the `ProjectManagement` site that you set up in Chapter 2.

Creating the Incoming Requirements Document Library

From the Site Actions menu, select the *More Options* link, as shown in Figure 3-11.

Figure 3-11. *Selecting the More Options link*

Select the Document Library template and enter the name **Incoming Requirements**.

Enabling Incoming E-Mails

Click the Library Settings button in the Library ribbon, as shown in Figure 3-12.

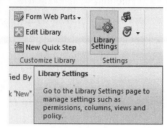

Figure 3-12. *Selecting the library settings*

The Document Library Settings page is shown in Figure 3-13.

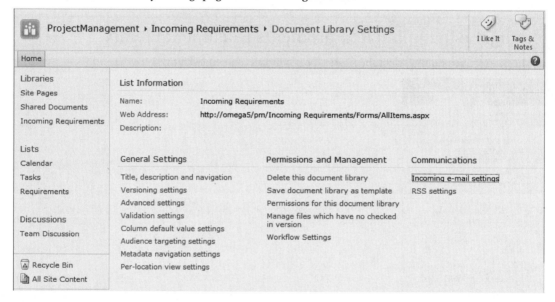

Figure 3-13. *The Incoming e-mail setting slink*

Select the *Incoming e-mail settings* link, which can be found in the Communications section. This will display the Incoming E-Mail Settings page shown in Figure 3-14.

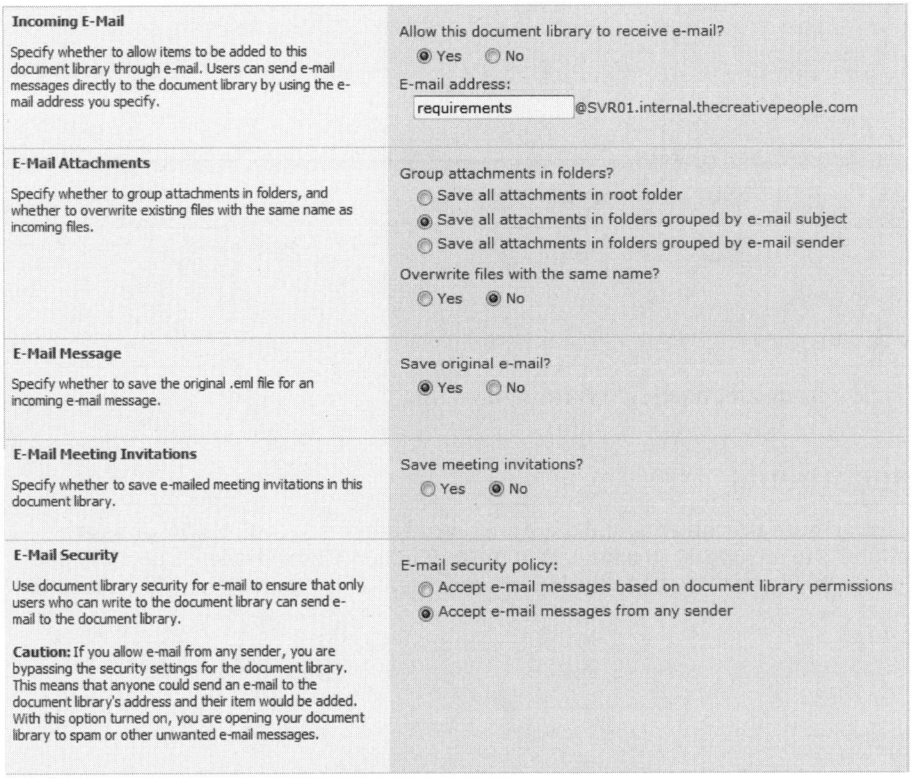

Figure 3-14. *Configuring incoming e-mails*

To enable this list to receive e-mails, select the Yes radio button in the Incoming E-Mail section. You will also need to specify a unique e-mail address. The portion of the e-mail address to the right of the @ symbol is fixed and cannot be changed. This is the address of the SharePoint server (or an SMTP server that is receiving mail on behalf of this SharePoint server). This address was configured previously using the SharePoint 2010 Central Administration application. The SMTP server puts all e-mails into a single drop folder and ignores the portion of the e-mail address to the left of the @ symbol.

SharePoint, however, *only* looks at the left-hand potion of the e-mail address. It uses this to determine which list the e-mail should be stored in. A single drop folder will be used for this server. Because of this, the address entered here must be unique across the entire server. This includes all sites and subsites on this server. If you enter an address that has been used somewhere on this server, you'll see the error shown in Figure 3-15.

Error
Unable to assign this e-mail address to the list, because the address is in use.
Troubleshoot issues with Microsoft SharePoint Foundation.
Correlation ID: 87e70123-5538-48c1-95af-83da4e42e722
Date and Time: 6/26/2010 8:49:06 PM
Go back to site

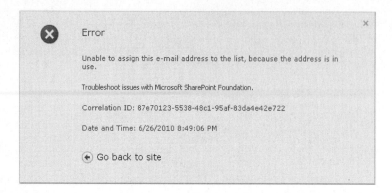

Figure 3-15. *Error indicating that the address has already been used*

Handling Attachments

The incoming e-mails can have attachments, and there are several options to control how these are handled. The first option is to include all attachments in the root folder. This will create a document in the list for each attachment. Figure 3-16 shows the library contents after two e-mails have been received.

Type
Name
Modified
Modified By
Another Requirement NEW
6/27/2010 4:00 PM
INTERNAL\mark
Feature NEW
6/27/2010 4:00 PM
INTERNAL\mark
New Requirement NEW
6/27/2010 4:00 PM
INTERNAL\mark
Test NEW
6/27/2010 4:00 PM
INTERNAL\mark
Test2 NEW
6/27/2010 4:00 PM
INTERNAL\mark
Add document

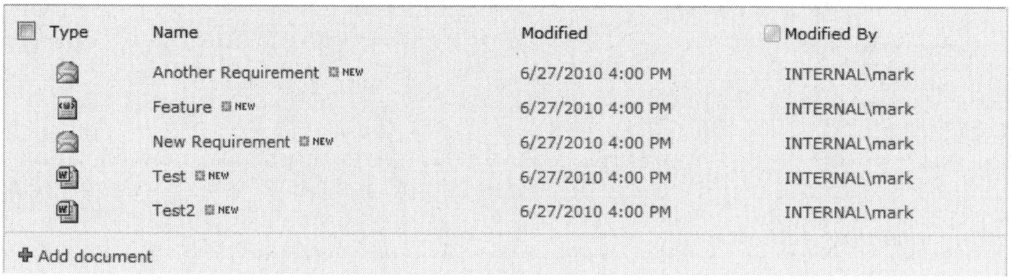

Figure 3-16. *The library contents with two incoming e-mails*

The drawback of this approach is that the attachments are not linked together; they are each listed as individual documents. For this reason, it is generally preferred to group attachments into a folder. You can group these by subject or by sender. Grouping by subject is the most common approach. Figure 3-17 shows the contents of the library with subject grouping after the same two e-mails have been received. Notice that both items are folder objects.

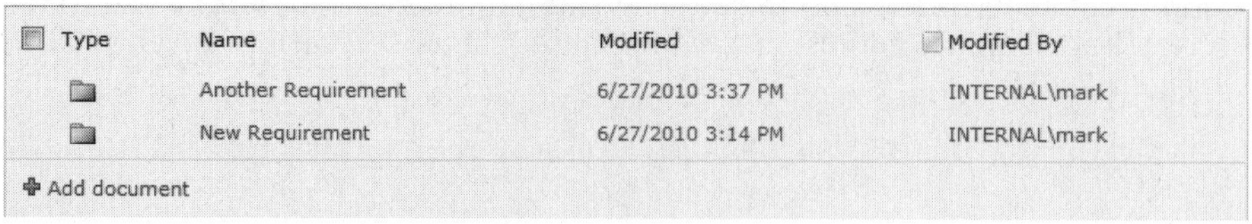

Type
Name
Modified
Modified By
Another Requirement
6/27/2010 3:37 PM
INTERNAL\mark
New Requirement
6/27/2010 3:14 PM
INTERNAL\mark
Add document

Figure 3-17. *The library contents with subject grouping*

If you click one of these items, you'll see the contents of the folder, as shown in Figure 3-18.

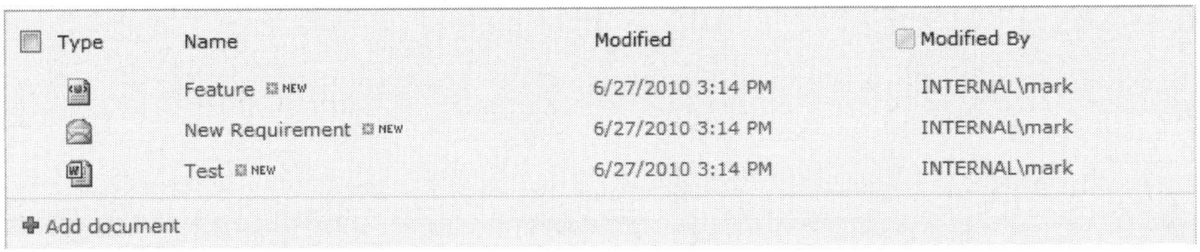

	Type	Name	Modified	Modified By
☐	📄	Feature ⊠ NEW	6/27/2010 3:14 PM	INTERNAL\mark
☐	📄	New Requirement ⊠ NEW	6/27/2010 3:14 PM	INTERNAL\mark
☐	📄	Test ⊠ NEW	6/27/2010 3:14 PM	INTERNAL\mark

✚ Add document

Figure 3-18. *Displaying the folder contents*

If another e-mail is received with the same subject, its attachments are stored in the same folder.

■**Caution**   You cannot have two documents in the same folder with the same name. If a subsequent e-mail is received that has the same subject as a previous e-mail, the attachments are "added" to the existing folder. However, if a file with that name already exists, the existing file is overwritten *or* the new file is ignored, depending on how the list is configured. The "Overwrite file with the same name?" radio buttons control this behavior.

The "Save original e-mail?" option is somewhat misleading. If this is set to Yes, the e-mail will be saved as a document in the library. If set to No, only the attachments are stored in the list, and the e-mail itself is ignored. If saved, the e-mail is stored as an EML file. Unfortunately, SharePoint does not have a built-in viewer for files of this type. If you select this document, a download dialog box will appear. To view the contents, save the file and then open it with Outlook.

You should think through how you expect people will use this feature to submit requirements and configure the incoming e-mails accordingly. For example, if the requirement will generally be in the e-mail itself and attachments rarely used, put all the documents in the root folder and make sure you choose to "save" the original e-mail. If the requirement is always specified in an attachment, you should put everything in the root folder and not save the e-mail. This is equivalent to uploading the requirements document to the library. If you can't rely on any consistency, your safest option is to group by subject, or perhaps sender.

■**Tip**   If you need to customize the way incoming e-mails are handled, you can implement your own custom event handler in Visual Studio. Override the `SPEmailEventReceiver` class to add your custom logic. Use other classes in the SharePoint object model to add or update list items as necessary.

Adding a Workflow

As a final step to this project, you'll add a simple workflow to this list to notify someone when a new e-mail is received. This workflow will add an item to their task list. Click the Workflow Settings button on the Library ribbon, as shown in Figure 3-19.

Figure 3-19. *Selecting the Workflow Settings button*

Associating the Approval Workflow

This will display the existing workflows associated with this list. The Workflows page shown in Figure 3-20 indicates that there are no existing workflows.

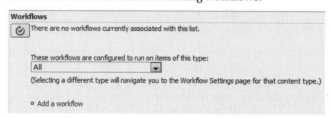

Figure 3-20. *The Workflows page showing no existing workflows*

Click the *Add a workflow* link, and the standard workflow association page shown in Figure 3-21 will be displayed.

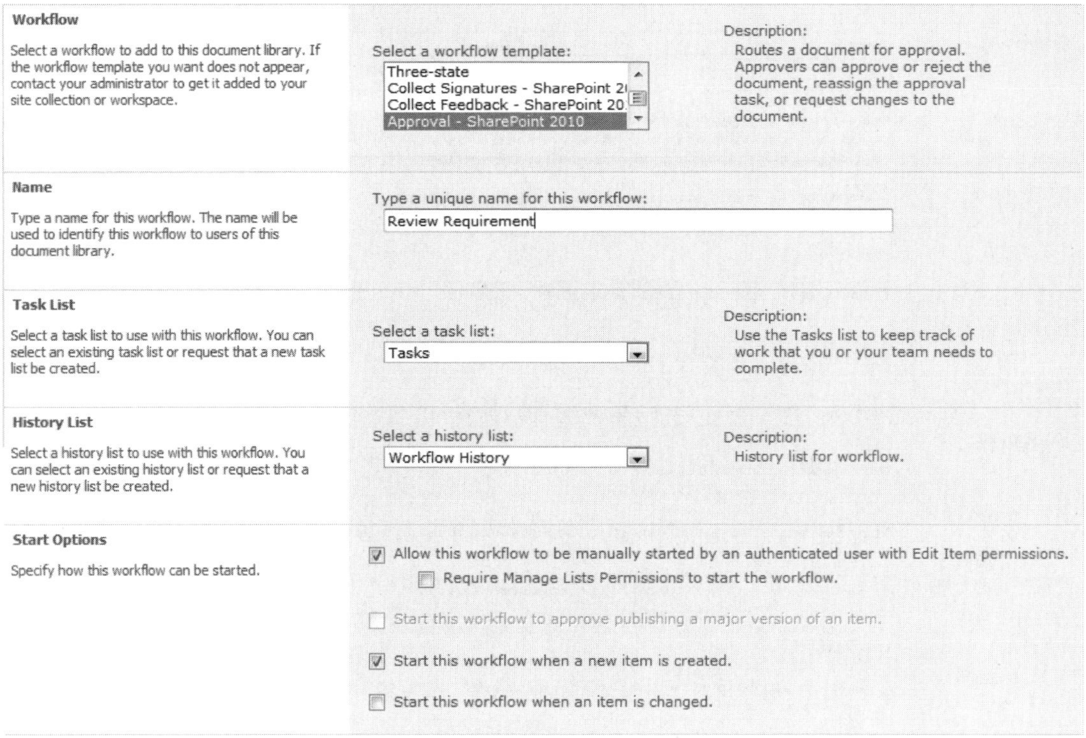

Figure 3-21. *The completed association page*

Select the Approval - SharePoint 2010 workflow. This workflow will create one or more tasks for someone to review and approve the document that the workflow is executed for. Enter the workflow name **Review Requirement**. You can use the default values for the task and history lists. The task list indicates the list that will contain the approval tasks that will be generated. The history list contains information about the execution of the workflow. Check the "Start this workflow when a new item is created" check box. This specifies that a workflow should be automatically started when a new item is added to the library. The completed form should look like Figure 3-21.

Click the Next button, which will display the workflow-specific page shown in Figure 3-22.

■**Note** When associating a workflow to a list or library, there are always two association forms. The first is a standard form (see Figure 3-21) that is used by all workflows. The second form is workflow specific (see Figure 3-22).

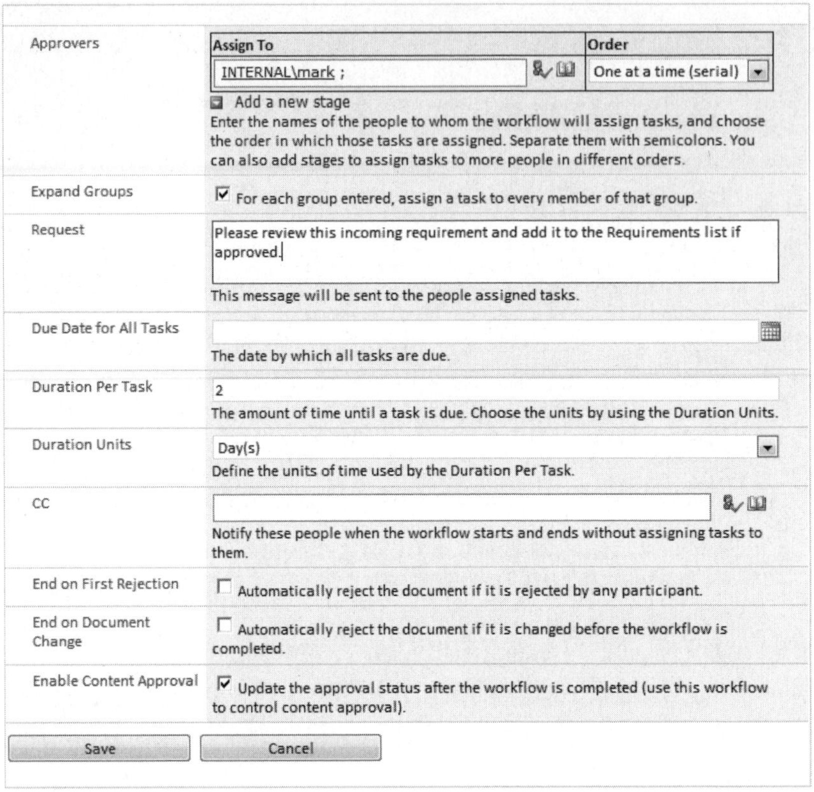

Figure 3-22. *The workflow-specific association page*

This workflow will create a task for each person that you have set up as a reviewer. In the Reviewers section, select a person or group that you want to review this requirement. If you select a group, the Expand Groups check box determines how the task should be assigned to the group. If Expand Groups is not selected, the task is assigned to the group, and anyone in the group can complete the task. If selected, a task is created for each person in the group. This means that every person in the group must review the document. If multiple tasks are created, the Order drop-down specifies whether they are assigned serially (one at a time) or in parallel (the reviews may be performed concurrently).

You can specify a due date for these tasks, either as a specific date or based on a duration from the time the task is assigned. I set this up for a duration of two days, which means that each reviewer will have two days to complete the task from the time it is assigned to them. Keep in mind that if you are using the serial option, the overall duration for the review process is compounded.

In the Reviewers section, you can also create additional stages. This allows you to fine-tune the review process. For example, you can have one person or group perform an initial review followed by a subsequent group once the first stage has completed.

Click the Save button to complete the association.

Testing the Workflow

The workflow is designed to start automatically when an item is added to the list. However, you can also start it manually. To start a workflow on an existing item, select the item in the list and then click the Workflow button in the Document ribbon. This will display the Workflows page shown in Figure 3-23.

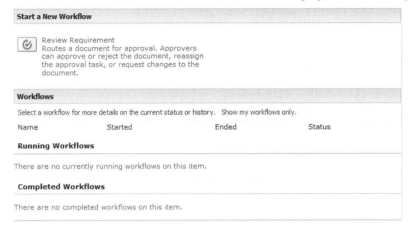

Figure 3-23. *The Workflows page*

This page shows all the workflows that have been associated with this list. Currently only the Review Requirement workflow is available. The page also shows the status of any currently running or completed workflow instances. Click the *Review Requirement* link to start this workflow.

Completing the Initiation Form

This will display a form that looks like the workflow-specific association form. This is called the *initiation* page, and it is often very similar to the association page. The association page defines all the default values for the workflow parameters. When starting a workflow manually, the initiation form is displayed so you can adjust the parameters that are sent to the workflow for this instance.

■**Note** When a workflow is started automatically, the initiation form is not used, and the values from the association form are used instead.

You can use all the default values on the initiation form or modify them if you prefer. Click the Start button to begin the workflow. After a few seconds, the Incoming Requirements library will be displayed. The Review Requirement column indicates the current status of that workflow. It should indicate In Progress, as shown in Figure 3-24.

Type	Name	Modified	Modified By	Review Requirement
📁	New Requirement	6/27/2010 7:39 PM	INTERNAL\mark	In Progress

✚ Add document

Figure 3-24. *The Incoming Requirements library showing an In Progress workflow*

Completing the Approval Task

The workflow should have created an approval task. Go to the Tasks list, and you should see a new item. Select this task, and the task form should look like Figure 3-25.

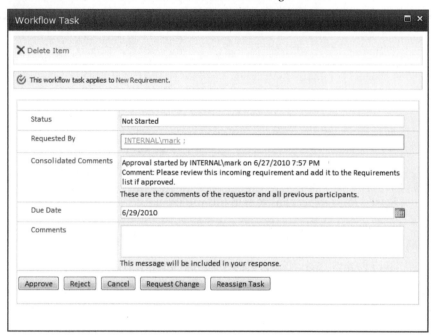

Figure 3-25. *The approval task form*

The top of this form states "This workflow task applies to *New Requirement*." If you click the *New Requirements* link, the folder containing the e-mail and its attachments will be displayed. The reviewer can examine the submitted requirements and add a new item to the Requirements list. When finished, they will click the Approve button on the task form. They could also choose to reject this requirement by clicking the Reject button. If the requirement is approved, the task will be marked Complete and the Incoming Requirements document will be marked Approved.

Summary

In this chapter you learned how to do the following:

- Create a document library that accepts incoming e-mails

- Implement a simple document approval workflow

You implemented these as part of the requirement-gathering process. As you work through the remaining chapters in this book, you will probably think of ways these techniques can be employed to facilitate other project management activities.

■■■

CHAPTER 4

Managing Requirements

In this chapter you'll enhance the `Requirements` list that you created in Chapter 2. First, you'll implement a way to score each requirement. This will provide a quantitative approach for determining which requirements should be implemented first. Then you'll add a feature to specify dependencies since some requirements will rely on other related requirements. With these enhancements you'll be able to more easily plan the project and decide which requirements are in scope.

Analyzing Requirements

As you start gathering requirements, you could have hundreds, even thousands of them. So how do you decide which to work on first?

Prioritizing Requirements

You should devise a mechanism for scoring each requirement based on a set of factors that fit your environment. A *factor* is an estimate of the impact that implementing this requirement would have. Some examples are:

- Improved customer service
- Time/money saved
- Increased market share

These factors can be either positive or negative. A factor such as time/money saved is a positive one; the more time saved, the better. You can also use negative factors such as required development or risk. Requirements that take more effort to implement would lower their overall score. This approach allows you to identify the low-hanging fruit; the items that have a big impact with relatively little effort.

The first step in this process is to decide on what factors work for you. When evaluating a requirement, what things about it would increase (or decrease) its importance? Ultimately, these should measure how implementing this requirement will help your organization fulfill its mission statement or operational objectives. Each factor should be assigned a relative weight, as some will have a bigger impact than others. I recommend using scale from –10 to 10 and assign the negative factors a negative weight. The most important positive factor should be given a 10 and all other factors should then be assigned a weight based on their relative importance.

■**Tip** If you use a scale with positive numbers only, such as 1 to 10, when computing an overall score, you'll need to remember to subtract the score for negative factors instead of adding them. Using negative numbers for the relative weight may seem a bit confusing, but it simplifies the subsequent computation.

The next step is to score each requirement against these factors. Use a score of 1 to 10. Again, assign a 10 to the highest requirement and then score the remaining ones relative to that one. This can be difficult to do because you may not have all the requirements identified yet. You may want to define scale to use for each factor. For example, for the development-required factor, you can specify the score to use for each predefined range of person-days to implement. For other factors this may be less quantitative, but it is a good idea to define some type of criteria so the scoring is consistent for all requirements.

There are some requirements that are, well, required. These are essential, non-negotiable requirements. These could be legal or operational constraints that are imposed on the project. Or they could be requirements that are so important that it would be pointless to implement the project without them. For these requirements, instead of scoring them, you'll just need to identify them as *required*.

Requirement Dependencies

Requirements should be detailed and specific. They may start out rather general, but as the process evolves they will be broken down into smaller, more specific requirements. At that level, requirements tend to be interrelated. For example, one requirement may be to collect sales tax and another to report the sales tax collected on the income report. In order to report on sales tax, the system must first collect it. In this case, the second requirement is dependent on the first.

When planning your project, you'll need to keep in mind how these requirements are related. A high-priority requirement may be dependent on a low-priority requirement. If the first is added to the project, the second must be also, even if it otherwise would fall below the cutoff line.

Another thing to be aware of is how breaking a requirement into smaller pieces can affect their individual scores. Take the sales tax scenario as an example. Collecting the tax may take a lot of effort and have little benefit, while the report may be easy and have more visibility. In this case, the first may get a low score and the second a much higher score. To compensate for this, you may want to score these together as a single requirement and give both the same score.

Adding Factors

You will need to add some columns to the Requirements list where you can score each of the factors. In the instructions that follow, I will use generic names like Factor1. You can do the same, but you will eventually need to decide on what factors you'll want to use and name these columns accordingly.

Using the List Settings Page

Open the `ProjectManagement` site that you used with the previous chapters and select the `Requirements` list. In the List ribbon, click the List Settings button, as shown in Figure 4-1.

Figure 4-1. *Selecting the list settings*

Scroll down to the Columns section and you'll see the columns that are currently defined for this list. This section should look like Figure 4-2.

Columns

A column stores information about each item in the list. Because this list allows multiple content types, some column settings, such as whether information is required or optional for a column, are now specified by the content type of the item. The following columns are currently available in this list:

Column (click to edit)	Type	Used in
Date Created	Date and Time	Requirement
Functional Area	Lookup	Requirement
Priority	Choice	Requirement
Requirement Description	Multiple lines of text	Requirement
Requirement Type	Choice	Requirement
Submitted By	Person or Group	Requirement
Title	Single line of text	Requirement
Created By	Person or Group	
Modified By	Person or Group	

Create column
Add from existing site columns
Indexed columns

Figure 4-2. *The Columns section of the Requirements list settings page*

Adding a Factor

Click the *Create column* link, which appears just after the list of existing columns. In the first section of the Create Column page, shown in Figure 4-3, you'll specify the name and the column type. For the column type, you have the same choices that you had when using SharePoint Designer in Chapter 2.

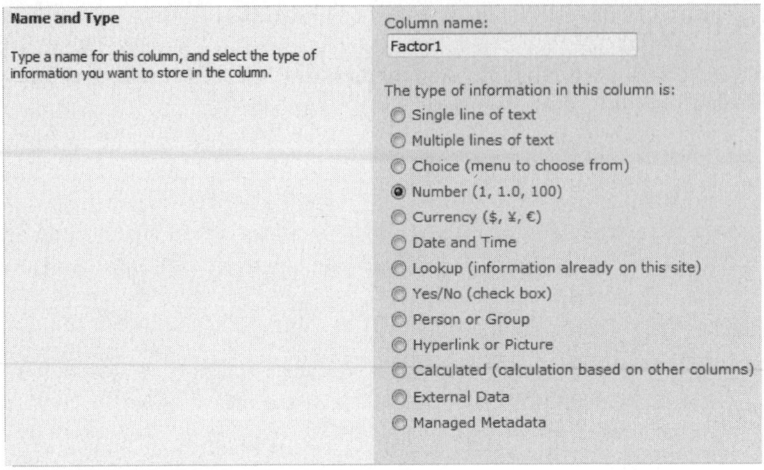

Figure 4-3. *Specifying the Name and Type*

Enter a name for this factor. I used Factor1, but you can choose a more meaningful name. For the type, select Number. Notice that the remainder of the page is updated based on your selection because each type has different options available. Enter the information in the Additional Columns Settings section, as shown in Figure 4-4.

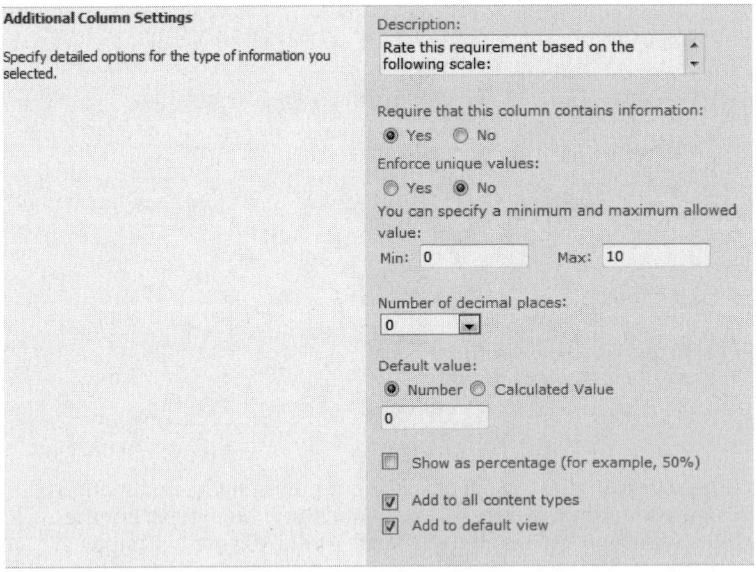

Figure 4-4. *The Additional Column Settings section*

The description only shows the first two lines of text, but you can have more than that. This is a good place to define the scale that should be used for this factor. Indicate that this column must have a value and specify the default value of 0. You can define the minimum and maximum values allowed for this column. Also, you should specify the number of decimal places to be zero since you're only working with whole numbers. If you click the "Add to all content types" check box, this column will also be added to the `Requirement` content type as well as the `Requirements` list. Click the OK button to add this column.

Adding Additional Factors

The List Settings page should be displayed, which will now include the new column. The columns are listed in alphabetical order, so the new column may not be at the end of the list. Repeat the following steps to add as many factors as you want:

1. Click the *Create column* link.

2. On the Create Column page, enter the name of the factor.

3. Specify the type as `Number`.

4. Enter a description for this factor (include scale information).

5. Require a value and set the default to 0.

6. Specify the minimum and maximum allowed values to 0 and 10, respectively.

7. Specify the number of decimal places as 0.

When you're done, the Column section of the List Settings page should look like Figure 4-5.

Columns

A column stores information about each item in the list. Because this list allows multiple content types, some column settings, such as whether information is required or optional for a column, are now specified by the content type of the item. The following columns are currently available in this list:

Column (click to edit)	Type	Used in
Date Created	Date and Time	Requirement
Factor1	Number	Requirement
Factor2	Number	Requirement
Factor3	Number	Requirement
Factor4	Number	Requirement
Factor5	Number	Requirement
Functional Area	Lookup	Requirement
Priority	Choice	Requirement
Requirement Description	Multiple lines of text	Requirement
Requirement Type	Choice	Requirement
Submitted By	Person or Group	Requirement
Title	Single line of text	Requirement
Created By	Person or Group	
Modified By	Person or Group	

Figure 4-5. *The updated column list*

Scoring a Requirement

Now that the factors have been added to the list, edit one of the existing requirements and specify the score for each factor. For each factor there should be a field that looks like Figure 4-6.

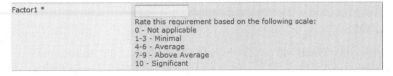

Figure 4-6. *Entering a factor score*

The description that you entered for this factor is displayed below the text box. You can place text here that will help the user enter consistent and accurate scores. The asterisk next to the factor name indicates that this is a required field.

■**Note** For new requirements, the score for each factor should default to 0. However, the default value logic is only applied when the item is first created. Since this is an existing record, the factors are all blank, and the edit form should require you to enter a value for each before you can save the record.

After entering a score for each factor, the requirement should look like Figure 4-7.

☐ ID	🔗	Title	Functional Area	Requirement Type	Date Created	Submitted By	Factor1	Factor2	Factor3	Factor4	Factor5
1		Income Report	Accounting	Deliverable	6/22/2010 2:15 PM	INTERNAL\mark	1	3	5	7	9

Figure 4-7. *A newly scored requirement*

Calculating the Overall Score

Now that you have scored the requirements using the defined factors, it would be very useful to compute an overall score based on relative weight of each of the factors. To do that, you'll use a calculated column.

The overall score is computed by multiplying the score for that factor by the relative weight assigned to the factor. These products are then summed to arrive at the overall score. The relative weights are fixed; they are the same for all requirements. The actual scores can be different for each requirement. For example, assume Factor1 has a relative weight of 10, Factor2 has a relative weight of 5, and Factor3 has a weight of –7. In this case Factor1 is twice as important as Factor2. Factor3 is somewhere between these but has a negative value because the higher the score, the less desirable this requirement is.

In this scenario, the overall score is computed by adding the score for Factor1 × 10, plus the score for Factor2 × 5, plus the score for Factor3 × –7.

Adding a Calculated Column

The value of a Calculated column is determined by a formula that you specify. This formula can include other columns in the list, as well as many built-in functions.

From the List ribbon, click the List Setting button. In the List Settings page, click the *Create column* link just like you did to add the factors. For the column name, enter **Overall Score** and select the Calculated column type. Enter the formula as follows:

=([Factor1]*5)+([Factor2]*7)+([Factor3]*10)+([Factor4]*-4)+([Factor5]*2)

This formula simply multiplies each factor score by the relative weight determined for that factor and then adds up the products. You may have different column names. Instead of these generic names, use the correct column names from your Requirements list. Also, the weights I used are just random numbers; you will need to use the weighted values that you determined for each factor.

■**Tip**   To add a column to the formula, you can select the column from the list box to the right of the formula and click the *Add to formula* link. When a column is used in a formula and the name contains spaces, it must be enclosed by square brackets (i.e., [ ]).

Change the data type returned to Number and set the number of decimal places to 0. The completed form should look like Figure 4-8.

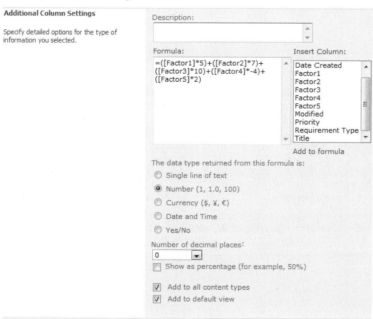

Figure 4-8. *Entering a Calculated column definition*

Click the Save button to add this column. Select the Requirements list and you should now see the Overall Score column in the view.

■**Tip** For more information about formulas in a Calculated column, go to http://msdn.microsoft.com/en-us/library/bb862071.aspx. This page provides lots of examples of formulas that perform string manipulation, mathematical and statistical functions, date comparisons and formatting, and conditional logic.

Modifying the View

The Overall Score should have been added to the default view. Now that you have this column, you probably don't need the individual factor scores in the view. From the List ribbon, click the Modify View button, as shown in Figure 4-9.

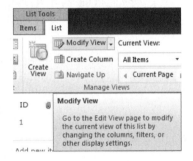

Figure 4-9. *Clicking the Modify View button*

On the Edit View page, unselect the factor columns (Factor1, Factor2, etc., or whatever you named your columns). Make sure you leave Overall Score checked. Click the OK button to save your changes. The Requirements list should now look like Figure 4-10.

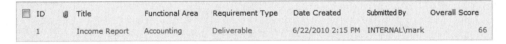

ID	ⓤ	Title	Functional Area	Requirement Type	Date Created	Submitted By	Overall Score
1		Income Report	Accounting	Deliverable	6/22/2010 2:15 PM	INTERNAL\mark	66

Figure 4-10. *The default view with the overall score*

The view form still shows the individual factor scores, as demonstrated in Figure 4-11.

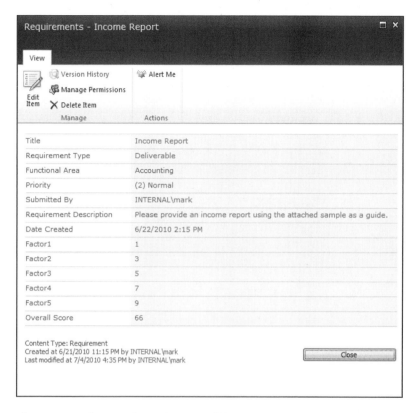

Figure 4-11. *The View form showing all factor scores*

Supporting Non-Negotiable Requirements

Before you finish up this feature, you'll add a flag to indicate that this is a required (or non-negotiable) requirement.

Adding the Required Flag

Go to the List Settings page and click the *Create column* link. On the Create Column page, enter the name as **Required** and choose the Yes/No column type. Select the default value of No because, hopefully, most of your requirements will not fall into this category. The completed form should look like Figure 4-12.

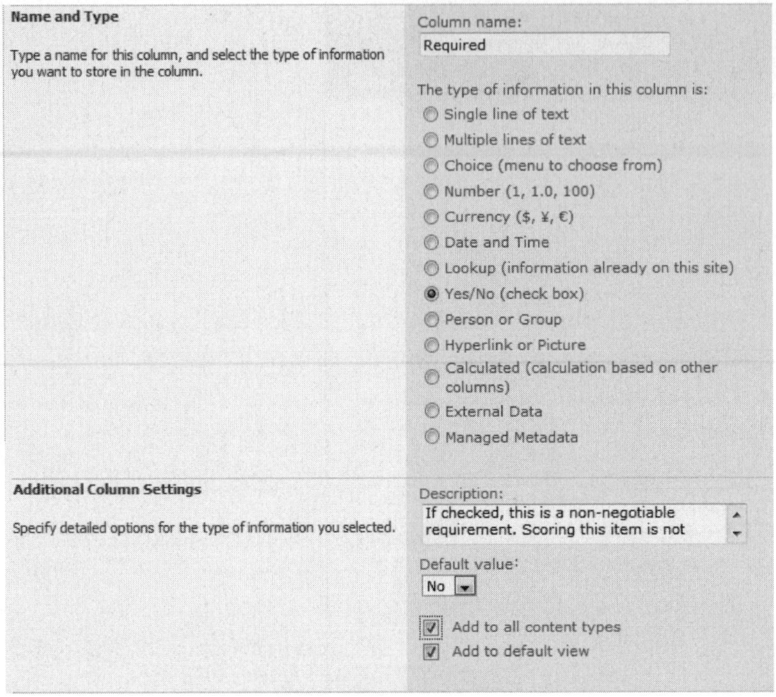

Figure 4-12. *Creating the Required column*

Modifying the Overall Score Formula

For required items, the score is not applicable. To avoid any confusion, it would be best to not display a score (even if the user enters values for one or more factors). To do that, modify the Overall Score formula to return 0 if it has the Required flag. From the List Settings page, select the Overall Score column. Modify the formula as follows:

=IF(Required,0,(Factor1*5)+(Factor2*7)+(Factor3*10)+(Factor4*-4)+(Factor5*2))

If the Required flag is set, the formula returns 0.

■**Note** The square brackets are not required if the column name does not have spaces. Notice that they have been removed from the formula that you originally entered.

Sorting the View

The last step is to sort the list so that required and higher-scoring items are at the top. Go back to the Requirements list and click the Modify View button from the List ribbon. In the Sort section, choose

Required as the first sort column and select the "Show items in descending order" option. Then choose Overall Score as the second sort column, and also use the descending-order option for this column. The completed section should look like Figure 4-13.

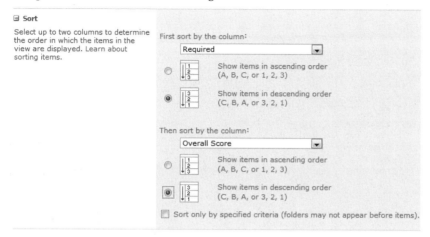

Figure 4-13. *Specifying the sort criteria*

The default view should now sort the requirements, putting the required items first and then sorting the remaining items based on their overall score. The view should look like Figure 4-14.

ID		Title	Functional Area	Requirement Type	Date Created	Submitted By	Overall Score	Required
2		Tax Reports ▣ NEW	Accounting	Legal Constraint	7/2/2010 12:00 AM	INTERNAL\mark	0	Yes
3		Disable Inactive Logons ▣ NEW	Human Resources	Use Case	7/5/2010 12:00 AM	INTERNAL\mark	153	No
1		Income Report	Accounting	Deliverable	6/22/2010 2:15 PM	INTERNAL\mark	66	No

Figure 4-14. *The sorted view*

Supporting Dependencies

The next feature that you'll implement is to provide the ability to define dependencies between individual requirements.

Adding a Lookup Column

You'll now enhance the Requirements list to allow you to specify dependencies. You'll do this using a multivalued Lookup column. From the List Settings page, click the *Create column* link. On the Create Column page, enter the name as **Dependencies** and select the Lookup column type.

In the Additional Column Settings section, select the Requirements list from the "Get information from" drop-down box. Select Title as the column to be used, which should be the default value. Check the "Allow multiple values" check box. This will allow a requirement to define multiple dependencies. The completed form should look like Figure 4-15.

Additional Column Settings

Specify detailed options for the type of information you selected.

Description:

List other requirements that this requirement is dependent on.

Require that this column contains information:
○ Yes ◉ No

Enforce unique values:
○ Yes ◉ No

Get information from:
Requirements ▾

In this column:
Title ▾
☑ Allow multiple values

Add a column to show each of these additional fields:
☐ Title
☐ Date Created
☐ Factor1
☐ Factor2
☐ Factor3
☐ Factor4
☐ Factor5
☐ ID
☐ Modified
☐ Created
☐ Version
☐ Title (linked to item)

☑ Add to all content types

☑ Add to default view

Figure 4-15. *Specifying the additional column settings*

Click the Save button to create the new column.

Adding a Dependency

Go to the Requirements list, select one of the items, and edit it. The edit form should include the Dependencies column, as shown in Figure 4-16.

Dependencies

Disable Inactive Logons
Income Report
Tax Reports

Add >

< Remove

List other requirements that this requirement is dependent on.

Figure 4-16. *Editing the dependencies*

Because the column supports multiple values, the edit form lists all the requirements (in alphabetical order) and provides an Add button to add an item to the Dependencies list. You can also select an existing dependency and use the Remove button to remove it from the Dependencies list.

Select one of the other requirements, click the Add button, and then save the form. The view will be displayed, and the selected requirement will be shown in the Dependencies list. The view should look like Figure 4-17.

ID		Title	Functional Area	Requirement Type	Date Created	Submitted By	Overall Score	Required	Dependencies
2		Tax Reports ☑ NEW	Accounting	Legal Constraint	7/2/2010 12:00 AM	INTERNAL\mark	0	Yes	Income Report
3		Disable Inactive Logons ☑ NEW	Human Resources	Use Case	7/5/2010 12:00 AM	INTERNAL\mark	153	No	
1		Income Report	Accounting	Deliverable	6/22/2010 2:15 PM	INTERNAL\mark	66	No	

Figure 4-17. *The updated view showing the dependencies*

Summary

In this chapter you provided a facility for scoring each requirement based on specific factors. The overall score was then calculated based on the weighted value of each factor. You also added a flag to indicate those requirements that are non-negotiable. Finally, the view was sorted to put higher-priority requirements at the top of the list. This allows you to easily see the more important requirements. You also implemented a feature for defining dependencies between individual requirements.

In this chapter, instead of using SharePoint Designer, you used the List Settings page in SharePoint to modify the Requirements list and the underlying Requirement content type. You used a Calculated column to compute the overall score and a multivalued Lookup column to specify dependencies.

CHAPTER 5

■ ■ ■

Supporting Discussions

Often during the requirement-gathering process there can be negotiation between individuals before arriving at the final requirement. While the final result is the primary artifact used for managing the project, sometimes the internal discussion can be a useful reference. In this chapter I'll show you how to add discussions to your SharePoint site. Specifically, you will do the following:

1. Create a discussion list, which will allow users to post comments and respond to previous posts.

2. Link a discussion to a specific requirement so you can organize the discussions.

3. Try different ways of displaying the various threads within a discussion.

4. Use web parts to display both a requirement and the related discussion on the same page.

5. Use Outlook to view the discussion and post replies.

■Note   A discussion board in SharePoint is implemented as a list containing the Discussion content type. The Discussion content type is derived from the Folder content type and is basically a specialized folder. The items that individuals post to a discussion use the Message content type and are stored in the Discussion folder. In addition to storing the contents of the posted message, the Message content type has several columns that are used for maintaining the discussion threads. Users don't always reply to the last post; sometimes they reply to a previous post, which starts another thread. SharePoint provides several view formats to allow you to see the posts and the threads they are part of.

Adding the Requirement Discussions List

Open the ProjectManagement site that you have been using. From the Site Actions menu, select the *More Options* link. Filter the options to List types, only and select the Discussion Board template. Enter the name **Requirement Discussions**, as shown in Figure 5-1.

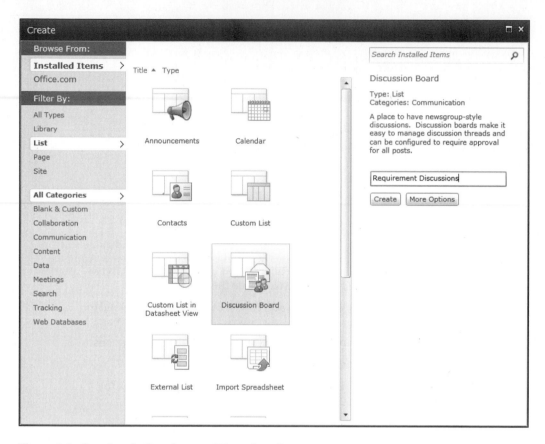

Figure 5-1. *Creating the Requirement Discussions list*

Open the List Settings page. Notice that this list supports two content types, Discussion and Message, as explained earlier and demonstrated in Figure 5-2.

Content Types

This list is configured to allow multiple content types. Use content types to specify the information you want to display about an item, in addition to its policies, workflows, or other behavior. The following content types are currently available in this list:

Content Type	Visible on New Button	Default Content Type
Discussion	✔	✔
Message	✔	

Figure 5-2. *Supported content types*

Discussion is the default content type. You normally start by adding a discussion and then adding messages (posts) to a discussion.

Linking the Related Requirement

Now you'll link the discussion with the related requirement. To do that, you'll add a Lookup column to
the new Requirement Discussions list. Click the *Create column* link. Enter the name **Requirement** and
select the Lookup column type. In the Additional Column Settings section, make this a required field, but
don't require unique values. At first it might seem like a good idea to require unique values, as it would
prevent someone from creating multiple discussions for the same requirement. However, this would
also prevent you from having multiple messages posted to the discussion. A discussion with only one
message is not very interesting.

Select Requirements as the related table and choose the Title column to be displayed. The
completed section should look like Figure 5-3.

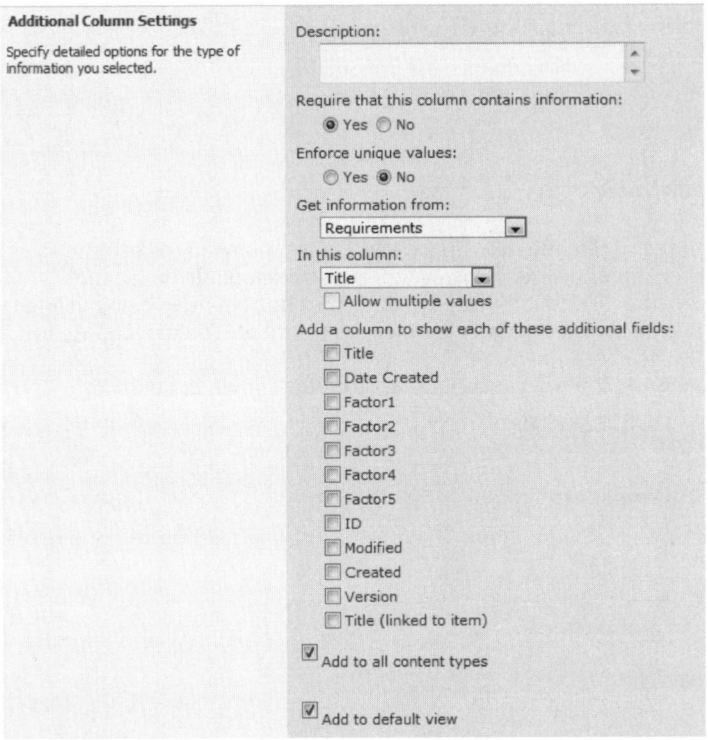

Figure 5-3. *Specifying the relationship*

Handling Deleted Records

The Relationship section at the bottom of the Create Column page provides options for enforcing
referential integrity. The new list, Requirement Discussions, will have a column that references a record
in the Requirements list. Referential integrity ensures that you can't remove the referenced requirement
without first removing the reference to it. By default, the "Enforce relationship behavior" check box is
unchecked. With this setting, referential integrity is ignored. If the related requirement is deleted, this list

will have a broken link. In other words, the `Requirement Discussions` item will refer to a `Requirements` item that no longer exists.

It is generally a good idea to handle this to avoid the broken-link scenario. SharePoint provides two options. The "Restrict delete" option will prevent users from deleting a `Requirements` item if it has a `Requirement Discussions` item referencing it. The "Cascade delete" option will delete all related objects. If the `Requirements` item is deleted, the related `Requirement Discussions` item, if there is one, will also be deleted. Figure 5-4 shows the options and the text provided to explain these options.

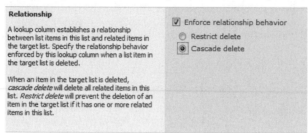

Figure 5-4. *Cascading deletes in the related table*

In this scenario, the cascade option seems like the right approach. There's no need to keep the discussion details if the requirement is no longer needed. However, it is also reasonable to use the restrict option to force the user to remove the discussion details first. If the requirement is being deleted because it is a duplicate, the discussion should be moved to the other requirement. You can choose to use the restrict option if you prefer.

Click the Save button to add this column. You will probably see the dialog shown in Figure 5-5.

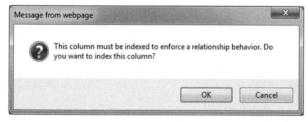

Figure 5-5. *Adding an index on the related column*

In order to efficiently enforce this relationship, the system requires an index on the new column so it can easily perform a reverse lookup. Click OK to allow the index to be created.

Adding a Discussion

Select the new `Requirement Discussions` list and click the *Add new discussion* link. Enter the subject and add a comment to the body. Select an existing item from the Requirement drop-down list, as shown in Figure 5-6. Click the Save button to add the record.

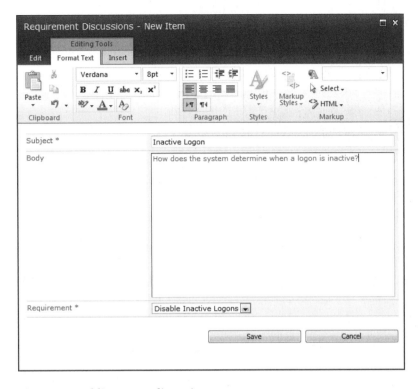

Figure 5-6. *Adding a new discussion*

A new discussion will be added to the list, as shown in Figure 5-7.

Figure 5-7. *The Requirement Discussions list with a newly added discussion*

Click the Subject, *Inactive Logon,* in the list, which is a link to open the discussion. The discussion will be displayed in *flat view,* as shown in Figure 5-8.

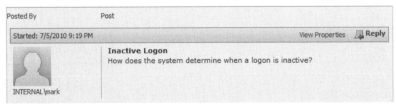

Figure 5-8. *Displaying the discussion in flat view*

Using the Discussion Feature

Click the *Reply* link on the post and enter a response. The edit form will look like Figure 5-9. You just need to type the response. The subject and related requirement are defaulted from the initial post. (In fact, the subject cannot be changed when posting a reply.)

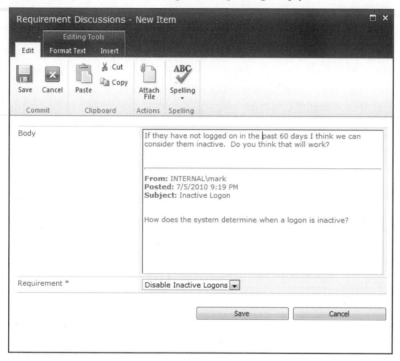

Figure 5-9. *Adding a reply*

Try creating several replies where at least one of them is replied from a previous post (not from the last post) to generate a new thread. The flat view lists all the posts in simple chronological order, as shown in Figure 5-10.

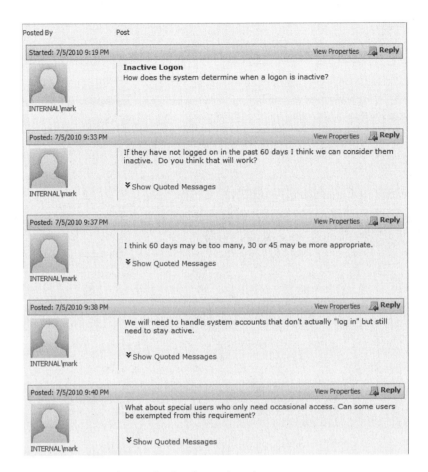

Figure 5-10. *Displaying the flat discussion view*

■**Note**   Please ignore the fact that it looks like I'm talking to myself in this thread. In a real scenario, these posts would be entered by different users.

From the List ribbon, switch to threaded view, as shown in Figure 5-11.

Figure 5-11. *Switching the discussion view*

The same discussion in threaded view is shown in Figure 5-12.

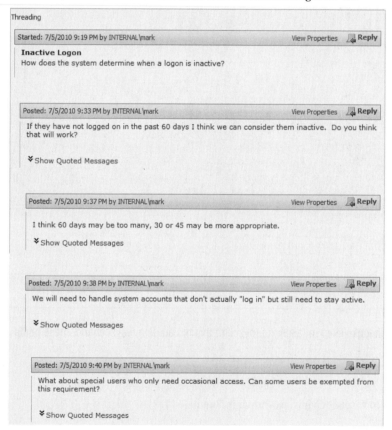

Figure 5-12. *Displaying the discussion in threaded view*

Apart from the fact that the user's picture is not shown, you should also note the indentation, which helps to show the message threads. Notice that the third and fourth posts are indented the same amount. That is because both of these were replies to the second post. If you click the *Show Quoted*

Messages link, the full message chain is displayed so you can see exactly which message chain this reply was made to.

Choosing the Default View

The `Requirement Discussion` list was created with three standard views. You can see these listed in the Views section of the List Settings page, which should look like Figure 5-13.

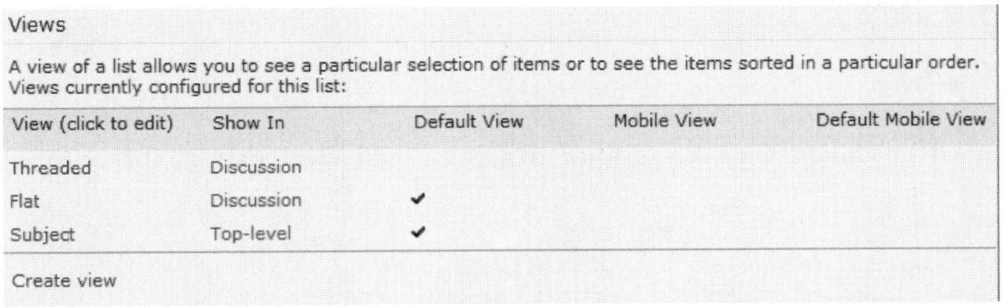

Figure 5-13. *Listing the standard views*

When the list is first selected, the `Subject` view is used to display the top-level information. This view lists each of the discussions along with general information, such as the number of replies. An example of this is shown in Figure 5-7. The two other views, `Threaded` and `Flat`, are used when a discussion is selected. These views show the details of the messages that were posted in this discussion. As you can see, flat view is selected as the default view for discussion mode.

To change the default view, click the *Threaded* link, which will display the Edit View page. Check the "Make this the default view" check box, as shown in Figure 5-14.

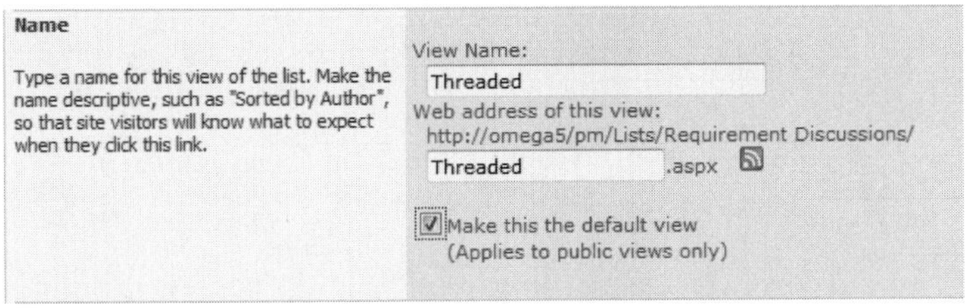

Figure 5-14. *Selecting the default view option*

Now when you select a discussion from the `Requirements Discussions` list, threaded view will be displayed by default.

Combining Lists

At this point you have the `Requirements` list, which contains the details of the actual requirement, and the `Requirement Discussions` list, which includes the history of posts related to this requirement. It would be really helpful to combine these into one list, or at least put both on one page. I'll now show you two ways you can accomplish that.

Adding a Web Part

Select the Requirements list, and from the List ribbon, select the Modify Form Web Parts button, as shown in Figure 5-15. In the context menu, select the *Default Display Form* link.

Figure 5-15. *Modifying the Web Parts*

The existing display form will be shown, with the addition of a link to add a web part, as shown in Figure 5-16.

Main

Add a Web Part

Requirements	▾ ☑
Title	Title field value.
Requirement Type	Other
Functional Area	
Priority	(2) Normal
Submitted By	
Requirement Description	Requirement Description field value.
Date Created	7/5/2010 5:42 PM
Factor1	0
Factor2	0
Factor3	0
Factor4	0
Factor5	0
Overall Score	
Required	Yes
Dependencies	

Content Type: Requirement
Created at 7/5/2010 5:42 PM by
Last modified at 7/5/2010 5:42 PM by

Close

Figure 5-16. *The existing display form*

Click the *Add a Web Part* link. The top part of the form allows you to search for an existing web part that can be added to the form. From the Lists and Libraries category, select the Requirement Discussions list, as shown in Figure 5-17.

Figure 5-17. *Adding the Requirement Discussions list*

Defining the Connection

This will add the entire list to the form. However, you only want the discussion that is related to the current requirement. To accomplish that you'll now set up a filter.

■**Tip** SharePoint provides a sophisticated framework that allows web parts to communicate with other web parts. The work is done primarily in the web parts themselves, so assembling existing web parts is a fairly easy task. For more information and web part connections, see the article at http://msdn.microsoft.com/en-us/library/ms178187.aspx.

If you hover the mouse over the Requirement Discussions list, a down arrow will appear. Click it to display the context menu. Select the *Connections* link, then the *Get Filter Values From* link, and finally the *Requirements* link, as shown in Figure 5-18.

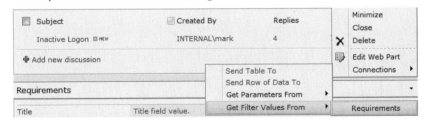

Figure 5-18. *Selecting the filter menu*

The will display the Configure Connection dialog box shown in Figure 5-19. Choose the ID column for the provider field name and the Requirement column for the consumer field name.

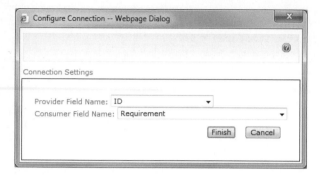

Figure 5-19. *Specifying the connection properties*

■Note The `Requirement Discussions` web part is the consumer of the connection. It uses the information provided to it to filter the discussion list. The `Requirements` list in the bottom web part is the provider, passing the `ID` of the current requirement to the discussion list.

Click the Finish button to update the connection. The `Requirement Discussions` list will now be empty because there is no currently selected requirement, as shown in Figure 5-20.

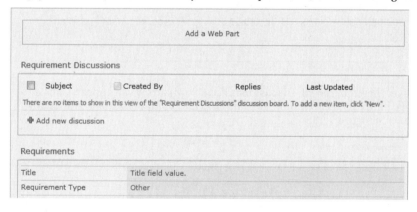

Figure 5-20. *The updated form with the new web part*

Testing the Display Form

Click the Stop Editing button in the ribbon to go back to the `Requirements` list. Select the requirement that you added the discussion to and choose the *View Item* link from the context menu. The display form should look like Figure 5-21.

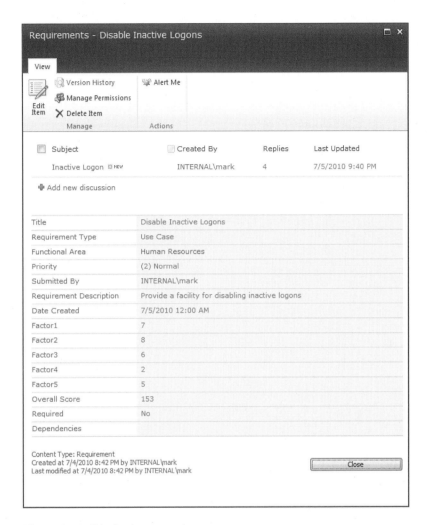

Figure 5-21. *Displaying a requirement*

The bottom portion looks like it used to, but the top now shows the summary of the related discussion. If you click *Inactive Logon*, which is a link to view the discussion, the threaded discussion view should be displayed, as shown in Figure 5-22.

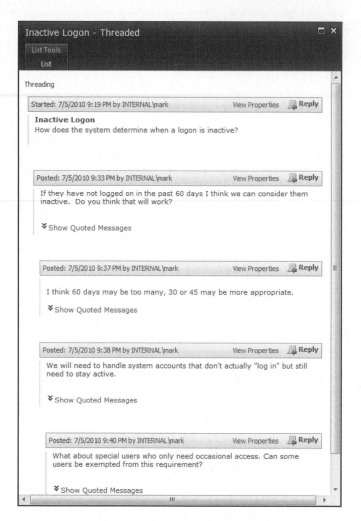

Figure 5-22. *Displaying the threaded discussion view*

■**Note** Now that you've added a web part to the display form, you could also follow these instructions to add the same web part to the edit form.

Creating a New Web Page

Another way to combine two lists is to create a new page and put two web parts on the page. This provides a little different approach for navigating the requirements, as you'll see.

Adding a Page to the SharePoint Site

From the Site Actions menu, click the *New Page* link, as shown in Figure 5-23.

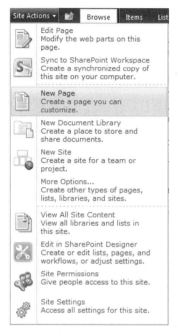

Figure 5-23. *Adding a new page to the site*

In the New Page dialog box, enter the page name **View Requirements**, as shown in Figure 5-24.

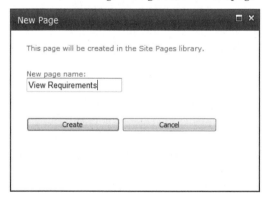

Figure 5-24. *Specifying the page name*

Click the Check Out button in the ribbon, as shown in Figure 5-25. This will allow you to edit the page.

Figure 5-25. *Checking out the new page*

From the Insert ribbon, click the Web Part button, as shown in Figure 5-26.

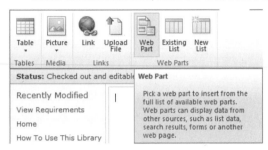

Figure 5-26. *Adding a web part to the page*

The top part of the form will allow you to select an existing web part. Select the `Requirements` list from the `Lists and Libraries` category and click the Add button.

Adding a Related List

Select the `Requirements` web part by clicking the check box in the upper right-hand corner of the web part. When you do that, the Web Part Tools ribbon should become available. Click the *Options* link and then click the Insert Related List button, as shown in Figure 5-27.

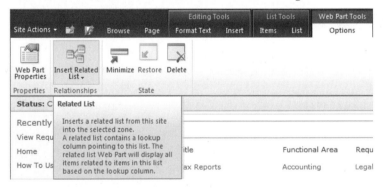

Figure 5-27. *Inserting a related list*

Select the `Requirement Discussions` list. You should now have both web parts loaded on the page, which should look like Figure 5-28.

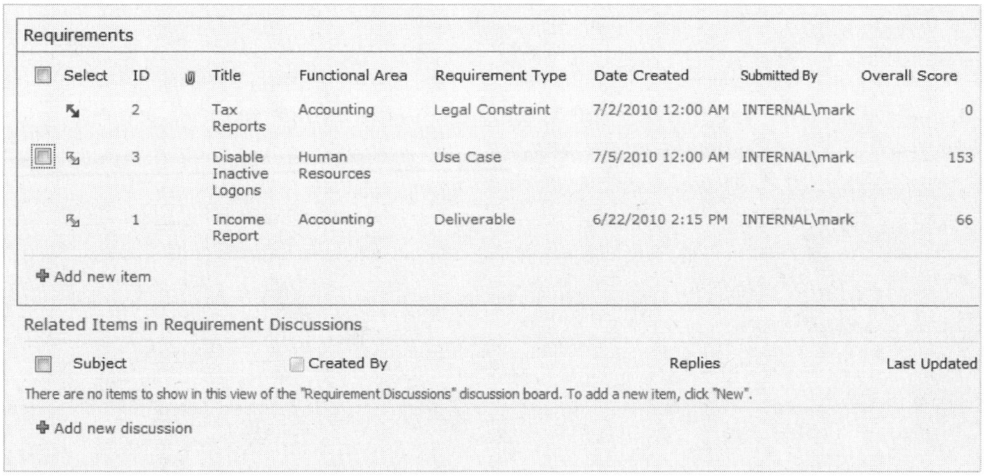

Requirements							
☐ Select	ID	🔗	Title	Functional Area	Requirement Type	Date Created	Submitted By	Overall Score
↖	2		Tax Reports	Accounting	Legal Constraint	7/2/2010 12:00 AM	INTERNAL\mark	0
☐ ⎙	3		Disable Inactive Logons	Human Resources	Use Case	7/5/2010 12:00 AM	INTERNAL\mark	153
⎙	1		Income Report	Accounting	Deliverable	6/22/2010 2:15 PM	INTERNAL\mark	66

✚ Add new item

Related Items in Requirement Discussions

☐ Subject	☐ Created By	Replies	Last Updated

There are no items to show in this view of the "Requirement Discussions" discussion board. To add a new item, click "New".

✚ Add new discussion

Figure 5-28. *The new page with both web parts*

From the Editing Tools ribbon, click the Save & Close button to save the changes, as shown in Figure 5-29.

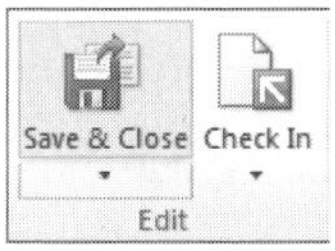

Figure 5-29. *Saving the changes to the web page*

To test the web part connection, select the requirement that you added the discussion to. The related Requirement Discussions item should be displayed below the Requirements list, as shown in Figure 5-30.

Figure 5-30. *The related discussion displayed below the Requirements list*

If you click the *Inactive Logon* link, the threaded view will be displayed, showing all the messages that have been posted.

■**Caution**   Make sure you check the page back in. The checked-out banner will continue to be displayed to remind you until the page is checked in.

Using Outlook

Before I finish this chapter, I want to show you how you can use Outlook to view and post messages to the discussions.

Configuring the Outlook List

Select the Requirement Discussions list. From the List ribbon, click the Connect to Outlook button, as shown in Figure 5-31.

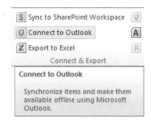

Figure 5-31. *Connecting the discussion to Outlook*

You will probably see a pop-up dialog box like the one shown in Figure 5-32. Click the Allow button to allow the SharePoint site to update your Outlook client.

Figure 5-32. *Dialog box requesting permission to update Outlook.*

This will be followed by another dialog box displayed by Outlook, shown in Figure 5-33, confirming that you want to add this discussion to Outlook. Click the Yes button to associate the list. You can also click the Advanced button if you want to configure this discussion list.

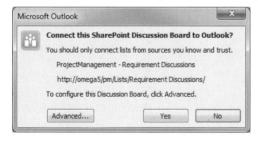

Figure 5-33. *Outlook's confirmation dialog box*

Viewing Discussions in Outlook

Within a few seconds, an offline copy of the `Requirement Discussions` list will be created in Outlook. You can select a discussion and expand the message details to see all the messages that have been posted. The Outlook list will look like Figure 5-34.

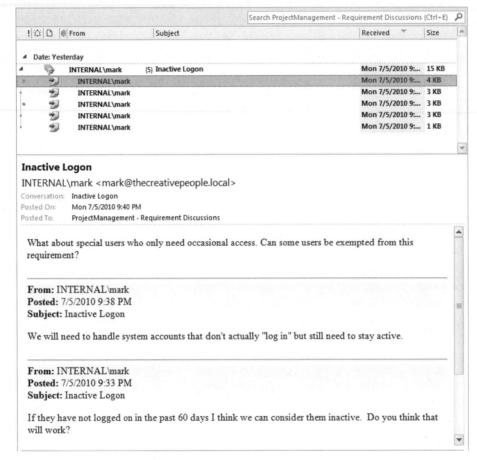

Figure 5-34. *Outlook's view of the Requirement Discussions list*

Outlook has a different way of showing the message threads. Notice the color-coded dots in the top portion of this page.

Posting a Reply

You can also post a reply from Outlook. Select one of the messages and click the Post Reply button. Enter a comment, as shown in Figure 5-35.

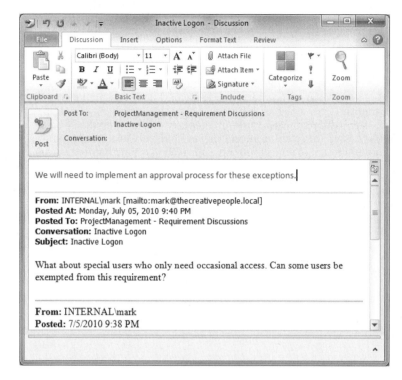

Figure 5-35. *Posting a reply from Outlook*

Outlook uses an offline cache of the data in SharePoint. When you post a reply, it is stored in the local cache, but the server is not updated until a send-and-receive operation is performed. This will synchronize all changes between the server and the local cache. If you refresh the SharePoint page, the new post should be displayed, as shown in Figure 5-36.

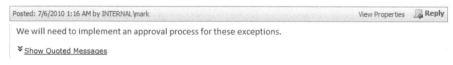

Figure 5-36. *New post from Outlook updated in SharePoint*

■**Tip**   Keep in mind that Outlook uses a local copy of the discussion list, which is automatically synchronized with the server. This allows you to view and even post responses while disconnected from the network. Changes are synchronized with the server when the client has been reconnected with the server.

Summary

In this chapter you created a discussion list to record the internal comments that naturally occur when defining requirements. Using Outlook to view and send messages, this process is just as easy as the traditional method of sending e-mails. However, with this approach the comments are stored in a central location and automatically tied to the related requirements. You won't have to search through your inbox to find a particular comment.

You also used web parts to provide two different ways to simultaneously display both the requirement and the discussion details. Using web parts is a great way to build very useful forms and web pages by combining existing SharePoint data. You will use this approach in other chapters as well.

■ ■ ■

PART 2

Managing Development

In this section, I'll address the activities that typically occur when managing the project implementation. This includes organizing the requirements into appropriately sized pieces, prioritizing and planning the development of those pieces, and tracking the overall progress of both the work performed and the work remaining. This represents a major part of the resource expenditure and often receives a great deal of management attention. Knowing how much work is left to do and when you're likely to finish is the dream of every project manager. The techniques presented here will help you accomplish that.

I have chosen to design the solutions in this section around the agile methodology. This is a widely adopted approach with lots of successful agile projects to its credit. If you've done any agile development, the process and terminology should be familiar to you. If you're not using the agile approach, the techniques provided here can be adapted to suit your environment. Read through these chapters and apply the pieces that fit.

In Chapter 6 you'll provide a list that will contain user stories, which is a way of breaking the project into implementable and deliverable chunks. These can be linked to the requirements, which allow you to trace the mapping between requirements and implementation. In Chapter 7 you'll add a project backlog as a view into these stories. This is sometimes called the *stack* and represents the work left to be done. In Chapter

8 you'll provide the ability to group these into iterations (also called *sprints*).

In Chapter 9 you'll support the remaining work items, which include tasks, issues, and defects. Finally, in Chapter 10, you'll provide various metrics to provide visibility into the overall project progress, including burn-down charts.

CHAPTER 6

■ ■ ■

User Stories

In this chapter you'll provide a facility for defining user stories, which is a handy technique for capturing the functionality of the project. I'll first explain what user stories are and then show you how to create a SharePoint list to store them.

Defining User Stories

In agile development, a user story is used to describe a piece of the system. It may be thought of as a specific feature that should be implemented or a particular interaction that needs to occur. The approach is to divide the entire project into a set of user stories. If you were building a house, for example, the list of user stories might look something like this:

- Pour footings.

- Lay the foundation.

- Frame the first floor.

- Frame the second floor.

- Rough-in the electrical service.

Each of these is a demonstrable piece of the finished work. You can visually inspect and verify that the unit of work is indeed complete. You can't say that the foundation is 95 percent complete. If you have obtained a construction loan, the bank will want proof that the planned user stories have been completed before additional funds are released.

In the same way, user stories are an effective way to access the status of a project. When writing the user stories for your project, try to find items that demonstrate real progress. Each user story should deliver something of value. The initial stories may be somewhat trivial. Even displaying "Hello, World!" can sometimes be meaningful if it proves that some particular infrastructure is working.

A user story must be small enough so that it can be completed by a single person in a short amount of time (usually one to four weeks). At the risk of oversimplifying, a user story defines a piece of demonstrable work. Throughout the project, these pieces are refined, prioritized, scheduled, and completed.

Describing User Stories

With the agile methodology, a user story is initially written at a very high level. It's almost like a placeholder or a reminder to do something. For example, it might be as simple as, "Provide an order entry form." The initial definition must be sufficient, however, to communicate the general idea; both users and developers can visualize an order-entry form without needing to define the specific fields or tab order.

In a "pure" agile project, user stories are written on a 3×5-inch index card. Using a small card forces the information to be kept at a very high level. The cards can then be reordered by simply rearranging them in the stack. We will, of course, implement this electronically. A sample user story is shown in Figure 6-1.

Provide the ability to create a login
Who: Public user
What: Create a login
Why: To access provided services
Priority: **Must**
Story Points: **2**
Details:

Figure 6-1. *A sample user story*

The user story definition must be sufficient to allow the users or stakeholders to define a priority for the user story. Priority can be defined as simply as high, medium, or low, or you could assign a number from 1 to 5. Three or four levels should be sufficient. One particularly creative definition is Must, Should, Could, and Won't. These properties provide a connotation that may help your users specify the appropriate priority.

Some agile approaches require a more formal approach to defining user stories. For example, they might require that each story be defined in terms of *who* is doing *what* and *why* they are doing it. The preceding story could be written in a more formal style, as "A salesperson (*who*) needs to enter an order (*what*) to fulfill a customer's needs (*why*)." The formal approach tends to force you to think a little bit before writing the user story.

User stories can be grouped into *themes*. This will help you organize the stories, especially on larger projects. Themes can be based on functional areas, technology, or any other logical grouping that works for you.

An important aspect of user stories is that a developer should be able to provide a high-level estimate of work required to complete it. This is because user stories are implemented in relatively short iterations. (I'll cover iterations in more detail in Chapter 7.) If you're using two-week iterations and have a five-person team, you'll have a total of 50 person-days to complete the iteration. Throw in a holiday and you're down to 40 days. So the stories need to be fairly small and easily quantified. One approach that is often used is to assign story points to each story. A story point is based on an arbitrary (but consistent) scale that reflects the relative work required to implement a user story. With a little practice you'll be able to determine that the average iteration can complete a certain number of story points.

Before the work begins, the details will need to be defined. This is generally deferred until just before the implementation starts. This is referred to as *just-in-time (JIT)* analysis. This is the general approach to agile development. Rather than doing all the analysis up-front before beginning the implementation, the development is started right away and the analysis is done as needed, throughout the project.

Sometimes you may have a rather large story that is too big to be called a story. This is referred to as an *epic*. These must be further detailed into stories at some point. An epic allows you to save a placeholder for the big piece that you don't quite have a handle on yet. For example, "Reconcile the sales data with the accounting system" would likely be an epic. You will eventually need to define the specific stories that must be implemented, but you can defer that until more of the system's features have been identified.

Often the user story details are provided as the acceptance criteria. In a *test-first* approach, the test cases are provided first and are then used to drive the implementation. This is like studying for a test and being given the questions ahead of time. The developer knows exactly how their work will be tested. This makes a lot of sense but does rely on someone doing a good job defining the test cases.

Linking to Requirements

Agile pundits may say that you can capture your requirements solely by defining user stories. With this approach, the collection of user stories becomes the requirements definition. There are scenarios where this will work and actually work quite well. For small projects that require a less formal definition, starting with the user stories can be a great way to jump-start your project.

However, in many cases you will need to perform a more formal requirement definition process using some of the techniques explained in the previous chapters. User stories are still a great way to drive the implementation activities, as you'll see throughout the next few chapters. So you'll need to provide an audit trail between the requirements and the user stories. This will ensure that all of the requirements have been addressed, and will allow you to easily reference the associated requirement when providing details to a user story.

You'll need to allow for a many-to-many relationship between requirements and user stories. A single requirement can generate multiple user stories. Likewise, a user story can satisfy more than one requirement.

Implementing User Stories in SharePoint

You'll now build a SharePoint list that you can use to capture user stories. To summarize the content of the list, you will need the following data elements:

- Brief description

- Who, what, and why (to support a formal style)

- Theme

- Priority

- Story points

- Epic—a Boolean flag to indicate this needs to be broken down further

- Details

- Acceptance criteria

- Linked requirements

- Attachments

You will also modify the New form, which is used to add a user story. The initial form will include only high-level data elements, such as description, theme, and priority.

Defining Themes

First, you'll need to create a list of themes, which will be used as a lookup when creating a new user story. You don't need any details about the themes, just a name to populate the drop-down. This is pretty easy to do by creating a custom list and using only the default columns.

Open the `ProjectManagement` SharePoint site that you have been using. From the Site Actions menu, select the *More Options* link, as shown in Figure 6-2.

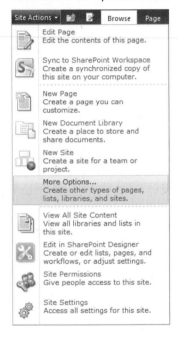

Figure 6-2. *Selecting the More Options page*

In the dialog that is displayed, select the Custom List template, which can be found in the Blank & Custom group. Enter the list name as **Themes**, as shown in Figure 6-3, and click the Create button.

Figure 6-3. *Creating the Themes list*

This will create the list and then display the empty list. Using the *Add new item* link, create several themes for you to choose from when adding user stories. The completed list should look like Figure 6-4.

Figure 6-4. *The Themes list with sample data*

Creating New Site Columns

Now you'll need to define some new site columns to store the data elements needed for the User Stories list. From the Site Actions menu, select the *Edit in SharePoint Designer* link, which will launch SharePoint Designer. Select the *Site Columns* link on the Navigation pane to list all of the existing site columns. These are organized into groups. Scroll to the end of the list and you should see a Project Management group that contains all of the custom columns that you have created so far.

Using the New Column button in the ribbon, add the columns listed in Table 6-1. Select the Project Management group, as shown in Figure 6-5, so that these will be included in your custom group. Most of these columns require only basic information, which is listed in the table. Some of the more complex columns are described following in more detail.

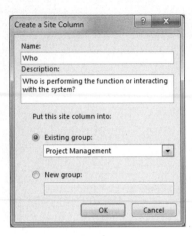

Figure 6-5. *Choose the existing Project Management group.*

■**Tip**　The Description column that is entered when defining the site column is displayed on the data entry form. This is a good place to put brief instructions so the user will know what data is expected in this field.

Table 6-1. *Required Site Columns*

Name	Column Type	Description
Who	Single line of text	Who is performing the function or interacting with the system?
What	Single line of text	What function or interaction is being executed?
Why	Single line of text	Why is this action being taken? What is the desired result?
Theme	Lookup	
Story Priority	Choice	Which word best describes the priority of this user story?
Story Points	Number	Enter a number reflecting the relative size of this user story.
Epic	Yes/No	Does this user story need to be broken down further?
Story Details	Multiple lines of text	Provide implementation details (use attachments if necessary).

Name	Column Type	Description
Acceptance Criteria	Multiple lines of text	How will this story be tested? What is the success criteria?
Story Requirements	Lookup	Which requirement(s) are satisfied by this user story?

Defining the Theme Column

The Theme column provides a lookup for the Themes list. When creating this, select the Title field as shown in Figure 6-6. This will display the theme title on the view and data forms.

Figure 6-6. *Configuring the Theme column*

Also, I left the "Allow blank values?" check box selected to make this field optional. You can uncheck this box if you want to ensure that every user story has a theme.

Defining the Story Priority Column

Story Priority is a Choice column where the user can select from the choices you define. You can use whatever naming convention works for you. I used **1 Must**, **2 Should**, **3 Could**, and **4 Won't**, as shown in Figure 6-7.

Figure 6-7. *Configuring the Story Priority column*

You can use high, medium, and low, or some other values that will be meaningful to the users.

■**Note**   You could make the Story Priority a numeric field. One useful advantage of doing this is that it makes sorting easier. You could simply sort by this field, and the higher-priority stories would be displayed at the top. Sorting Must, Should, Could, and Won't doesn't put them in actual priority order. However, I think using words instead of numbers will help the users select the appropriate value. One way to compromise between the two is to define the choices as **1 Must**, **2 Should**, and so on. This provides the textual connotation while still allowing a numerical sort.

I also unselected the "Allow blank values?" check box and specified the default value as 2 Should. This will require a value but default it to 2 Should. The user will only need to change the selection when Should is not appropriate. This is a matter of personal preference. You might rather allow null values and not default a selection. Then you would know that the value was set intentionally, instead of being defaulted by the system.

Defining the Story Points Column

I set a default value of 0 for the Story Points column and limited the maximum value to 10, as shown in Figure 6-8.

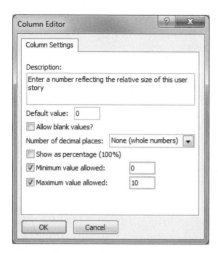

Figure 6-8. *Configuring the Story Points column*

Using this approach, zero means "undefined." Again, you might prefer to simply allow null values. Also, depending on the scale you're using to determine the store points, 10 may not be an appropriate maximum. You should consider entering the scale information in the column description to help the user enter an accurate value.

Defining the Epic Column

After creating the Epic column, you'll need to edit it to change the default value to No, as shown in Figure 6-9. The initial form doesn't give you a place to change the default value.

Figure 6-9. *Changing the default value of the Epic column*

Defining the Story Requirements Column

The Story Requirements column is a Lookup column just like the Theme column. However, it allows multiple values since the user story could address more than one requirement. Make sure you select the Requirements list and the Title field, as shown in Figure 6-10. You should also allow null values, since you may not be using the Requirements list.

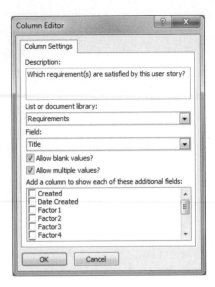

Figure 6-10. *Configuring the Story Requirements column*

Summarizing the Site Columns

When you have created all the new site columns, the list in your custom `Project Management` group should look like Figure 6-11.

Project Management			
Acceptance Criteria	Multiple lines of text	Project Management	http://omega5/pm
Epic	Yes/No (check box)	Project Management	http://omega5/pm
Functional Area	Lookup (information already on this site)	Project Management	http://omega5/pm
Requirement Description	Multiple lines of text	Project Management	http://omega5/pm
Requirement Type	Choice (menu to choose from)	Project Management	http://omega5/pm
Story Details	Multiple lines of text	Project Management	http://omega5/pm
Story Points	Number (1, 1.0, 100)	Project Management	http://omega5/pm
Story Priority	Choice (menu to choose from)	Project Management	http://omega5/pm
Story Requirements	Lookup (information already on this site)	Project Management	http://omega5/pm
Submitted By	Person or Group	Project Management	http://omega5/pm
Theme	Lookup (information already on this site)	Project Management	http://omega5/pm
What	Single line of text	Project Management	http://omega5/pm
Who	Single line of text	Project Management	http://omega5/pm
Why	Single line of text	Project Management	http://omega5/pm

Figure 6-11. *The list of all custom site columns*

The value of the URL for your columns will be different from what is shown here.

Creating the User Story Content Type

Now you're ready to create the `User Story` content type. From SharePoint Designer, select the *Content Types* link in the Navigation pane. In the Create a Content Type dialog box, enter the name **User Story**.

Select Item as the parent type and add this to the existing Project Management group, as shown in Figure 6-12.

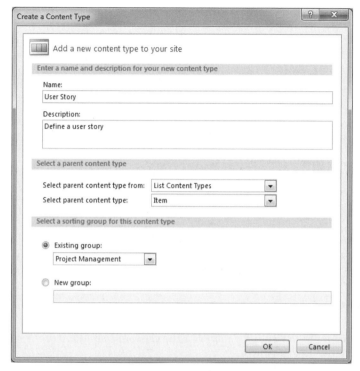

Figure 6-12. *Creating the User Story content type*

This will add the new content type to the list. Select it to display the content type editor. Click the *Edit content type columns* link in the Customization section. The User Story content type will have a single column, Title, which is inherited from the Item content type. This column will store the brief description. You'll need to add all the custom site columns that you just created. Using the Add Existing Site Column button in the ribbon, add the following columns:

- Who
- What
- Why
- Theme
- Story Priority
- Store Points
- Epic
- Story Details

- Acceptance Criteria

- Story Requirements

When you have finished, the column list for the User Story content type should look like Figure 6-13.

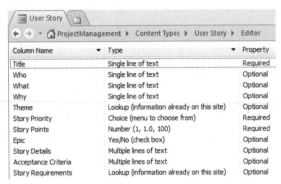

Figure 6-13. *User Story content type columns*

Creating the User Stories List

The last step is to create the User Stories list based on the User Story content type. From SharePoint Designer, select the *Lists and Libraries* link in the Navigation pane. Click the Custom List button in the ribbon. Enter the name **User Stories**, as shown in Figure 6-14.

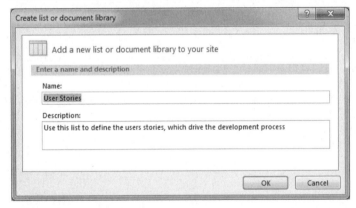

Figure 6-14. *Creating a new User Stories list*

This will create a new list that will be added to List section. Click the *User Stories* link to edit the new list. In the Settings section, select the "Allow management of content types" check box, as shown in Figure 6-15. This will allow you to add the User Story content type.

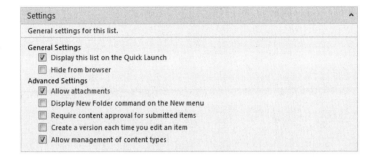

Figure 6-15. *Allowing management of content types*

In the Content Types section, click the Add button to add a new content type. Choose the User Story content type from the Content Types Picker control shown in Figure 6-16.

Figure 6-16. *Selecting the User Story content type*

In the list editor, select the Item content type and click the Delete button in the ribbon. This will remove the Item content type from the User Stories list and should set the User Story content type as the default content type.

■**Tip**　In the Content Type section of the list editor, the content type name is a link. If you click it, the content type editor will be displayed to edit that content type. To select the Item content type to remove it, don't click the *Item* link. Instead, click somewhere else on that row. That will select the content type so you can remove it.

The Content Type section should look like Figure 6-17.

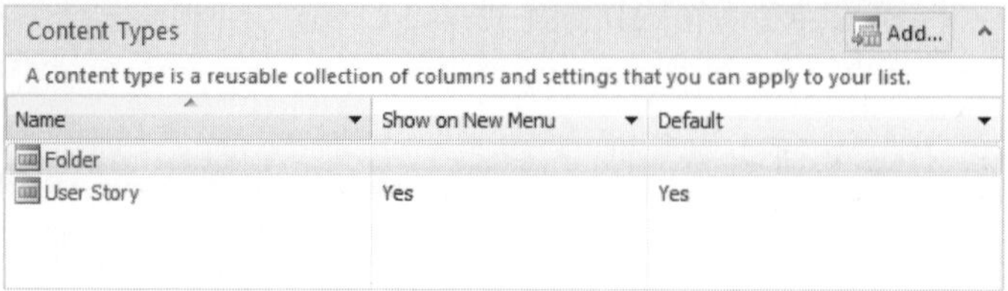

Figure 6-17. *The Content Type section*

Defining the View

The default view that was created was based solely on the Item content type. You'll need to modify the view to add the appropriate columns from the User Story content type. Open the SharePoint site and select the User Stories list, which should be an empty list. From the List ribbon, click the List Settings button. Scroll down to the bottom of the page and click the *All Items* link in the Views section.

In the Columns section, add the following columns:

- Epic
- Story Points
- Story Priority
- Theme

Change the position of the Theme column to 3, so it will be displayed just after the Title. Click the OK button to save the changes. The empty list will then be displayed with the additional columns. Click the *Add new item* link and fill out the initial part of the form, as shown in Figure 6-18.

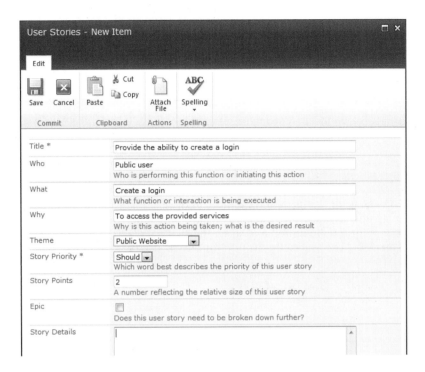

Figure 6-18. *Adding a new user story*

Click the Save button to add the user story. The list should now look like Figure 6-19.

		Title	Theme	Epic	Story Points	Story Priority
☐	📎	Provide the ability to create a login ☐ NEW	Public Website	No	2	Must
➕ Add new item						

Figure 6-19. *The default User Stories view*

Modifying the New Form

The default New form that is generated for you contains all the columns supported by the list. User stories, however, are usually created a very high level. The details are then filled in later as the project progresses. To simplify the initial creation of user stories, you'll now modify the form to accept only the few fields that are likely to be used when a user story is first identified.

From the List ribbon, click the Edit List in SharePoint Designer button, as shown in Figure 6-20.

Figure 6-20. *Launching SharePoint Designer*

This will launch SharePoint Designer (if not already running) and display the list editor. Click the List Form button in the ribbon. In the Create New List Form dialog box, enter the form name as **InitialUserStory**. Select the New item form radio button and select the "Set as default form for selected type" check box, as shown in Figure 6-21. This will cause the new form to be used whenever a new item is created.

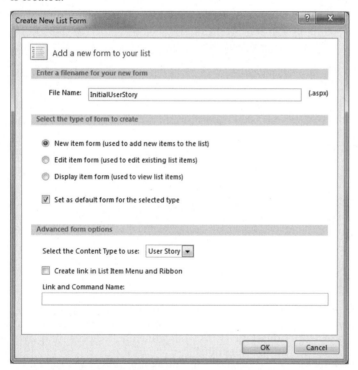

Figure 6-21. *Creating a new list form*

This will create a new form named InitialUserStory.aspx, which is actually a copy of the existing NewForm.aspx. It will be listed in the Forms section of the list editor, as shown in Figure 6-22.

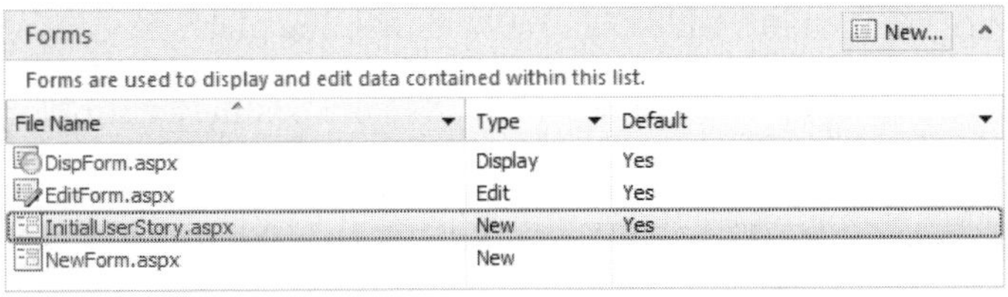

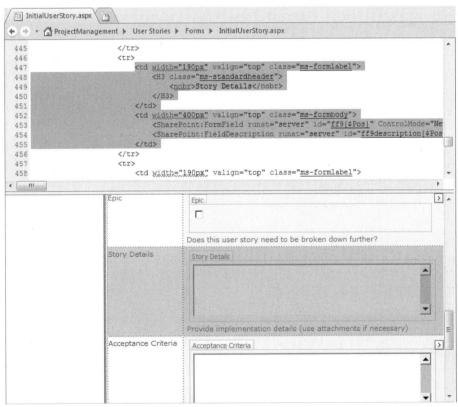

Figure 6-22. *The Form section with the new form added*

Click the *InitialUserStory.aspx* link to edit this form. This will display the form editor. The top portion of the windows shows the actual markup code and the bottom contains a preview of what the form will look like. Each row in the form contains two columns. If you select one of the rows, the corresponding code will be highlighted, as demonstrated in Figure 6-23. I will show you how you can remove rows, which will delete the referenced columns from the form. If you have experience working with XAML files, you can also do more advanced formatting.

Figure 6-23. *The form editor in SharePoint Designer*

Each row on the form starts with a `<tr>` tag and ends with a closing `</tr>` tag. The highlighted code in Figure 6-23 includes two sections wrapped in `<td>` and `</td>` tags. These sections represent the columns. The first column includes the label, Story Details, and the second contains the control for editing the Story Details column. Delete the highlighted code along with the preceding `<tr>` and subsequent `</tr>` tag. That will remove the Story Details row from the form.

Repeat this step to also remove the Acceptance Criteria, Story Requirements, and Attachments rows. If you're not using the formal style (who, what, and why), you can also remove these rows as well. When you save your changes, the preview pane will be refreshed to reflect the changes you've made.

When you're done, close SharePoint Designer and create a new user story in the SharePoint site. The New form should look like Figure 6-24.

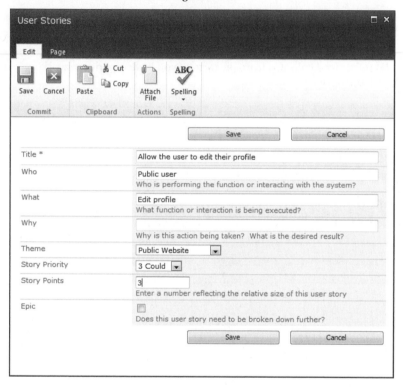

Figure 6-24. *The revised New form*

When you view or edit an existing item, the initial form that includes all the columns will be used, as demonstrated in Figure 6-25.

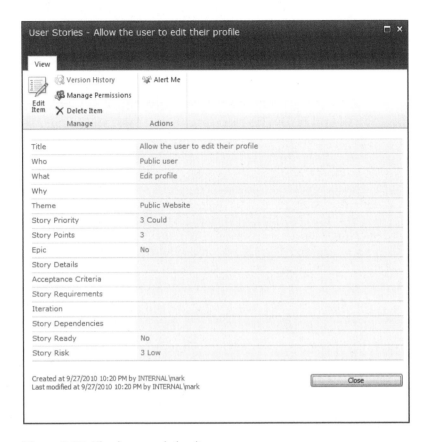

Figure 6-25. *Viewing an existing item*

Summary

In this chapter you learned about user stories, which provide a useful technique for breaking a system down into smaller pieces that will be later prioritized and scheduled. You then implemented a simple list in SharePoint that you'll use to enter and view these user stories. I also showed you how to edit the New form to display only a subset of the columns. This allows you to have a fairly simple form when creating user stories. The Edit form still allows for all the columns to be viewed and edited.

In the next two chapters, you'll organize these user stories and plan the iterations that will implement them.

CHAPTER 7

Project Backlog

In the last chapter you created a User Stories list, which you'll use to collect the features of the project. Once these have all been identified, the collection of user stories will now be the definition of the work to be done. In this chapter you'll begin using these to start planning the project.

Describing Agile Methodology

A key principle in agile methodology is dividing the work into a series of iterations.

Using Iterations

Here is a simple analogy to help you envision this process. You go to the mall on a serious shopping spree and fill up your car with boxes, bags, and packages of all shapes and sizes. You arrive home and are faced with the task of bringing everything into the house. You quickly realize that you can't carry everything in one trip, so you start planning the loads. Perhaps on the first trip you bring in the box of ice cream that's starting to melt. On the next trip you carry the big heavy box. On subsequent trips you carry several lighter-weight items. As the car begins to empty, you find yourself figuring how many loads are left.

You just applied the agile methodology to manage the project of unloading the car. The things you brought in are the user stories, and each trip represents an iteration. You can only carry a certain amount with each trip so at the beginning of the each trip you review what is left and plan the next load. You can estimate how many trips (iterations) you'll need, which will give you a good idea of when you'll be done.

Note In some agile variations, like Scrum, iterations are called *sprints*. The connotation is that, as in track and field, a sprint is short and fast. During a sprint, it's "all hands on deck," as everyone is focused on the single goal of completing the sprint. Throughout this book I will use the more generic term *iteration*, but the solutions provided here will work just as well for sprints.

Iterations are fairly short, about one to four weeks in duration. Each user story must be completed in a single iteration; this includes testing. Iterations are never late; they always end on the prescribed date. If one or more user stories were not completed, they are simply moved to a future iteration.

The important thing to know about iterations is that you only plan the next one. You first decide which users stories will be completed in the next iteration. Based on that, you plan the activities solely around completing that iteration. During the iteration, you are likely to identify new user stories and adjust existing ones. As we all know, during a project, priorities will change, assumptions turn out to be incorrect, and resources are realigned. So rather than planning the entire project in detail only to change it on a regular basis, with the agile methodology, you only plan the next iteration.

Defining the Project Backlog

A *backlog* is simply a list of items that still need to be completed. In this chapter I'll address the *project backlog*, which is the list of user stories that have not been completed. In the next chapter I'll cover the *iteration backlog*, which is the list of tasks left to complete the iteration. While these two are similar in concept, in practice they are very different.

■**Note**   The project backlog is sometimes called the *product backlog*. I will use the term *project* as it is, again, more generic. Also, the iteration backlog is often called the *sprint backlog*.

The first step in planning the next iteration is to decide which user stories will be included. The project backlog provides the information necessary to determine which items should be chosen. I discussed a few of these in the previous chapter. Priority and estimated effort (defined by story points) are the main factors that will be used. There are a few more that you'll add in this chapter, as follows:

- *Dependencies*: Often a group of user stories need to be implemented in a certain order. On each one you can specify one or more other stories that must be completed first. The backlog can then indicate which items have unfulfilled dependencies.

- *Risk*: When analyzing a project there are usually a few items that have some risk associated with them. They may require something that has not been done before and has some unknowns about it. Or a particular story might be critical to the overall success of the project. It is a good idea to address the riskier user stories first. This gives you more time to adjust the remainder of the project should something unexpected occur.

- *Readiness*: As I explained in the previous chapter, a user story often starts as a high-level description. The details are filled in later as the project progresses. The implication of this approach is that not all user stories are ready to be implemented. Some may still be an epic that needs to be broken down further before the work can be scheduled. Others may lack sufficient detail to start implementation. The project backlog should provide some insight into the readiness of each user story. Those that require more analysis should be pushed back for future iterations.

■**Note** I mentioned that during an iteration everyone is focused on completing the current iteration. That is true for the developers. However, the stakeholders, business analysts, and architects are busy working to refine the remaining user stories. That is an ongoing process. In addition to defining the existing user stories, often during an iteration, additional user stories are identified, requiring more analysis and readjusted priorities.

In this chapter you'll implement a project backlog. This is basically the User Stories list that you created in the previous chapter. However, you'll need a few more data elements and a specialized view that only returns the user stories not already assigned to an iteration.

Implementing Iterations

The first thing you'll do is define iterations. You'll start by creating an Iteration content type and then creating a list based on this. You'll then modify the User Stories list to allow each item to be assigned to an iteration.

Defining Iterations

For each iteration, you'll record basic information, including the following:

- Iteration number
- Status (planned, current, or complete)
- Start date
- End date

Open the SharePoint site that you have been working with. From the Site Actions menu, click the *Edit in SharePoint Designer* link.

Adding Site Columns

You'll need to create site columns to store the iteration number and status. From the Navigation pane in SharePoint Designer, click the *Site Columns* link. Then click the New Column button in the ribbon and select the Number column type. Enter the name **Iteration Number** and select the Project Management group, as shown in Figure 7-1.

Figure 7-1. *Creating the Iteration Number column*

Click the Column Settings button in the ribbon. In the Column Editor dialog box, enter **0** for the default value and unselect the "Allow blank values?" check box. Specify whole numbers only, as shown in Figure 7-2.

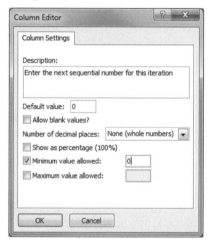

Figure 7-2. *Modifying the column settings*

Create an additional site column named **Iteration Status**. Use the Choice column type and select the Project Management group. In the Column Editor dialog box, enter the choices as **Planned**, **Current**, and **Complete**. Enter **Planned** for the default value and unselect the "Allow blank values?" check box. I used the "Radio buttons" display option, but you can also you the "Drop-down menu" option, if you prefer. The completed dialog box should look like Figure 7-3.

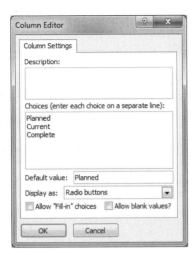

Figure 7-3. *Configuring the Iteration Status column*

Creating the Iteration Content Type

Now you're ready to create the content type. Click the *Content Types* link in the Navigation pane. Then click the Content Type button in the ribbon. Enter the name **Iteration**, as shown in Figure 7-4.

Figure 7-4. *Creating the Iteration content type*

This will display the Content Type Settings page. Click the *Edit content type columns* link in the Customization section. Add the following site columns:

- Iteration Number

- Iteration Status

- Start Date

- End Date

The list of columns for the Iteration content type should look like Figure 7-5.

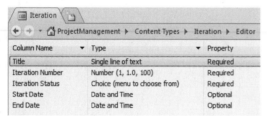

Figure 7-5. *The columns in the Iteration content type*

■**Tip** The Title column is inherited from the base Item content type. All lists and content types require this. This is also a required field, meaning that you must supply a value before you can create the iteration. I recommend that you enter the Title as **Iteration <n>**, with n being the iteration number. That's a little bit of extra data entry. You could store the iteration number in the Title field and not have a separate Iteration Number column. However, I prefer having a separate numeric field, as it helps with sorting. In a text field, 2 comes *after* 11.

Creating the Iteration List

Select the *Lists and Libraries* link in the Navigation pane and then click the Custom List button in the ribbon. Enter the name **Iterations**, as shown in Figure 7-6.

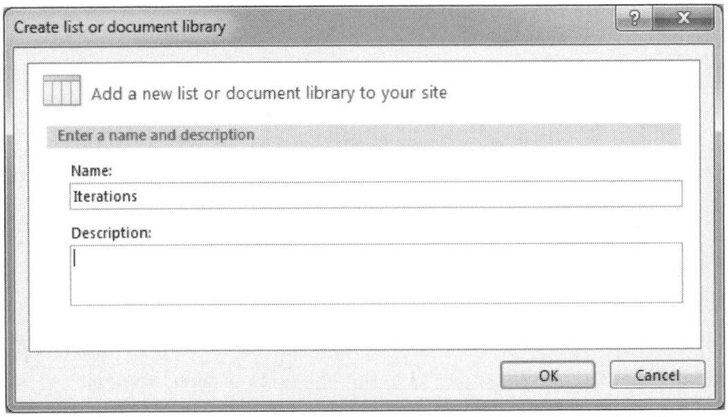

Figure 7-6. *Creating the Iterations list*

The page will then show all of the existing lists. Click the Iterations list to modify it. In the Settings section, click the "Allow management of content types" check box. Then click the Add button in the Content Types section. In the Content Type Picker that is displayed, select the Iteration content type that you just created. Remove the Folder and Item content types from this list and save your changes. The Iterations list is now available.

Go to the SharePoint site and select the Iterations list. Use the *Add new item* link to add an iteration. The completed form should look like Figure 7-7.

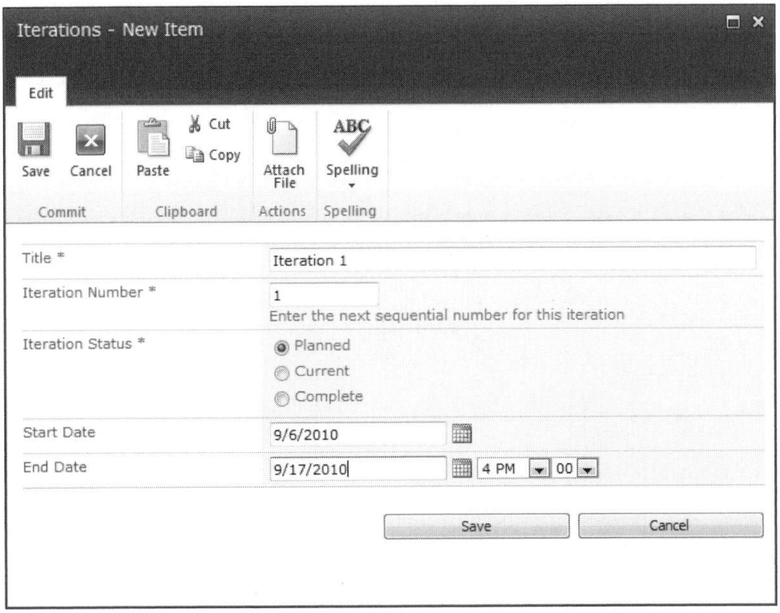

Figure 7-7. *Adding a new iteration*

Assigning an Iteration

The next step is to modify the User Stories list to allow each story to be assigned to an iteration. You'll need to first create a Lookup column for the Iterations list and then add this to the User Story content type.

■Caution Because the content type you're modifying is already being used, you must push these changes so the list will be updated as well. When you assign a content type to a list, SharePoint creates a copy of the content type definition. This creates two separate definitions: one in the site's Content Type list and one in the list's Content Type list. If you look at the content type in both places using SharePoint Designer, you'll notice that they have different ID values. Actually, the list content type is created as a child of the site content type. You can modify the list's content type, but these changes are *not* propagated to the site content type, nor is any other list that may use this content type. When you edit a list using the List Settings page, it only updates the list's content type. However, when you change the site's content type, you can choose to *push* these changes to all child content types. You should update the site's content type and push the changes to all child objects. This will keep everything in sync.

Creating a Site Column

Instead of using SharePoint Designer, you'll use the Site Settings page to create a site column and to modify the content type. From the Site Actions menu, click the *Site Settings* link, as shown in Figure 7-8.

Figure 7-8. *Navigating to the Site Settings page*

There are links in the Galleries section of the Site Settings page for creating and modifying site columns and content types. Click the *Site columns* link, as shown in Figure 7-9.

Figure 7-9. *Displaying the Site Columns page*

On the Site Columns page, click the *Create* link to create a new site column. The New Site Column page, shown in Figure 7-10, will be displayed.

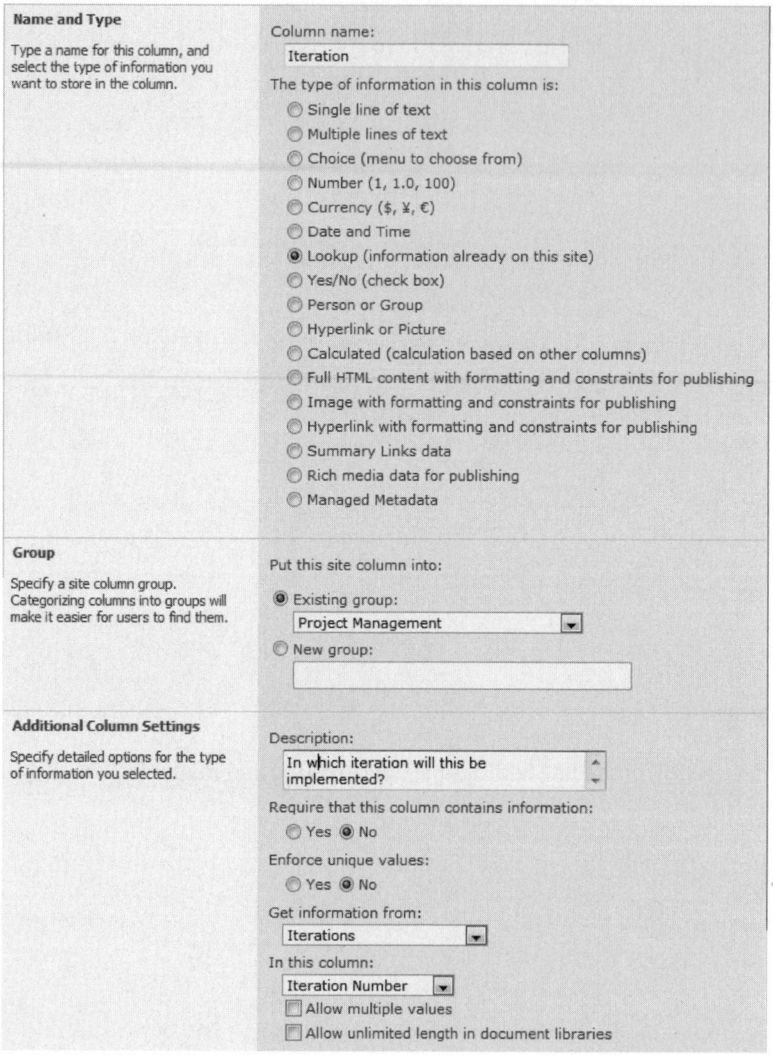

Name and Type

Type a name for this column, and select the type of information you want to store in the column.

Column name:

Iteration

The type of information in this column is:

- ○ Single line of text
- ○ Multiple lines of text
- ○ Choice (menu to choose from)
- ○ Number (1, 1.0, 100)
- ○ Currency ($, ¥, €)
- ○ Date and Time
- ● Lookup (information already on this site)
- ○ Yes/No (check box)
- ○ Person or Group
- ○ Hyperlink or Picture
- ○ Calculated (calculation based on other columns)
- ○ Full HTML content with formatting and constraints for publishing
- ○ Image with formatting and constraints for publishing
- ○ Hyperlink with formatting and constraints for publishing
- ○ Summary Links data
- ○ Rich media data for publishing
- ○ Managed Metadata

Group

Specify a site column group. Categorizing columns into groups will make it easier for users to find them.

Put this site column into:

- ● Existing group:

  Project Management

- ○ New group:

Additional Column Settings

Specify detailed options for the type of information you selected.

Description:

In which iteration will this be implemented?

Require that this column contains information:
- ○ Yes ● No

Enforce unique values:
- ○ Yes ● No

Get information from:

Iterations

In this column:

Iteration Number

- ☐ Allow multiple values
- ☐ Allow unlimited length in document libraries

Figure 7-10. *Creating the Iteration site column*

This is basically the same information that you would enter using SharePoint Designer. Enter the name **Iteration** and select the Lookup column type. The page will be updated to reflect the options that are appropriate for this type. Select the Iterations list and the Iteration Number column. This will cause the associated iteration number to be displayed on the User Stories form. The completed page should look like Figure 7-10. Click OK to create the new site column.

Modifying a Content Type

Go back to the Site Settings page and click the *Site content types* link. On the Site Content Types page, select the Project Management group to filter the content types that are listed on the page. The page should look like Figure 7-11.

Site Content Type	Parent	Source
Project Management		
Functional Area	Item	ProjectManagement
Iteration	Item	ProjectManagement
Requirement	Item	ProjectManagement
User Story	Item	ProjectManagement

Show Group: Project Management

≝ Create

Figure 7-11. *The Site Content Types page*

Click the *User Story* link to modify the content type. Then select the *Add from existing site columns* link near the bottom of the page. This will list all the existing site columns. Select the Project Management group to filter this list. Select the Iteration column and click the Add button. Make sure that the Update List and Site Content Types radio button is set to Yes. The completed page should look like Figure 7-12. Click the OK button to save the changes.

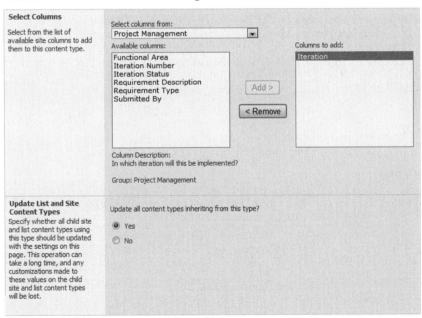

Figure 7-12. *Adding a column to the User Story content type*

■**Tip** SharePoint Designer also provides the ability to push content type changes to all child objects. However, in practice I have found that to not work reliably. Perhaps a future release will fix this. In any case, making the changes from the SharePoint UI seems to work fine.

Assigning User Stories

Go to the User Stories list and edit one of the records. There should be a drop-down list at the bottom of the form that allows you to select the iteration, as shown in Figure 7-13.

Figure 7-13. *Selecting an iteration*

Select the iteration that you just created and save your changes.

Enhancing the Iteration Form

Now that you have the ability to assign user stories to an iteration, it would be really useful to list the user stories when displaying an iteration. You'll add that now by adding a web part to the Display form just like you did in Chapter 5. Go to the Iterations list. In the List ribbon, click the Modify Form Web Parts button. This will list the existing forms for this list. Click the *Default Display Form* link, as shown in Figure 7-14.

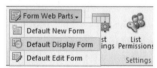

Figure 7-14. *Selecting the Display form*

Click the *Add a Web Part* link near the top of the form. From the Lists and Libraries category, select the User Stories list and click the Add button, as shown in Figure 7-15.

Figure 7-15. *Adding the Iteration list web part*

The list of user stories is now added to the Iteration form. But it is showing all of them, and you only want to include the stories that have been assigned to this iteration. To do that, you'll need to set up a filter. If you hover over the User Stories list, a drop-down icon will appear at the top-right corner. Click this and then select the *Connections, Get Filter Values From,* and *Iterations* links, as shown in Figure 7-16.

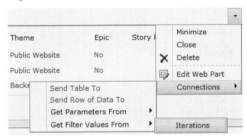

Figure 7-16. *Adding a connection between web parts*

In the Configure Connection dialog box, select the ID column as the provider field and Iteration as the consumer field, as shown in Figure 7-17. Click the Finish button to create the connection.

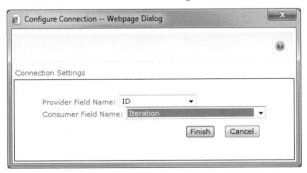

Figure 7-17. *Configuring the connection*

Click the Stop Editing button in the ribbon to save the changes. Now, display the iteration and you should also see the list of user stories assigned to that iteration, as demonstrated in Figure 7-18.

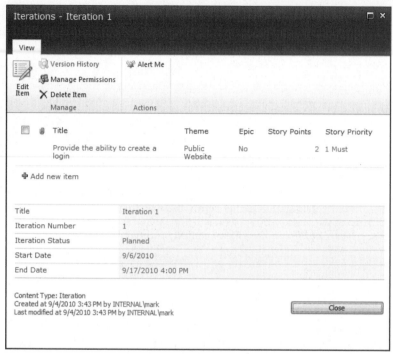

Figure 7-18. *The Iterations Display form with user stories*

Implementing a Project Backlog

With these changes, you now have the ability to assign user stories to an iteration. When displaying an iteration, the page also shows which user stories are included. Now you'll implement a project backlog.

Adding User Story Details

There are a few more details that you'll need to add to the User Stories list to help. Again, you'll be modifying an existing content type, so you'll use the Site Settings page instead of SharePoint Designer since it better handles pushing down to child objects. From the Site Actions menu, click the *Site Settings* link. In the Site Galleries section, click the *Site columns* link. Select the Project Management group to limit the list to only show your custom columns.

Creating the Story Dependencies Column

Click the *Create* link to add a new site column. Enter the column name **Story Dependencies** and select the Lookup column type. Select the Project Management group. For the additional column settings, select the User Stories list, the Title column, and the "Allow multiple values" check box, as shown in Figure 7-19. Click the OK button to create the site column.

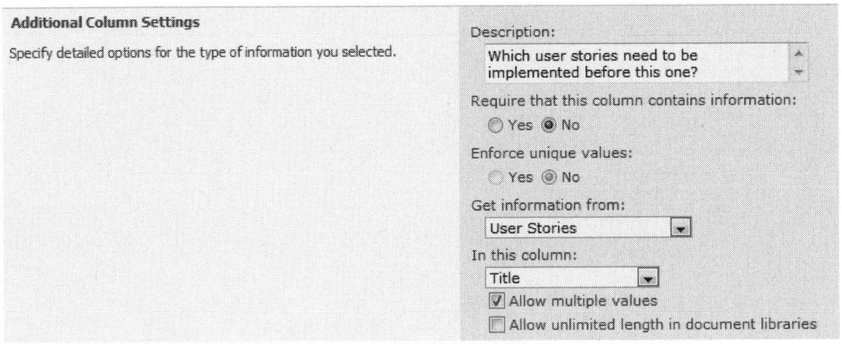

Figure 7-19. *Configuring the Story Dependencies column*

Creating the Story Risk Column

Click the *Create* link again to create another site column. Enter the column name **Story Risk** and select the Choice column type. Again, select the Project Management group. Enter the choices as **1 High**, **2 Medium**, and **3 Low**. Select the "Require that this column contains information" radio button and enter **3 Low** for the default value, as shown in Figure 7-20. Click the OK button to save the changes.

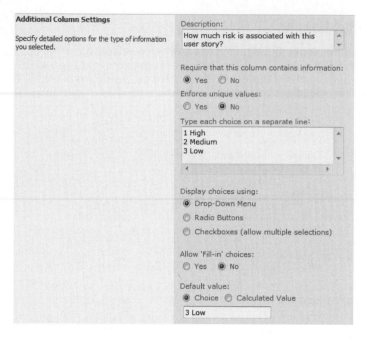

Figure 7-20. *Configuring the Story Risk column*

Creating the Story Ready Column

Create another column with the name **Story Ready** using the Yes/No column type. Select the Project Management group and specify No for the default value, as shown in Figure 7-21.

Figure 7-21. *Configuring the Story Ready column*

Modifying the User Stories List

Go back to the Site Settings page and click the *Site content types* link. Click the *User Story* link to view this content type. Then click the *Add from existing site columns* link near the bottom of the page. The page will list the site columns that are not currently included in this content type. Select the Project Management group to limit the list to only show the custom columns. Select the Story Dependencies, Story Ready, and Story Risk columns, and click the Add button. Make sure the "Update all content types inheriting from this type?" radio button is set to Yes, as shown in Figure 7-22. Click the OK button to update the content type.

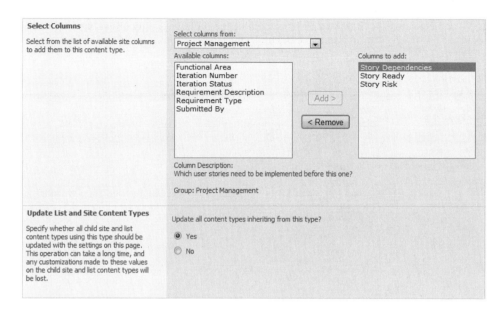

Figure 7-22. *Adding columns to the User Story content type*

Now go to the User Stories list and add a few items. Populate these new columns on some of the user stories.

Creating the Project Backlog View

As I mentioned, the project backlog is simply the list of user stories that have not yet been assigned to an iteration. You will implement this as a custom view of the User Stories list by adding a filter to the view.

Adding a View Filter

Go to the User Stories list. In the List ribbon, click the Create View button, as shown in Figure 7-23.

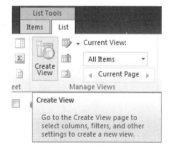

Figure 7-23. *Creating a new view*

On the Create View page, click the *Standard View* link. Enter the name as **Project Backlog**. In the Filter section, select the Iteration column and leave the operation as "is equal to." Also leave the value blank, as shown in Figure 7-24.

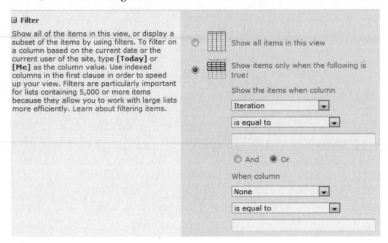

Figure 7-24. *Specifying the iteration filter*

This will cause the view to only include the user stories that do not have an iteration assigned.

Specifying the Content

The product backlog will be used to view the user stories and decide which ones to include in the next iteration. To support that, the view should include the columns that would be most useful for that purpose. I recommend including the following columns:

- Title—which is also a link to display this user story
- Theme
- Epic
- Story Ready
- Story Risk
- Story Priority
- Story Points
- Story Dependencies

In the Columns section, make sure these columns (and only these columns) are checked. Also, modify the Position value so the columns will appear in this order.

Also, it would be helpful to sort these so the most likely candidates are near the top of the list. SharePoint only allows you to specify two columns to sort on. Which columns will work best to sort on is somewhat dependent on how you will use them. I suggest sorting first by Story Ready (in descending order) and then by Story Risk. This will put the stories that are not ready at the bottom of the list and the higher-risk items (that are ready) at the top. The Sort section should look like Figure 7-25.

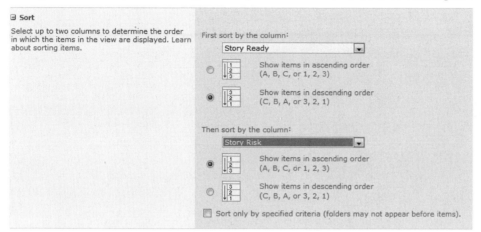

Figure 7-25. *Specifying the sort criteria*

You can use different columns and sort criteria to fit the way you will be using this list. The project backlog should look like Figure 7-26.

Title	Theme	Epic	Story Ready	Story Risk	Story Priority	Story Points	Story Dependencies
Allow the use to change their password	Public Website	No	Yes	2 Medium	2 Should	1	Provide the ability to create a login
Provide a report of inactive logins ☑ NEW	Backend Processing	No	No	1 High	4 Won't	2	

Figure 7-26. *The Project Backlog view*

Summary

In this chapter you added a facility in your system to assign user stories to an iteration. Specifically, you did the following:

- Created an Iterations list to define the iterations

- Modified user stories so you can assign each user story to a specific iteration

- Enhanced the Iterations Display form to show the user stories that have been assigned to this iteration

- Provided a product backlog that lists all user stories that have not been scheduled yet

This will enable you to start the process of planning an iteration. In the next chapter, you'll implement an iteration backlog, which provides the ability to plan items that are specific to the current iteration.

■ ■ ■

CHAPTER 8

Iteration Backlog

The iteration backlog is the primary tool that the development team uses to manage its activities. In this chapter, you'll add an iteration backlog to your SharePoint site.

Review

In Chapter 6 you implemented a facility for defining user stories, which are a great way to divide a project into smaller, deliverable units. The key point to remember about user stories is that each one represents a piece of functionality that can be delivered to the customer and verified. It may not be very useful by itself, but it does demonstrate tangible implementation progress.

In Chapter 7 you then provided a way to define iterations. An iteration is a relatively short time period (usually one to four weeks) that is focused on implementing a set of user stories. You also implemented the ability to assign user stories to an iteration. You provided a project backlog, which lists the user stories not yet scheduled in an iteration. This is used at the beginning of an iteration to choose the set of user stories to be included.

So now you have the current iteration defined with a set of user stories to work on. In this chapter, you'll implement an iteration backlog, which you will use to plan the work needed to complete the assigned user stories.

Populating the Iteration Backlog

The iteration backlog can contain the following items:

- Tasks

- Defects

- Issues

Defining Iteration Tasks

Each user story needs to be broken down into a series of *tasks*. Tasks describe the actual work items that must be completed. During the iteration planning, the following question is answered: "What tasks are required to be completed in order to deliver this functionality?" These tasks should include any necessary design or analysis tasks as well as testing and documentation tasks.

For each task, the amount of work should be estimated. This is generally done in terms of person-hours. When all the tasks have been identified, you'll have a pretty good estimate of how long it will take to complete this iteration. At this point, before the iteration begins, you may need to add or remove some user stories from the iteration. This is a normal part of the iteration-planning process.

Once the iteration has started, the list of tasks can fluctuate. New tasks may be identified and existing tasks may be determined to be unnecessary, or redundant. Even more likely, however, the task estimates can change as you progress through the iteration.

Managing Defects

An iteration is supposed to deliver verified functionality. This requires that testing occur during the iteration. Testing will undoubtedly identify defects. These defects are also added to the iteration backlog. So, in addition to the initially planned the tasks, the team must also correct the defects that have been identified.

■Note There is some disagreement about how to deal with defects. The consensus is that, if possible, defects should be corrected in the iteration in which they were identified. This is reflected in my approach of adding them to the iteration backlog. However, what should you do if there are unresolved defects when the iteration is finished? There are basically two options. First, you could create a new user story to address the defect. This would defer the resolution to a future iteration. The second option is to state that the user story was not completed, since it has known defects, and put the user story back on the project backlog. The argument for the latter approach is that you can't really say the user story is complete. Ultimately, you'll probably need to decide this on a case-by-case basis.

Some defects can significantly affect the ability to work on other tasks. These should be identified as such to help with the prioritization of tasks. The term I'll use to describe this is *blocking*.

Handling Issues

The third item type that can be added to the iteration backlog are *issues*. Issues are generally dependencies outside of the development team. An issue could be a question about a requirement that needs to be clarified. Or perhaps some third-party component is not working as expected. Each issue should also indicate if this is blocking development. This is somewhat subjective, since all issues will become blocking eventually. The blocking attribute should be used if most development is currently stopped due to this issue.

While issues may not actually require work by the development team (as tasks and defects do), they still impact the ability to deliver the iteration in time. So they are included in the iteration backlog. As with defects, issues should be resolved before the iteration is complete. Unresolved issues will likely lead to moving the affected user story back to the project backlog.

Using the Iteration Backlog

The iteration backlog defines all the work items that the development team needs to complete. Team members use this to decide which item to work on next. Each item should have the following information:

- *Iteration*: This is used to restrict the view to only the items in the current iteration.

- *Short description*:

- *User story*: This is optional, as some tasks may not be assigned to a single user story. However, where possible, the user story should be identified, as it will help with tracking.

- *Status*: Pending (not started), In Progress, Complete

- *Effort*: For items that are in progress, this should reflect the amount of work remaining, usually expressed in person-hours.

- *Details*: Optional

At the beginning of each day, the iteration backlog is reviewed to plan the day's activities. As tasks are started, the status should be changed from Pending to In Progress. This indicates that someone has started working on this task. As tasks are completed, the status should be changed to Complete. Throughout the iteration, tasks can be added or removed as needed.

At the end of every day, developers should update the items that they have worked on to make sure the status is correct and to reestimate the work remaining. This is always expressed as the amount of work remaining, regardless of how much time has been spent already. For example, assume a task was estimated to take 12 hours to complete. You worked 6 hours today, but there is still more to do. You should estimate how much time is left and not just subtract the time already spent from the estimate.

Also, pending tasks should be updated if a more accurate estimate is available. The goal is to make the iteration backlog present an accurate picture of how much work needs to be done before the iteration ends.

Implementing an Iteration Items List

You'll create an iteration backlog in SharePoint as a list called Iteration Items, which will contains tasks, defects, and issues. You'll use a separate content type for each type of item. This will allow you to have a different set of columns for each, while still being included in the same list.

Creating New Site Columns

You'll first need to define some new columns that will be included in the Iteration Items list. Open the SharePoint site. From the Site Actions menu, select the *Edit in SharePoint Designer* link. This will launch SharePoint Designer and open this site. Click the *Site Columns* link in the Navigation pane. Add the following columns, making sure to add them to the Project Management group:

- User Story: Lookup

- Item Status: Choice (Pending, In Progress, Complete)

- Hours Left: Number

- Blocking: Yes/No (set the default value to No)

- Task Details: Multi Lines of Text

- Defect Details: Multi Lines of Text

- Issue Details: Multi Lines of Text

For the User Story column, select the User Stories list and the Title column. Select the "Allow blank values?" check box, as shown in Figure 8-1, since not all items can be assigned to a user story.

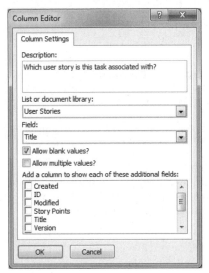

Figure 8-1. *Configuring the User Story column*

For the Item Status column, enter the choices as **Pending**, **In Progress**, and **Complete**. Unselect the "Allow blank values?" check box and specify the default value of **Pending**, as shown in Figure 8-2.

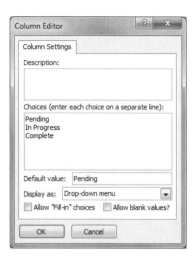

Figure 8-2. *Configuring the Item Status column*

For the Hours Left column, unselect the "Allow blank values?" check box and set the default to **0**. Select whole numbers only and set the minimum value to **0**, as shown in Figure 8-3. This will prevent the users from entering negative numbers.

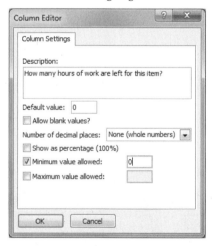

Figure 8-3. *Configuring the Hours Left column*

For the Blocking column, after creating the column, click the Column Settings button in the ribbon and change the default value to No. For the remaining columns, you can use all the default values.

Creating the Content Types

The iteration backlog will contain three types of objects, and you'll use a different content type for each. Since the columns of these content types are similar, you'll create a base content type called Iteration Item, from which the other three will be derived.

Creating the Base Content Type

In SharePoint Designer, click the *Content Types* link in the Navigation pane. Then click the Content Type button in the ribbon. In the Create a Content Type dialog box, enter the name **Iteration Item**, select Item for the parent type, and select the Project Management group, as shown in Figure 8-4.

Figure 8-4. *Creating the Iteration Item content type*

Select the *Iteration Item* link from the list of content types to edit the content type. Click the *Edit content type columns* link in the Customization section. Using the Add Existing Site Column button in the ribbon, add the following site columns to this content type:

- Iteration
- User Story
- Item Status

- Hours Left

Make sure you save your changes. The column list should look like Figure 8-5.

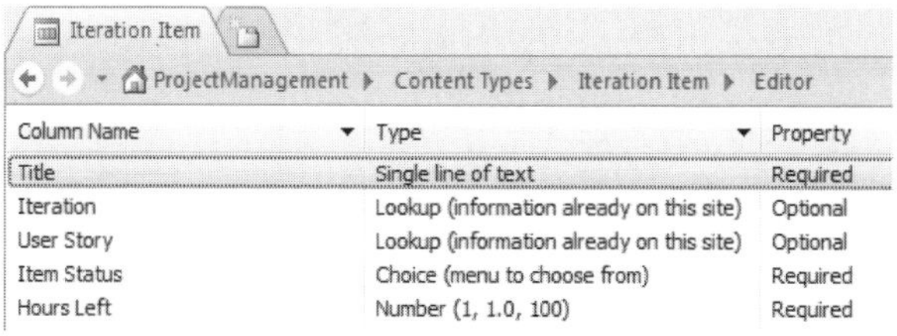

Figure 8-5. *The column list for the Iteration Item content type*

Creating the Iteration Task Content Type

Click the *Content Types* link in the Navigation pane. Then click the Content Type button in the ribbon. In the dialog box, enter the name **Iteration Task** and select the Iteration Item as the parent content type. Make sure to select the Project Management group, as shown in Figure 8-6.

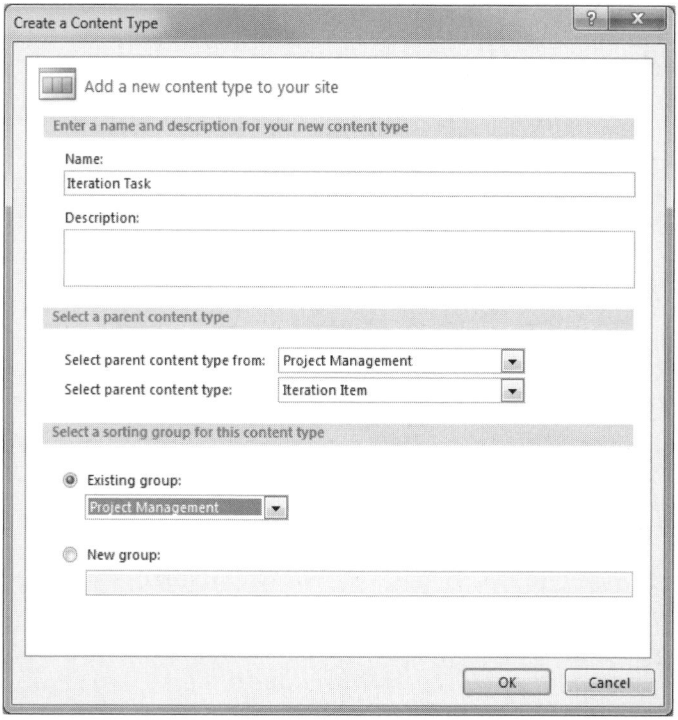

Figure 8-6. *Creating the Iteration Task content type*

Select the Iteration Task content type from the content type list and edit the column list. Notice that all the columns you added to the Iteration Item content type are automatically included. Add the Task Details column and save your changes. The completed column list should look like Figure 8-7.

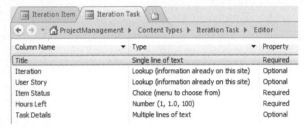

Figure 8-7. *The Iteration Task column list*

Creating the Remaining Content Types

In the same way, create the Iteration Defect and Iteration Issue content types. Both of these will require the Blocking column. The Defect Details and Issue Details columns, respectively, should be added as well. The column list for these content types should look like Figure 8-8 and Figure 8-9.

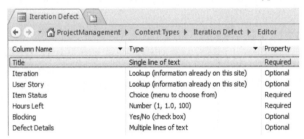

Figure 8-8. *The Iteration Defect column list*

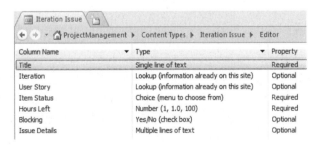

Figure 8-9. *The Iteration Issue column list*

Creating the Iteration Items List

Now you're ready to create the Iteration Items list. In SharePoint Designer, click the *Lists and Libraries* link in the Navigation pane. Then click the Custom List button in the ribbon. Enter the name **Iteration Items** and click the OK button.

   You will add all three content types to this list. This will enable you to add tasks, defects, and issues in the same list. Click the *Iteration Items* link to edit this list. In the Settings section, select the "Allow management of content types" check box. Then click the Add button in the Content Types section. In the Content Types Picker dialog box, select the Iteration Task content type and click the OK button. Repeat this step to also add the Iteration Defect and Iteration Issue content types. Also remove the Folder and Item content types.

■**Tip**   Make sure the Iteration Task content type is set as the default. It is a little easier to add the default content type, and you are likely to add far more tasks that the other two types.

Using the Iteration Items List

Open the SharePoint site and display the Iteration Items list. You'll notice that it only displays the Title column. You'll now modify the default view to include the other columns.

Modifying the Default View

From the List ribbon, click the Modify View button. In the Columns section, remove the Attachments column and then add the following columns:

- Content Type
- Item Status
- Blocking
- Title
- Hours Left
- User Story

   Also update the position so they will be displayed in this order. The Columns section should look like Figure 8-10.

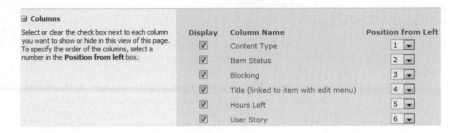

Figure 8-10. *The updated Columns section*

In the Sort section, sort by the Item Status column and then by the Blocking column, both in descending order, as shown in Figure 8-11.

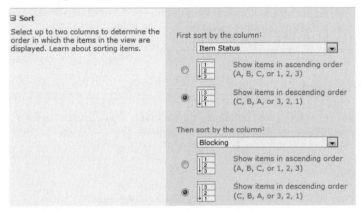

Figure 8-11. *The updated Sort section*

In the Filter section, only include items where the Item Status is not Complete. The Filter section should look like Figure 8-12.

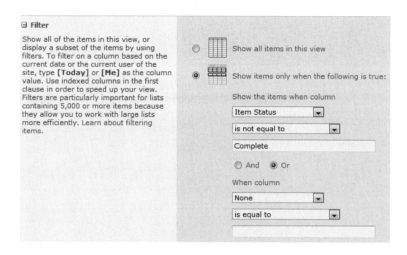

Figure 8-12. *The updated Filter section*

In the Totals section, add the sum of the Hours Left column, as shown in Figure 8-13.

Figure 8-13. *The updated Totals section*

Click the OK button to save the changes to the default view.

Adding Tasks

Click the *Add new item* link to create a new task for the list. Since Iteration Task is set as the default content type, when creating items through this link, this content type will be used. The New form will look like Figure 8-14.

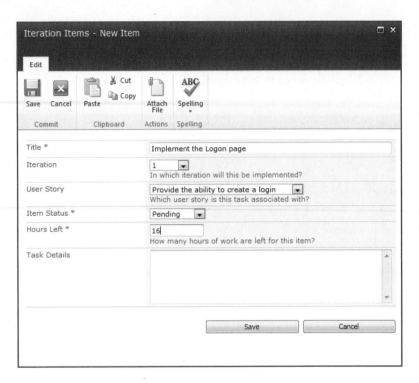

Figure 8-14. *Creating a new iteration task*

After adding a few tasks, the view will look like Figure 8-15.

	Content Type	Item Status	Blocking	Title	Hours Left	User Story
					Sum= 35	
	Iteration Task	Pending		Design the database schema to support web logons ⊞ NEW	4	Provide the ability to create a login
	Iteration Task	Pending		Implement the business rules to support web accounts ⊞ NEW	12	Provide the ability to create a login
	Iteration Task	Pending		Implement the Logon page ⊞ NEW	16	Provide the ability to create a login
	Iteration Task	In Progress		Mockup the UI for the Logon page ⊞ NEW	3	Provide the ability to create a login

Figure 8-15. *The default view*

Adding Defects and Issues

To add the other content types, use the Item ribbon. If you click the bottom portion of the New Item button, a menu will appear for you to select the content type to use. Click the *Iteration Defect* link to enter a new defect, as shown in Figure 8-16.

Figure 8-16. *Selecting the Iteration Defect content type*

■**Tip**   Notice that the description for all of these content type is the same. This is the description that was entered for the base type. No description was entered for the child types, so they defaulted to the parent's description. You might want to add a description for these content types.

The New form will look like Figure 8-17. Notice that the Blocking and Defect Details fields are included in the form.

Figure 8-17. *Entering a new defect*

You can control which content types can be selected and the order in which they are listed with the New Item button. From the List ribbon, click the List Settings button. In the Content Type section, click the *Change new button order and default content type* link. The page shown in Figure 8-18 is then displayed, which you can use to adjust the order of the content types.

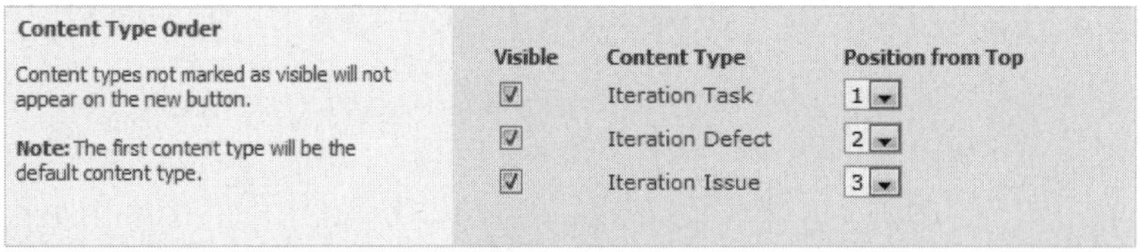

Content Type Order	Visible	Content Type	Position from Top
Content types not marked as visible will not appear on the new button.	☑	Iteration Task	1
Note: The first content type will be the default content type.	☑	Iteration Defect	2
	☑	Iteration Issue	3

Figure 8-18. *Modifying the content type order*

After adding some defects and issues, the view should now look like Figure 8-19. Notice the Pending items are listed at the top with the Blocking items listed first.

Content Type	Item Status	Blocking	Title	Hours Left	User Story
				Sum= 44	
Iteration Defect	Pending	Yes	There is no password field on the login page ☒ NEW	2	Provide the ability to create a login
Iteration Issue	Pending	Yes	The password required are not defined ☒ NEW	6	Allow the use to change their password
Iteration Defect	Pending	No	Pleese is spelled wrong on the login page ☒ NEW	1	Provide the ability to create a login
Iteration Task	Pending		Design the database schema to support web logons ☒ NEW	4	Provide the ability to create a login
Iteration Task	Pending		Implement the business rules to support web accounts ☒ NEW	12	Provide the ability to create a login
Iteration Task	Pending		Implement the Logon page ☒ NEW	16	Provide the ability to create a login
Iteration Task	In Progress		Mockup the UI for the Logon page ☒ NEW	3	Provide the ability to create a login

Figure 8-19. *Default view containing multiple content types*

Creating the Iteration Backlog

The Iteration Items list can now be used as the iteration backlog. However, there's one more thing you'll need to do. The list needs to be filtered to only show the items for a single iteration. I'll show you two ways you can accomplish that.

■**Note** In theory, all items on the iteration backlog should be complete by the time the iteration has ended. So, if everything is done as expected, you would not need to add a filter for the iteration. However, if Murphy's Law holds true, you should not count on this. It is a good practice to filter out other iterations just in case some items were left over.

Creating an Iteration Backlog View

You'll now create a new view called Iteration Backlog, which will specifically include only one iteration. From the List ribbon, click the Create View button. Then click the *Standard View* link. This will display the Create View page.

Enter the name as **Iteration Backlog**. This new view should have the same column settings as the default view. However, the other sections default to the initial values. Set the Sort and Totals sections just like you did for the default view. In the Filter section, filter by Item Status not equal to **Complete** and also by Iteration equal to **1** as shown in Figure 8-20.

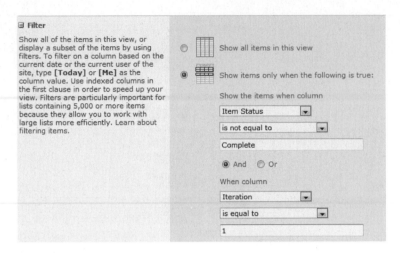

Figure 8-20. *Defining the view filter*

■**Caution**   This view is hard-coding the iteration to filter on. The disadvantage of this approach is that you'll have to change the view with every new iteration. That's not a big price to pay, but it is still worth considering. If you forget, you'll probably have an empty backlog until this is corrected.

Enhancing the Iteration Form

The second approach is to display the iteration backlog on the Iterations list's Display form. In the previous chapter you used a web part to display the list of user stories included in an iteration. You'll now use the same approach to add the iteration backlog.

Go to the Iterations list. In the List ribbon, click the Modify Form Web Parts button and then select the *Default Display Form* link, as shown in Figure 8-21.

Figure 8-21. *Selecting the default display form*

Click the *Add a Web Part* link near the top of the form. From the Lists and Libraries category, select the Iteration Items list and click the Add button. This will add the Iteration Items list to the top of the form. Now you'll need to set up a connection to the web part so it can be filtered based on the selected iteration. Hover the mouse over this web part, and the drop-down icon will appear near the top-right corner. Click this, and then click the *Connections, Get Filter Values From,* and *Iterations* links, as shown in Figure 8-22.

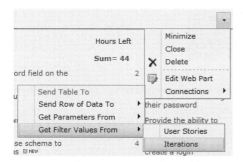

Figure 8-22. *Setting up a connection to the web part*

In the dialog box, select the ID column for the provider and the Iteration column for the consumer, as shown in Figure 8-23.

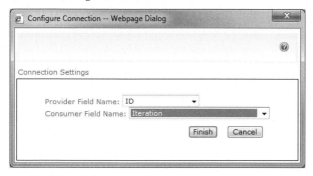

Figure 8-23. *Specifying the connection columns*

Click the Stop Editing button in the ribbon to save your changes. Now select the first iteration. The Display form should now include the iteration backlog, as demonstrated in Figure 8-24.

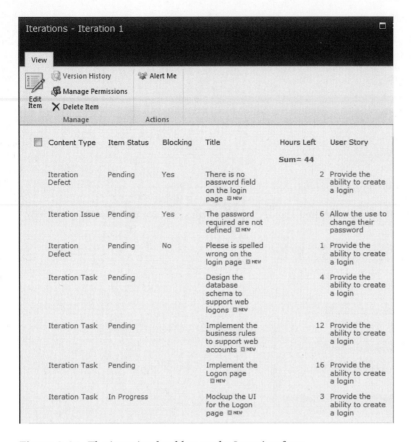

Figure 8-24. *The iteration backlog on the Iteration form*

The display form for the Iterations list now contains some very useful information. In addition to the iteration details such as start and end dates, it shows all the user stories that are included in the iteration. It now also includes the iteration backlog.

Summary

In this chapter you provided a place to list all the work items that need to be included in the current iteration. This includes the following:

- *Tasks*: Implementation items needed to complete the user stories

- *Defects*: Bugs found during the iteration

- *Issues*: Problems that could affect the success of the iteration

These are included in the `Iteration Items` list, which is used as the iteration backlog. This is used initially to plan the work of the upcoming iteration. The development team will also use this on a daily basis to track progress and to know what items are left to complete.

In the next chapter, you'll use the details captured here to present metrics that will give an accurate representation of how the iteration is going.

■■■

CHAPTER 9

Burndown Charts

In the previous chapters you provided mechanisms for organizing the project, breaking it down into relatively short iterations and then planning the activities of the current iteration. In this chapter, you'll implement facilities for tracking progress, both for the current iteration as well as the overall project. You will also build a developer's portal page that will include most of the features of your SharePoint site that developers will use on a daily basis.

Review

You expressed the project's requirements as a set of user stories. Each user story represents a deliverable unit of functionality. You then implemented the project as a series of iterations, where each iteration delivers a subset of the user stories. So you delivered a working system with the first iteration, and each subsequent iteration provides additional functionality. For example, the first iteration might provide the ability to log in. The second might allow you to change your password. The third might provide a way for your password to be e-mailed to you if you've forgotten it.

For the current iteration, you listed all the tasks necessary to implement the assigned user stories. These tasks were stored in an iteration backlog. The backlog can also include defects that need to be corrected and issues that need to be resolved. The iteration backlog is a convenient place to quickly see all the items that still need to be worked on. Each item also contained an estimate of the amount of work remaining to complete that item. The sum of these estimates represents the amount of work to be completed before the end of the iteration.

Using Burndown Charts

In agile methodology, the iteration *burndown* is a useful graphical representation of the progress of the iteration. The concept is quite simple. At the end of each day, an estimate is made of the amount of work remaining. This is done by adding up the estimates for each of the items in the iteration backlog. These data points are the tracked over time. An example of a burndown chart is shown in Figure 9-1.

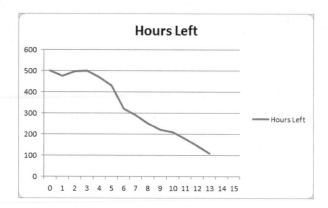

Figure 9-1. *A sample iteration burndown chart*

Understanding a Burndown Chart

In this iteration, the initial estimate was made at 500 hours. In an ideal situation, you would see a straight line from 500 at day 0 to 0 on day 15. (This is a three-week iteration, so there are 15 work days to complete the iteration.) To complete 500 hours of work in 15 days, the development team needs to complete an average of 100 hours every three days. As you can see from this burndown chart, this iteration was less than ideal.

In a couple of days, after making good progress, the remaining work actually increased. This is typical, because once you start the actual implementation, additional tasks are often identified or initial estimates need to be revised. After three days, while the remaining work should have dropped by 100 hours, there was still 500 hours left.

Around day 6, there was a sharp drop in the remaining work. The project manager realized that the iteration was in trouble and decided to remove one or more user stories from the iteration. These were put back on the project backlog to be included in a future iteration. When the user stories were moved from the iteration, the tasks associated with those user stories were also removed. This decreased the remaining work to just over 300 hours, putting the iteration back on track.

On day 10, there was another setback, where progress seems to have slowed. In this case, the team completed the same amount of work, but additional items were added to the backlog. This is because the testers found several serious defects that will require some effort to correct.

It is now the end of day 13 and there are just over 100 hours of work left and 2 days remaining in the iteration. The average production has been about 35 person-hours per day, and you'll probably need 3 days to complete the remaining work. So what do you do? Remove one or more user stories? Call for mandatory overtime? Deliver the iteration late?

As you can see, the iteration burndown chart can quickly communicate how the iteration is progressing. It is based solely on the amount of work remaining, which is reestimated every day. As the iteration proceeds, the estimate becomes more accurate.

Using a Project Burndown

A project burndown works much like an iteration burndown, except the remaining work is expressed as the number of story points that have not yet been delivered. Recall from Chapter 6 that each user story is assigned a number of story points. This is way of specifying the relative *size* of the user story.

> **■Note** The size of a user story is not necessarily based on the amount of work required, and this should not be construed as an estimate of effort. The estimate is only done for the current iteration when all the tasks have been identified. Rather, a story point is just a subjective assessment, along the lines of, "This one is twice as big as that one."

After each iteration is complete, the number of story points remaining is tracked over the course of the project. The project backlog provides the details of the remaining user stories and should tell you the number of story points remaining. A sample project burndown chart is shown in Figure 9-2.

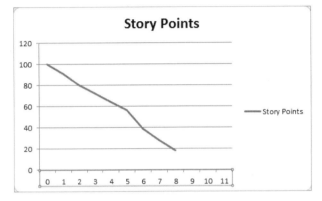

Figure 9-2. *A sample project burndown chart*

This project started out with 100 story points. After five iterations, more than half of the story points remained. Based on this progress, it was estimated that the project would take another six or seven iterations. Since this project is using 3-week iterations, the project would take between 18 and 21 more weeks to complete. The stakeholders decided to remove some of the lower-priority user stories in order to complete the project in ten iterations. The sharp drop after iteration six reflects this change.

After eight iterations, there are 18 story points remaining. The team has been delivering between eight and ten story points per iteration. Based on this burndown chart, the project appears on schedule to be completed in a total of 30 weeks.

Implementing an Iteration Burndown

To implement an iteration burndown chart, you'll first define a list to hold the data points. I'll then show you two ways to enter the data. First, you'll use a datasheet view that will allow you to quickly enter several data points. I'll then show you how to create a specialized form for entering new data points. Once the data has been captured, you'll use a Chart web part to display the data in SharePoint as a line chart.

Defining the Iteration Burndown Stats List

You'll create this list by first defining the content type and then adding it to a custom list. Open the SharePoint site and then, from the Site Options menu, click the *Edit in SharePoint Designer* link. This will launch SharePoint Designer and open the current site. You will need to define an additional site column. Click the *Site Columns* link in the Navigation pane, and then click the Site Column button in the ribbon. Choose the Number column type and enter the name **Iteration Day**. Make sure you select the Project Management group, as shown in Figure 9-3.

Figure 9-3. *Creating the Iteration Day site column*

Click the Column Settings button in the ribbon and unselect the "Allow blank values?" check box. Set the default and minimum values to **0**, as shown in Figure 9-4, and save your changes. Day 0 will represent the initial value before the iteration has started.

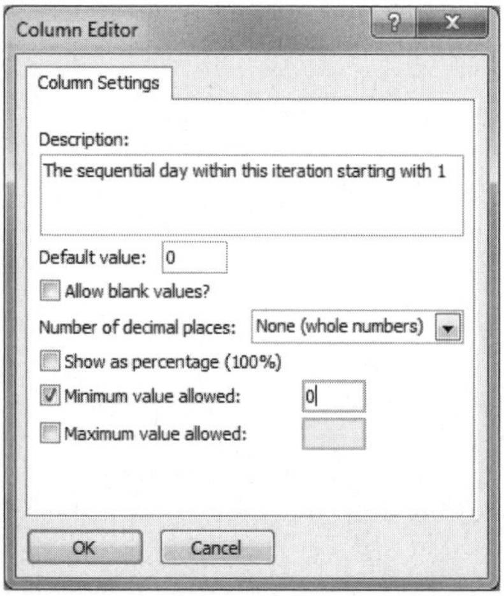

Figure 9-4. *Modifying the Iteration Day column*

Creating the Iteration Burndown Content Type

Click the *Content Types* link in the Navigation pane and then click the Content Type button in the ribbon. Enter the name **Iteration Burndown** and select Item for the parent type, as shown in Figure 9-5. Click the OK button to create the content type.

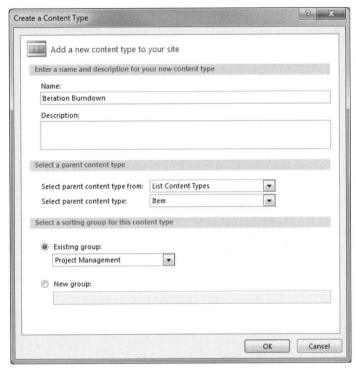

Figure 9-5. *Creating the Iteration Burndown content type*

Select the *Iteration Burndown* link from the list to define the content type. In the content type editor, click the *Edit content type columns* link in the Customization section. Using the Add Existing Site Column button, add the following site columns:

- Iteration Number
- Iteration Day
- Hours Left

Make sure you save your changes.

Creating the Iteration Burndown Stats List

Click the *Lists and Libraries* link in the Navigation pane, and then click the Custom List button in the ribbon. Enter the list name **Iteration Burndown Stats**. Click the *Iteration Burndown Stats* link in the list to define this list. In the Settings section, unselect the "Allow attachments" check box and select the "Allow management of content types" check box. Save the changes. The Settings section should look like Figure 9-6.

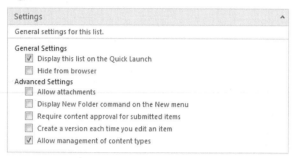

Figure 9-6. *The Iteration Burndown Stats list settings*

Click the Add button in the Content Types section and select the Iteration Burndown content type from the Content Type Picker. Remove the Folder and Item content types from this list. Save your changes.

Creating a Datasheet View

Go to the SharePoint site and select the new Iteration Burndown Stats list. Now you'll create a datasheet view that will allow you to quickly enter multiple data points. From the List ribbon, click the Create View button and then click the *Datasheet View* link.

■**Tip**   If you are using a 64-bit version of Office on the client, you may get an error stating "A datasheet component compatible with Microsoft SharePoint Foundation is not installed." SharePoint uses a datasheet component that is provided in the Office client to display a datasheet view. However, this is not included in the 64-bit version of Office. For more information you can view the article at http://support.microsoft.com/kb/2266203. Basically, Microsoft provides two options. The first is to uninstall the 64-bit version and use the 32-bit version instead. The second is a workaround where you can install the 32-bit version of the datasheet component. There are a few restrictions, the biggest of which is that you must use a 32-bit version of Internet Explorer.

Enter the view name **Data Entry**. Select the following columns to be displayed:

- Title

- Iteration Number

- Iteration Day

- Hours Left

Select the position value so these columns will be displayed in this order. Specify the sort criteria to sort by Iteration Number in descending order (so the most recent iteration will be first), and then sort by Iteration Day. The Sort section should look like Figure 9-7.

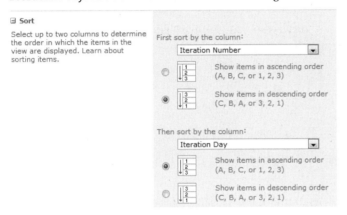

Figure 9-7. *Specifying the sort criteria*

Click the OK button to create the view. The form should look like Figure 9-8.

Title	Iteration Number	Iteration Day	Hours Left

Figure 9-8. *The empty Data Entry view*

You should modify the All Items view to include these same columns as well. You will be using this default view later in this chapter. You can remove the Title column from the All Items view. Also, in the Sort section, sort by Iteration Number in descending order, and then by Iteration Day, also in descending order. For the Data Entry view, the Iteration Day was sorted in ascending order, but for the default view, you'll want these in reverse order.

Populating the Data

In order to have some data to test the iteration burndown chart, use the Data Entry view to populate some data points.

Note The Title column is required, even though it is not used. All lists must include a Title column, as this is inherited from the base Item content type. The form will require you to specify a Title. To satisfy this requirement, you can just enter an asterisk (*) or any other character.

When you have entered some data points, the view should look like Figure 9-9.

Title	Iteration Number	Iteration Day	Hours Left
*	1	0	500
*	1	1	470
*	1	2	490
*	1	3	500
*	1	4	465
*	1	5	425
*	1	6	305
*	1	7	270
*	1	8	230
*	1	9	195
*	1	10	160
*	1	11	150
*	1	12	180
*			

Figure 9-9. *The Data Entry view with data points*

Creating Iteration Views

There are some views of the Iteration list that will be useful later in this chapter. There are only two iterations that are you will normally be interested in:

- The *current* iteration that is being implemented
- The next iteration that is being *planned*

You'll create a Current and a Planned view, which will filter the Iterations list based on the Iteration Status column. This will provide a convenient way to retrieve the desired iteration without having to hard-code the iteration number.

Modifying the Default View

The default view only includes the Title column. You'll add the additional columns now so they will automatically be included when you create the new views. Go to the Iterations list. From the List ribbon, click the Modify View button. Unselect the Attachments and Title columns. Then add the following columns:

- Iteration Number

- Iteration Status

- Start Date

- End Date

Select the position value so these columns are included in this order. The Columns sections should look like Figure 9-10. Click OK to save the changes.

Figure 9-10. *Selecting the columns for the default view*

Adding New Views

From the List ribbon, click the Create View button and then click the *Standard View* link. Enter the name **Planned**. In the Filter section, select the Iteration Status column and enter the value **Planned**. The Filter section should look like Figure 9-11.

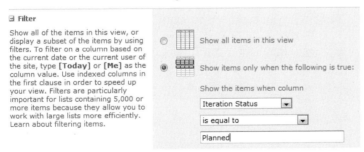

Figure 9-11. *Specifying the filter criteria*

Repeat these steps to create a view named **Current**. For this view, however, select the "Make this the default view" check box, as shown in Figure 9-12.

Name

Type a name for this view of the list. Make the name descriptive, such as "Sorted by Author", so that site visitors will know what to expect when they click this link.

View Name:

Current

☑ Make this the default view
   (Applies to public views only)

Figure 9-12. *Making this the default view*

The current iteration is the one that will most often be used. By making the Current view the default view, only the current iteration will be displayed when viewing the Iterations list. The Planned and All Items views are available if other iterations are needed.

■**Tip**   If the status of the iteration that you entered in the previous chapter is not Current, change its status now. It should be displayed when the Current view is used. The remaining enhancements in this chapter are designed to work with the current iteration.

Customizing the New Form

Now, back to the Iteration Burndown Stats list. You now have a Data Entry view, which allows you to enter multiple data points through a datasheet form. However, a single data point should be entered at the end of each day, after each of the items has been updated. As I promised, I'll now show you how to modify the New form when adding a single data point. You will modify the form to include some additional web parts that will provide the information needed when entering the data point.

Go to the Iteration Burndown Stats list. From the List ribbon, click the Modify Form Web Parts button, as shown in Figure 9-13. This is the same button you used in previous chapters. In this case, however, choose the *Default New Form* link.

Figure 9-13. *Selecting the Modify Form Web Parts button*

Click the *Add a Web Part* link near the top of the form. From the Lists and Libraries category, select the Iterations list and click the Add button. Select the check box at the top-right corner of the web part. Then from Web Part Tool ribbon, click the Web Part Properties button. Change the toolbar type to No Toolbar. In the Appearance section, change the title to **Current Iteration** and specify the height as **55** pixels, as shown in Figure 9-14. Click the OK button in the properties pane to save these changes.

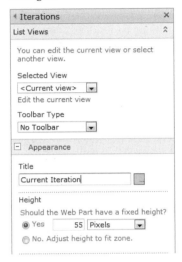

Figure 9-14. *Editing the web part properties*

Click the *Add a Web Part* link to add another web part. For this web part, select the `Iteration Items` list. Edit the web part like you did for the previous one. Select the `Iteration Backlog` view, select `No Toolbar`, and enter **Iteration Backlog** for the title. Enter **60** for the height, as shown in Figure 9-15.

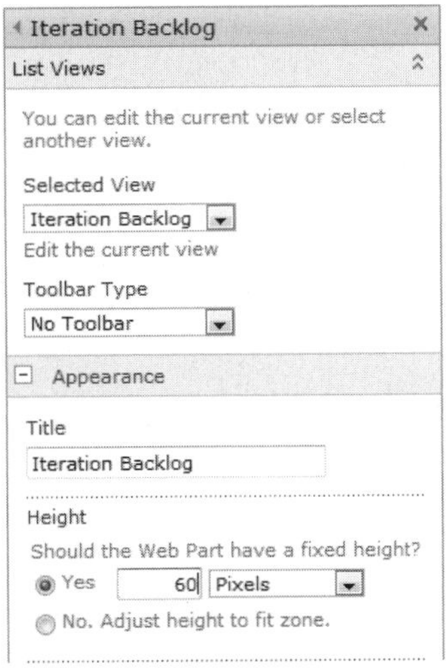

Figure 9-15. *Editing the backlog web part*

Click the *Add a Web Part* link to add a third web part. Select the Iteration Burndown Stats list. Edit the web part properties and enter the title as **Last Data Point**. Also, select No Toolbar and enter the height as **55** pixels, as shown in Figure 9-16.

Figure 9-16. *Editing the Last Data Point web part*

Now you'll need to set up the connections to filter for the current iteration. Hover the mouse over the Iteration Backlog web part and then click the drop-down icon. Click the *Connections, Get Filter Values From,* and *Current Iteration* links, as shown in Figure 9-17.

Figure 9-17. *Creating a web part connection*

In the dialog box, select the ID column for the provider and the Iteration column for the consumer, as shown in Figure 9-18.

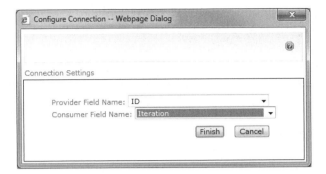

Figure 9-18. *Configuring the connection*

In the same way, create a connection for the `Last Data Point` web part. Connect it to the `Current Iteration` web part just like the previous web part. For this web part, however, you'll need to connect them using the `Iteration Number` column, as shown in Figure 9-19.

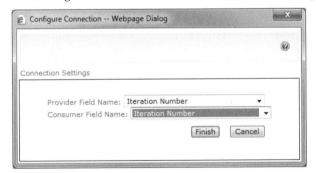

Figure 9-19. *Configuring the connection using the Iteration Number column*

Click the Stop Editing button to save the form changes. Now add a new data point using the *Add new item* link at bottom of the list. Notice the New form shown in Figure 9-20.

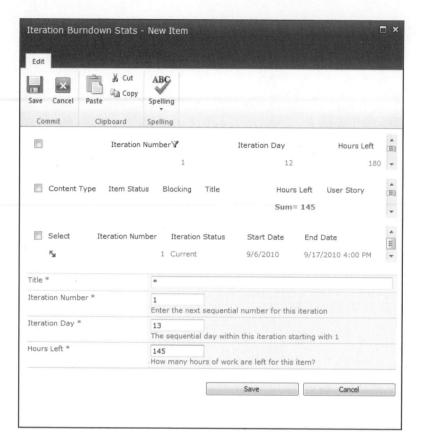

Figure 9-20. *Adding a new data point using the enhanced form*

In addition to the normal data entry form, the additional web parts are providing

- The current iteration number and the iteration start and end dates
- The iteration backlog showing the current estimate
- The iteration day of the last data point
- The hours left as of the last data point

By simply assembling a few extra web parts, the default New form now contains all the details you'll need to enter the data point for today. The web parts were configured with a fixed height so only the top row (or summary line) is visible. There are scroll bars on the form so you can see the rest of these lists if you need to.

Creating a Developer's Portal

So far, I still haven't shown you how to display the iteration burndown chart. This can be added as a web part to an existing page, such as the Iterations list default view page. However, this page is already fairly busy with several web parts on it. Instead, you'll create a new web page and assemble the web parts that are useful to the development team. This will include the iteration backlog and the iteration burndown chart.

Creating a Web Part Page

From the Site Actions menu, click the *More Options* link, as shown in Figure 9-21.

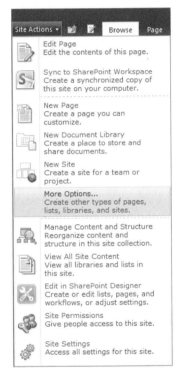

Figure 9-21. *Selecting the More Options link*

This will display the Create form. Filter the list to only include pages, and then select the Web Part Page template, as shown in Figure 9-22. Click the Create button.

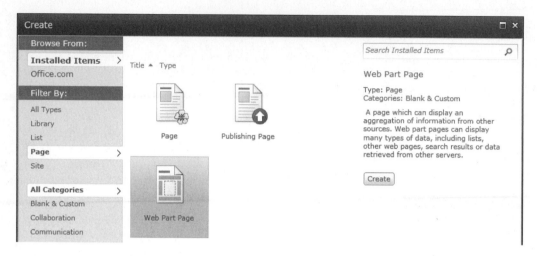

Figure 9-22. *Selecting the Web Part Page template*

Enter the page name **Portal**. You can choose from a variety of formats, as shown in Figure 9-23. The `Header, Footer, 3 Columns` layout will work well for this page.

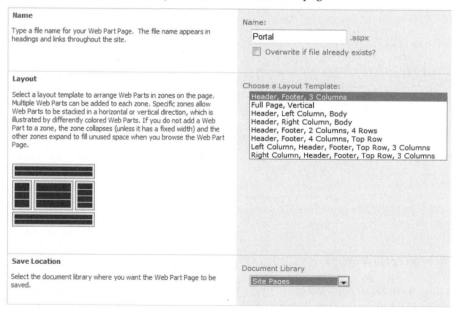

Figure 9-23. *Configuring the web page*

You will also need to select the document library where this page should be stored. I added this to the `Site Pages` library. You might want to create a new library to store this page. You can control access at the library level, so if you want to grant or restrict access to this page, you'll need to create a library for it. Click the OK button to create the web page. This will display the empty page shown in Figure 9-24. The form has links to add web parts to the various sections based on the layout that was chosen.

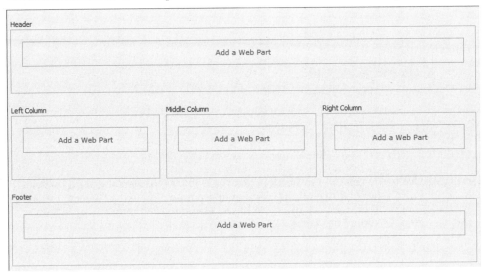

Figure 9-24. *The initial web page*

Building the Web Page

As you can see, the web page is built by assembling a collection of web parts. Put the `Iterations` list in the Header section and make sure that you select the `Current` view. This will ensure that this page always shows the current iteration. To save space, you can edit the web part to select the No Toolbar option and enter a fixed height of about 55 pixels, just like you did previously.

Add the `Iteration Items` list to the Footer. Edit the web part and select the `Iteration Backlog` view, and also change the title to **Iteration Backlog**. Leave the Summary Toolbar option as is, since the developers will need to add and update the items in this list. Don't restrict the height, as you will want to display as many items as will fit on the page.

You will also need to set up a connection to the `Current Iteration` web part so the backlog will be restricted to the current iteration only. The filter should use the `ID` column of the provider and the `Iteration` column of the consumer, as shown in Figure 9-25.

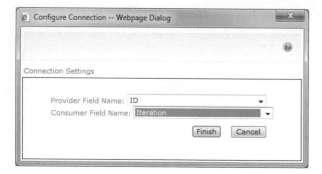

Figure 9-25. *Configuring a web part connection*

Add the User Stories list to the Left Column section. Edit the web part to select the All Items view and the No Toolbar option. This should be a read-only list. Set up a connection to the Current Iteration web part just like you did for the other web part, using the ID and Iteration columns. Click the Stop Editing button, and the new page should be displayed. It should look similar to Figure 9-26.

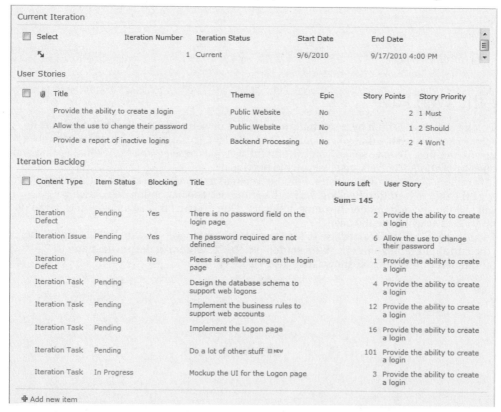

Figure 9-26. *The partial web page*

Adding a Chart

Now you'll finally add the burndown chart to this page. You will use the Chart web part that is provided with SharePoint 2010 Enterprise edition.

Enabling the Enterprise Features

If you install the Enterprise edition of SharePoint 2010, you have to specifically enable the enterprise features. The Chart web part can be found in the Business Data category. This category will only be available if the enterprise features have been enabled.

■**Tip** If you don't have Enterprise edition, there are a couple free products that you can install to provide charting ability. If you use one of these, follow the instructions provided with the documentation. The basic approach will be similar to the technique described here. For Fusion Charts, use this link:

http://charts4sharepoint.codeplex.com.

Also, you might want to check out this link as well for details about ChartPart:

http://chartpart.codeplex.com.

At the time of this writing, these products do not support SharePoint 2010, but this appears to be currently under development.

To enable the enterprise features, use the SharePoint 2010 Central Administration application, which you should have in your Start menu. From the main page, click the *Upgrade and Migration* link. Then click the *Enable Features on Existing Sites* link. This will display the page shown in Figure 9-27.

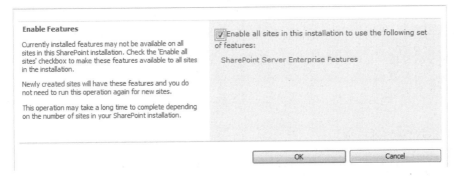

Figure 9-27. *Enabling the enterprise features*

Select the check box and click the OK button. This process may take several minutes to complete.

Adding the Chart Web Part

Go to the Portal page and from the Page ribbon, click the Edit Page button. Click the *Add a Web Part* link in the right column section. Select Chart Web Part from the Business Data category, as shown in Figure 9-28, and click the Add button.

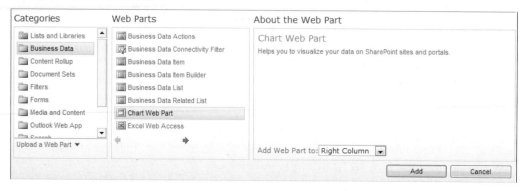

Figure 9-28. *Adding the Chart web part*

Hover the mouse over this web part, and then click the drop-down icon. Click the *Customize Your Chart* link, as shown in Figure 9-29.

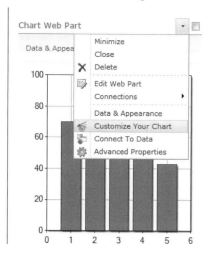

Figure 9-29. *Configuring the chart options*

On the first page that is displayed, choose the basic line chart, as shown in Figure 9-30.

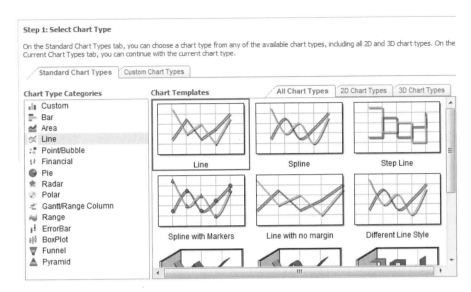

Figure 9-30. *Selecting the line chart option*

Click the Next button to go to the step 2. You can configure various appearance options here. The only one that I recommend is that you change the Chart Width to **500px**. Click the Next button to go to step 3. There are quite a few options here. I suggest that you add a chart title, as shown in Figure 9-31. You can use the default values for the remaining options. Click the Finish button to return to the Portal page.

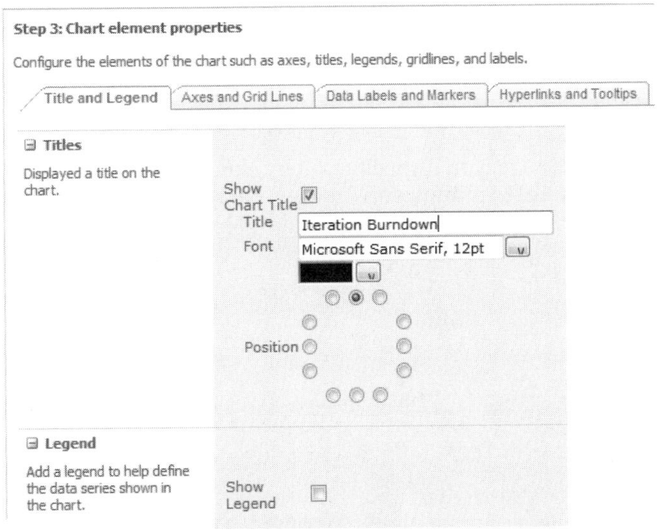

Step 3: Chart element properties

Configure the elements of the chart such as axes, titles, legends, gridlines, and labels.

| Title and Legend | Axes and Grid Lines | Data Labels and Markers | Hyperlinks and Tooltips |

⊟ **Titles**

Displayed a title on the chart.

Show Chart Title ☑

Title [Iteration Burndown]

Font Microsoft Sans Serif, 12pt [⌄]

Position ○ ● ○

⊟ **Legend**

Add a legend to help define the data series shown in the chart.

Show Legend ☐

Figure 9-31. *Adding a chart title*

Configuring the Chart Data

The Portal page will now display a line chart using canned data. The next step is to configure the chart to use the data from the Iteration Burndown Stats list. Click the Edit Page button in the Page ribbon, and then click the *Data & Appearance* link just above the chart. In the page that is displayed, click the *Connect Chart To Data* link.

The first page of the Data Connection Wizard shows the available data sources that you can connect the chart to. Choose the "Connect to a List" option and click the Next button to go to step 2. The site drop-down should already have the current site selected. In the List drop-down, select the Iteration Burndown Stats list. Then click the Next button, which will take you to step 3 and show a preview of the data in this list.

You'll need to set up a filter so only the data points from the current iteration are used. Expand the Filter Data section. Select Iteration Number for the first parameter and select Int32 for the type. You can enter 1 for the default value. The page should look like Figure 9-32. Then click the Preview Data button to verify the filter is working correctly.

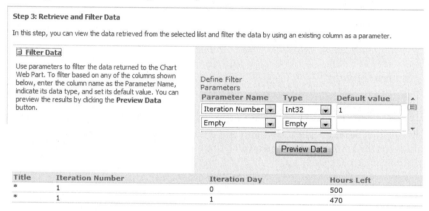

Figure 9-32. *Creating an Iteration Number parameter*

Click the Next button to go to the step 4. On this page, you'll specify which columns to use for populating the chart. For the Y field select the Hours Left column, and for the X field select the Iteration Day column, as shown in Figure 9-33. Click the Finish button close the wizard.

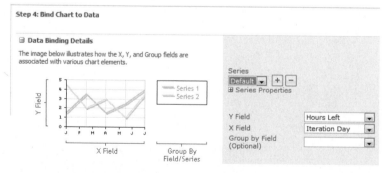

Figure 9-33. *Configuring the column bindings*

Adding a Connection

The last step is to set up a connection to this web part so the current iteration number is used to filter the data. Click the Edit Page button in the Page ribbon. Hover the mouse over the Chart Web Part and click the drop-down icon. Then click the *Connections, Get Parameters From,* and *Current Iteration* links, as shown in Figure 9-34.

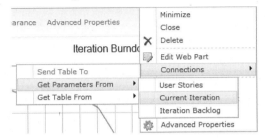

Figure 9-34. *Creating a connection to the Chart web part*

Then select the Iteration Number column for the provider and the Iteration_x0020_Number parameter for the consumer, as shown in Figure 9-35.

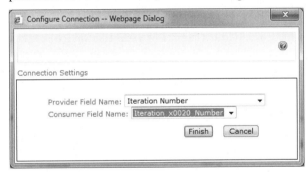

Figure 9-35. *Configuring the web part connection*

■**Note** When configuring the Chart web part, you selected the Iteration Number column to filter the data by. This created a parameter named Iteration_x0020_Number. This is the internal name assigned to this column. Since the column name had a space in it, the space was replaced with _x0020_ when defining the internal name. The parameter's name is used when setting up the connection.

Edit the Chart web part and change the title to **Iteration Burndown**.

Displaying the Portal Page

The Portal page is now complete. The page should look similar to Figure 9-36.

Figure 9-36. *The completed Portal page*

This page provides most of the information that developers will need. It has information about the current iteration, such as the end date. It also lists the user stories that will be completed in this iteration. The title of the user story is a link to the details about the user story. This is useful for finding reference information. The iteration burndown is displayed, giving everyone a snapshot of how the iteration is going. Finally, the iteration backlog is where developers can view the outstanding tasks and update their status.

Creating a Project Burndown

Before I end this chapter, I want to show you how to create a project burndown. This is very similar to the iteration burndown.

Collecting Data Points

The project burndown chart displays the number of remaining story points at the beginning of each iteration. The simplest way to capture this is to add a Story Points Remaining column to the Iterations list. Just before each iteration is started, the current number of story points not yet delivered is recorded on the iteration. This data will then be displayed in a chart.

From the Site Actions menu, click the *Site Settings* link. Then click the *Site columns* link, which will display a list of existing site columns. Click the *Create* link at the top of the page to define a new site column. Enter the name **Story Points Remaining**, select the Number column type, and select the Project Management group. In the Additional Column Settings section, enter a minimum value of **0** and select 0 for the decimal places, as shown in Figure 9-37.

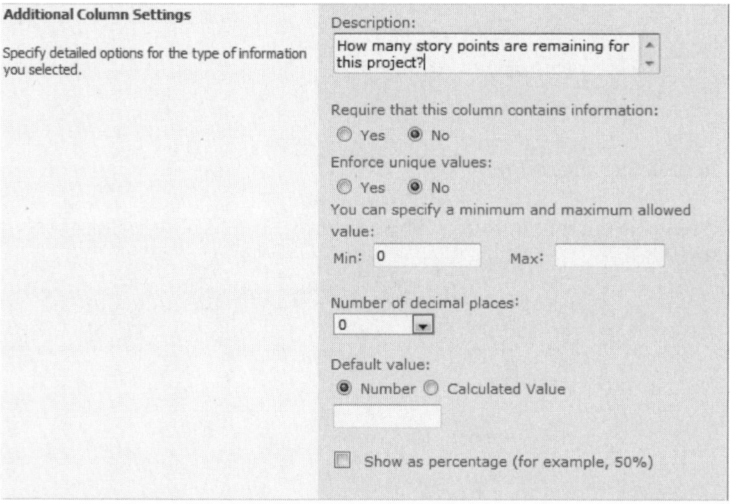

Figure 9-37. *Configuring the Story Points Remaining site column*

Then click the *Site content types* link in the Galleries section. The page will then list all the content types defined for this site. Select the *Iteration* content type, which will be in the Project Management group. Click the *Add from existing site columns* link near the bottom of the page. Select the Project Management group to filter the list of existing site columns. Select the Story Points Remaining column and click the Add button. Make sure the "Update all content types inheriting from this type?" option is set to Yes, as shown in Figure 9-38. Click the OK button to add the Story Points Remaining site column to both the Iteration content type and the Iterations list.

167

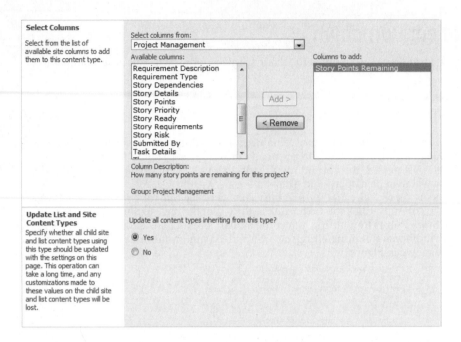

Figure 9-38. *Adding the Story Points Remaining site column*

Now go to the Iterations list and edit the current iteration. The edit form should now include the new column, as demonstrated in Figure 9-39.

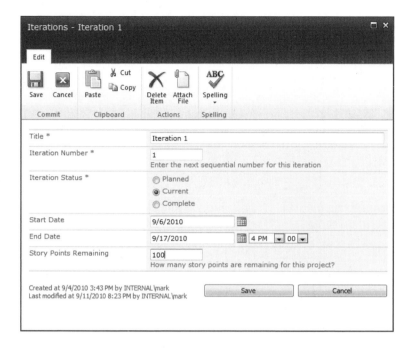

Figure 9-39. *Entering the story points remaining*

Create several more iterations so there will be some data points to graph. Make sure that you assign sequential iteration numbers. Also, set the Iteration Status to Planned so this won't interfere with the Portal page and other forms that are based on the current iteration.

Modifying the Project Backlog View

You'll need to make a minor enhancement to the Project Backlog view to add a total for the Story Points column. This will make it easy for you to determine the number of story points remaining. Go to the User Stories list. From the List ribbon, select the Project Backlog view and then click the Modify View button. In the Totals section, select Sum for the Story Points column, as shown in Figure 9-40.

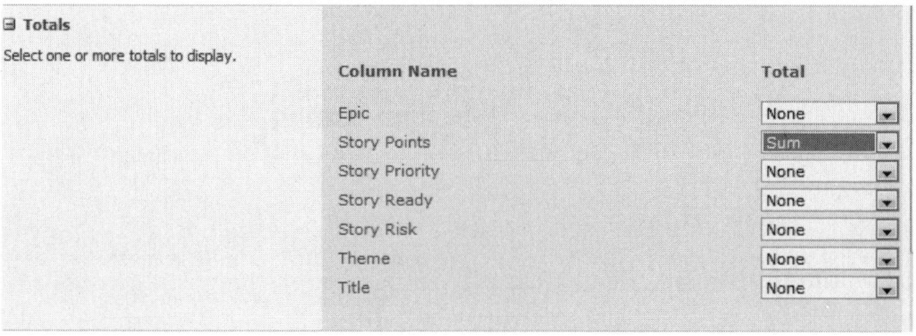

Figure 9-40. *Providing a sum of story points*

Adding a Project Page

The project burndown chart doesn't logically belong on any existing form, so you'll create a new page like you did for the Portal page. This page will have only a single web part, so you can create a simple web page. From the Site Actions menu, click the *New Page* link. Enter the page name **Project Info**, as shown in Figure 9-41.

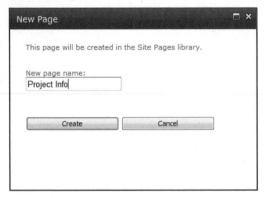

Figure 9-41. *Creating a new site page*

From the Insert ribbon, click the Web Part button. Select the Chart web part from the Business Data category and click the Add button. This will add the web part to the page. From the Page ribbon, click the Save & Close button. The page will display with a default chart. Click the *Data & Appearance* link to configure the chart.

Click the *Connect Chart To Data* link, and then select the Connect to a List option and select the Iterations list. No filter is required, so click the Next button to skip the next step. For the data binding, select Story Points Remaining for the Y field and Iteration Number for the X field, as shown in Figure 9-42.

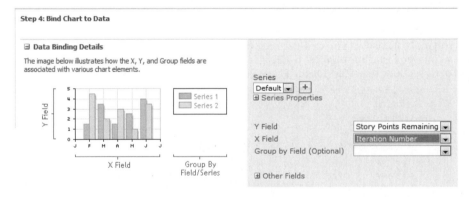

Figure 9-42. *Selecting the data bindings*

The page will now display the data points using the default chart configuration. Edit the web part and change the title to **Project Burndown**. Now you'll need to configure the appearance of the chart.

Click the *Data & Appearance* link again, but this time click the *Customize Your Chart* link. In step 1, select the standard line chart. In step 2, change the width to **500px**. In step 3, enter **Project Burndown** for the title and change the font to **14** pts. Then click the finish button. The page should look similar to Figure 9-43.

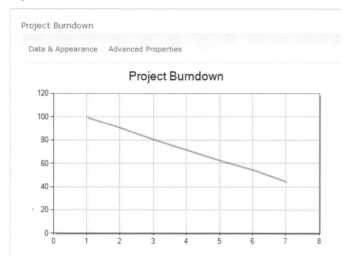

Figure 9-43. *The Project Info page*

By extrapolating this graph, you can estimate that it will take four or five more iterations to complete the project.

Summary

In this chapter you created web pages to display the iteration and project burndown charts. You used the Chart web part provided with the Enterprise edition of SharePoint 2010. The web part allowed you to easily add a graphical representation of your data. To support this feature, you provided a place to store the data points that are displayed in the charts. You also used some additional SharePoint techniques, including

- Creating a datasheet view for bulk editing
- Creating new web pages
- Modifying an existing data entry form to provide additional data
- Creating custom views to filter the list data

The solutions described in this chapter made heavy use of web parts. By simply assembling web parts for existing lists, you can easily implement useful pages and forms.

In the next section, you'll provide facilities to support the testing activities.

■ ■ ■

PART 3

Testing

In this section I'll describe some typical testing activities and explain how you can use SharePoint to facilitate these. Testing activities occur throughout the project. Testing is not a project phase like requirement gathering, implementation, and support. However, I have grouped these activities together as they are logically related. Also, all testing activities should be coordinated through a comprehensive test plan. My intention is not to teach you how to test, but to help you organize the test activities that you choose to include in your test plan.

A SharePoint site is a great place to store all kinds of information from documents, spreadsheets, calendars, contacts, and useful links. In Chapter 10, I'll show you some ways you can take advantage of these capabilities to organize your test planning and activities. None of this is rocket science, and the ideas I'll present can be used in other areas as well. Then, in Chapter 11, I will show you how to develop and organize your test cases.

Once the testing has started, the solution presented in Chapter 12 will allow you to record defects and track your test activities. Finally, in Chapter 13, I'll show you how to capture and report various testing metrics. These will not only provide insight into the overall testing progress but also the quality of the project.

CHAPTER 10

Getting Organized

In this chapter, I'll show you some useful techniques for organizing information in SharePoint. This is a very brief introduction to SharePoint, but it will get you started with some of the more useful features.

Using Document Libraries

A document library in SharePoint is a specialized list, where each item in the list contains some type of document. At its most basic level, a document library is a handy place to store your files and to keep related items in one place. Putting your documents in a library is a great way to share and organize them. SharePoint also provides some nice features—which I will demonstrate briefly—that you will probably find useful.

Creating a Document Library

The first step is to create a document library. From the Site Action menu, click the *New Document Library* link, as shown in Figure 10-1.

Figure 10-1. *Selecting the New Document Library link*

This will display the dialog box shown in Figure 10-2. Enter the name **Test Documents** and a description. The Navigation option is used to indicate if you want a link to this library in the Quick Launch area. Make sure you enable the Document Version History option. This will allow you to keep a record of each version of the document. I will demonstrate this feature later. Finally, select "Microsoft Word document" for your library template, as shown in Figure 10-2.

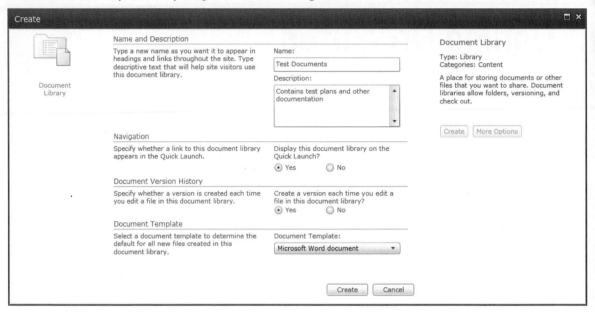

Figure 10-2. *Creating the Test Documents library*

■**Tip**   If you choose the Microsoft Word document as the library template, you are *not* limited to this type of document. In fact, you can store any type of file in any library. The choice of template, however, determines the additional columns in your library, which I'll explain later.

Click the *Add document* link to add a new document to the library. Use the Browse button to select the document that you want to add. You can also enter comments to describe the document, as shown in Figure 10-3.

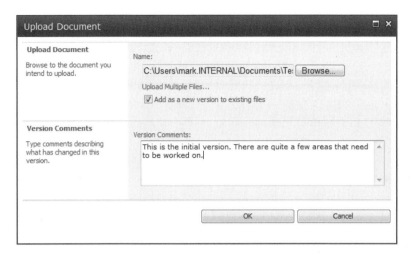

Figure 10-3. *Adding a new document to the library*

The library will now list this document along with information about its last modification, as shown in Figure 10-4.

Figure 10-4. *The document summary*

Providing Version History

One of the great features of a document library is that it can automatically keep previous versions. This is really helpful, especially when there are several people contributing content. To edit a shared document, the first thing you should do is check it out. Click the actions drop-down next to the document title and click the *Check Out* link, as shown in Figure 10-5.

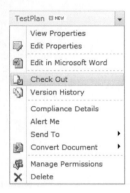

Figure 10-5. *Viewing the document options*

Click the OK button to confirm the check out. Notice that the icon in the list has changed. The arrow in the green box indicates that the file has been checked out. This will indicate to everyone else that the document is being edited and will prevent anyone else from checking it out.

Modify the document on your local disk (the same one that you added to the library initially). From the Documents ribbon, click the Upload button. This will display the same Upload Document dialog box that you used to add the file. Browse to the file and enter a description of the changes you made. Notice the "Add as a new version to existing files" check box. With this checked, it will add this as a new version to the existing document instead of creating a new document. For this to work, the file names need to be the same. Click the OK button to upload this revision.

The upload process will automatically check in the document for you. It will then display the Edit form, shown in Figure 10-6, where you can modify the document properties. You can click the Cancel button since you don't need to make any changes.

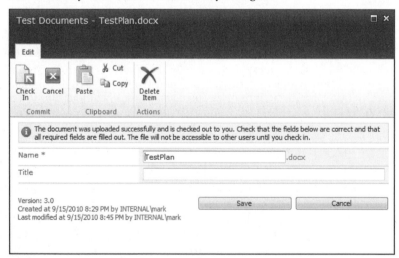

Figure 10-6. *After uploading a new revision*

From the actions drop-down beside the document title, click the *Version History* link. The dialog shown in Figure 10-7 will be displayed, listing all the versions that have been made. You can use this dialog to remove versions that you don't want to keep.

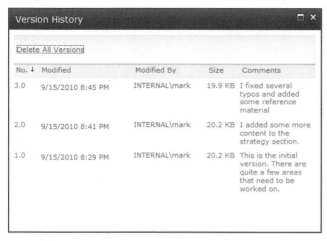

Figure 10-7. *Viewing the version history*

■**Note**   This feature does *not* provide change tracking; it simply archives each file that is uploaded. This will allow you to see previous versions of the document. It will allow you to compare versions, but if you need a full-featured change tracking facility, you should turn on the change-tracking feature in the Office document.

You may have noticed that SharePoint does not require you to check out a document before editing it or uploading a new version. This is the default setting. If you're working in a team environment, you should require a checkout before changing a shared document. To do that, click the Library Settings button in the Library ribbon. Click the *Versioning settings* link in the General Settings section. The versioning options are shown in Figure 10-8.

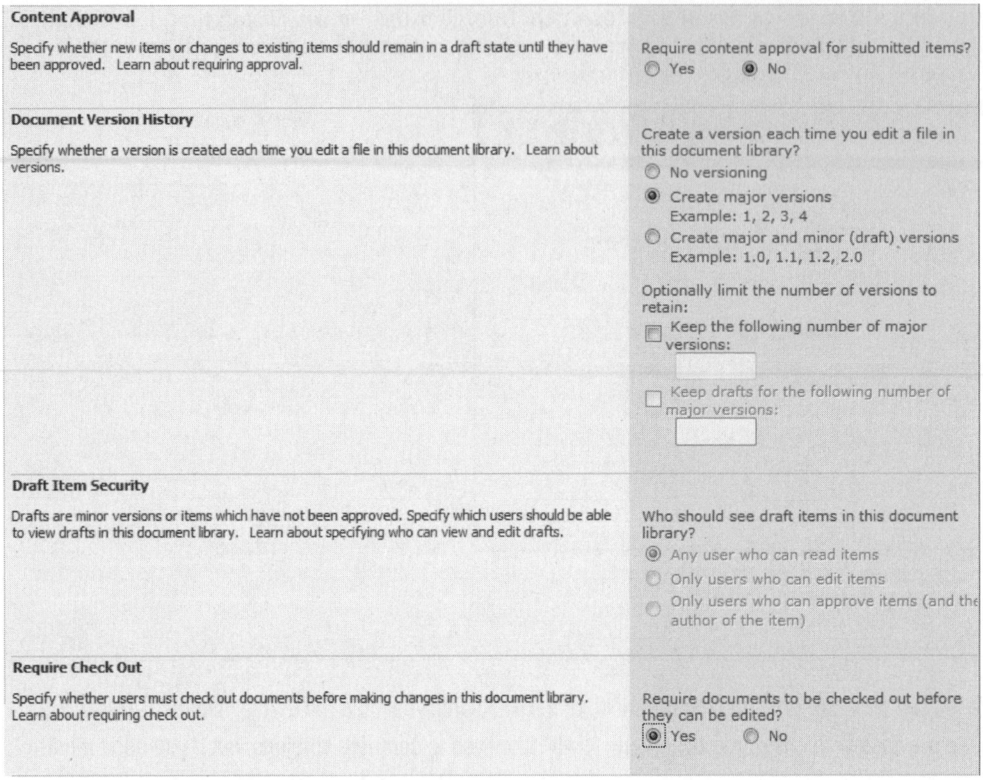

Figure 10-8. *Modifying the versioning settings*

At the bottom of this page, in the Require Check Out section, click the Yes radio button. This will require documents to be checked out before they can be modified.

There are a few other options on this page that you might be interested in. If you choose to require content approval, when a new version is uploaded, it will be saved as a draft. Most people will not have access to draft versions, so it will not be available to the general public. The document must be approved before it becomes available. Use this feature if you want to control the content that is being uploaded. If you enable this, the other options will control how the drafts are versioned and who is allowed to see them.

Viewing Library Documents in Office

If you are storing Office documents (such as Word or Excel documents), you can check out the file from within the Office document. From the SharePoint document library, click the document title, which is a link that opens the document. Depending on your system configuration, you may see the banner, shown in Figure 10-9, warning you about potentially unsafe documents. Just click the Enable Editing button.

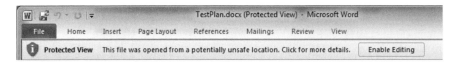

Figure 10-9. *The Protected View banner*

Because you turned on the option that requires a check out, you should see another banner telling you that the document must be checked out first, as shown in Figure 10-10. Click the Check Out button.

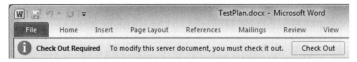

Figure 10-10. *Checking the document out from Office*

Click the File tab to see the document options that are available. The first section, shown in Figure 10-11, tells you that the document is currently checked out. When you have finished with your changes, you can click the Check In button to check the document in. You can also use the Discard Check Out button if you decide to not make any changes.

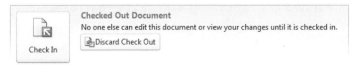

Figure 10-11. *Checking-in a document from the File tab*

You can also view the list of previous versions, as shown in Figure 10-12.

Figure 10-12. *Viewing the version history on the File page*

If you click one of the previous versions, the selected version will be displayed with a banner warning you that this is not the current version. This banner includes a Compare button so you can see the differences between this version and the current version.

Make some changes to the document and save your changes. From the File tab, click the Check In button. The Check In dialog box, shown in Figure 10-13, will appear. Enter a description of what was changed and click the OK button.

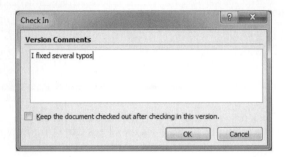

Figure 10-13. *Viewing the version history on the File tab*

You can select the "Keep the document checked out after checking in this version" check box. This will check in your changes, making them available for others to see, while keeping the document checked out so others cannot edit it.

Organizing Documents in Folders

A document library will allow you to create folders for organizing the contents. If you have a lot of documents, you might want to group them into folders. To add a new folder, click the New Folder button in the Documents ribbon, as shown in Figure 10-14.

Figure 10-14. *Adding a folder*

In the New Folder dialog box, enter the folder name. The folders will be listed along with the documents, as shown in Figure 10-15.

Figure 10-15. *The document library with folders*

Click the folder name to see the contents of the folder. A folder can also have subfolders.

Customizing Your Library

As I mentioned earlier, a document library is a specialized list. This means that, in addition to storing a document, each item can have data columns. The default columns already created for you include Type, Name, Modified, and Modified By. You can also add custom columns just like you can for lists. For example, suppose you created a document for each test scenario and you created a document library to store these. You could include columns to specify the ID assigned to that scenario, a brief description, and the current status.

To add a new column, click the Create Column button in the Library ribbon, as shown in Figure 10-16.

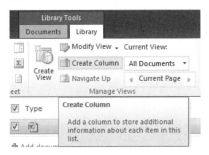

Figure 10-16. *Adding custom columns*

This will create a new column for this list only. If you want to include an existing site column, click the Library Settings button instead. On the Document Library Settings page, the existing columns are listed with links to modify the columns, as shown in Figure 10-17. Click the *Add from existing site columns* link to display a list of existing columns that can be added to your library.

Columns

A column stores information about each document in the document library. The following columns are currently available in this document library:

Column (click to edit)	Type	Required
Title	Single line of text	
Created By	Person or Group	
Modified By	Person or Group	
Checked Out To	Person or Group	

Create column
Add from existing site columns
Column ordering
Indexed columns

Figure 10-17. *Displaying the existing library columns*

You can also create additional views to filter the list of documents. For example, you might want a view that only shows the documents that you have currently checked out. You could also filter the view by one or more of the custom columns.

Using Calendars

Calendars are useful for displaying certain types of information. You might want to keep track of when staff members are unavailable. Or perhaps you need to use some special test equipment that is only available to your team at specific times. A calendar works well for these purposes.

You can create a new calendar by creating a list using the Calendar template. From the Site Actions menu, click the *More Options* link and then select the Calendar template, as shown in Figure 10-18.

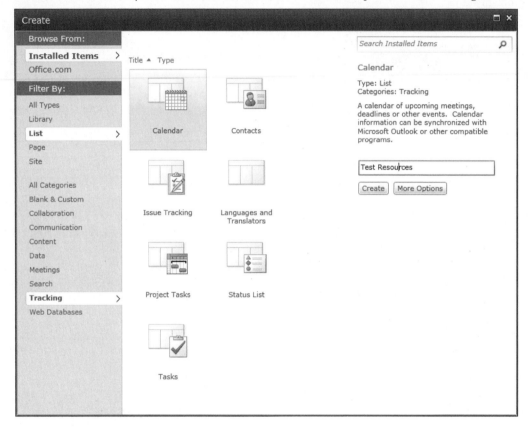

Figure 10-18. *Creating a new calendar*

■Tip   Because this site was creating using the Team Site template, a calendar has already been created for you. You can use this calendar for everything on your site, or you can create individual calendars for each area. A common calendar for everything related to this project can be useful. However, for large projects, specialized calendars may be more manageable.

Items in a calendar list are often referred to as *events*. To add events to the calendar, hover the mouse over the desired date and an *Add* link will appear. Click that link and fill in the event details, as shown in Figure 10-19.

Figure 10-19. *Entering a new event*

Events can span multiple days. You can also set up a recurring event such as weekly staff meetings. After you have saved the event, it is then included in the calendar, as shown in Figure 10-20.

Figure 10-20. *Displaying the Test Resources calendar*

As with all other lists, you can add columns to the list to store custom data. You can also create custom views to filter the events based on the type of event or even the custom columns. SharePoint provides standard views for displaying a single day, a week, or a month. If you have multiple calendars on your site, you can overlap up to ten calendars on a single view.

Organizing Links

SharePoint includes an out-of-the-box list that you can use to keep track of various links. You can use this list to store hyperlinks to documents or internal and external web sites. If you have multiple test environments, you can create links to them here so everyone will know where to find them. An advantage of using the Links list is that you only need to update them in one place should the link need to be changed.

A Links list was created for you when you created the site using the Team Site template. Click the *Lists* link in the Quick Launch pane to see all the lists that are available on the site, and then click the *Links* link. This will display an empty list. Click the *Add new link* link. Enter the link URL and description, as shown in Figure 10-21.

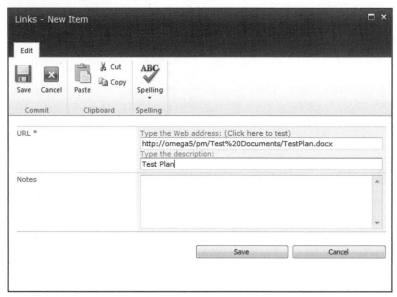

Figure 10-21. *Adding a link to the Test Plan document*

The default view includes the notes column as well as a link for editing the link, as shown in Figure 10-22.

Figure 10-22. *The default view*

I recommend removing the extra information from this view and just showing the URL column. The Notes column may be useful as well, depending on how clear the descriptions are.

■**Tip** The URL column contains two parts: the actual URL and a description. In the view, the description is displayed and the URL is not. This column is displayed as a hyperlink where the description is displayed and the URL defines the href command.

Add several other links to internal or external web sites. With the modified view, the Links list will look like Figure 10-23.

Figure 10-23. *The simplified Links view*

Putting It All Together

Now you'll create a portal page like you did for the developers that includes these reference lists. You'll create a web part page and include the lists and libraries so you can view them all from a single page.

From the Site Actions menu, click the *More Options* link. Select the Web Part Page template and click the Create button. Enter the name **Testing** and choose the Right Column, Header, Footer, Top Row, 3 Columns layout, as shown in Figure 10-24.

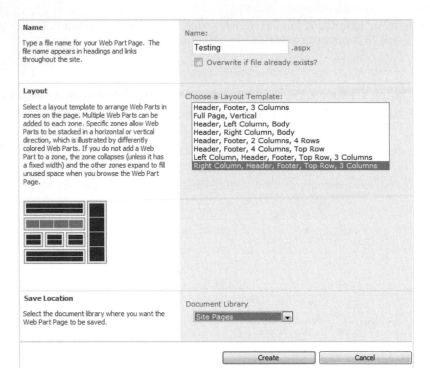

Name

Type a file name for your Web Part Page. The file name appears in headings and links throughout the site.

Name:

Testing .aspx

☐ Overwrite if file already exists?

Layout

Select a layout template to arrange Web Parts in zones on the page. Multiple Web Parts can be added to each zone. Specific zones allow Web Parts to be stacked in a horizontal or vertical direction, which is illustrated by differently colored Web Parts. If you do not add a Web Part to a zone, the zone collapses (unless it has a fixed width) and the other zones expand to fill unused space when you browse the Web Part Page.

Choose a Layout Template:

Header, Footer, 3 Columns
Full Page, Vertical
Header, Left Column, Body
Header, Right Column, Body
Header, Footer, 2 Columns, 4 Rows
Header, Footer, 4 Columns, Top Row
Left Column, Header, Footer, Top Row, 3 Columns
Right Column, Header, Footer, Top Row, 3 Columns

Save Location

Select the document library where you want the Web Part Page to be saved.

Document Library

Site Pages ▼

Create   Cancel

Figure 10-24. *Selecting the page layout*

Click the *Add a Web Part* link in the Right Column section. From the Lists and Libraries category, select the Links list. Edit the web page and select the All Links view. In the same way, add the Testing Resource list to the Header section. Finally, add the Test Documents library to the Footer section. Click the Stop Editing button to display the page, which should look like Figure 10-25.

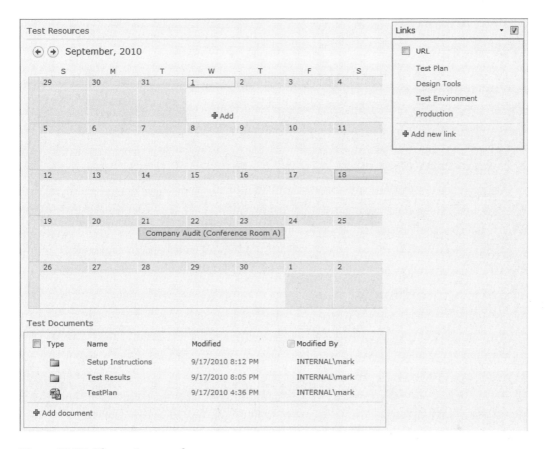

Figure 10-25. *The testing portal page*

Summary

In this chapter you used some of the basic features of a SharePoint site to organize your project information. The techniques described in this chapter could also be used in many other areas of your project. A document library provides

- A common location for storing documents

- Automatic document versioning

- Simple integration with Office applications

- The ability to customize data and views

You created a calendar to track events and resources that affect your project. You also used a Links list to keep useful links to internal and external documents and web sites. Finally, you created a portal page that included these lists and libraries for easy reference.

CHAPTER 11

■ ■ ■

Creating Test Cases

In this chapter, you'll build the test cases that will be used to verify your project. Defining a set of test cases to verify all of the requirements can be a daunting task. I'll explain some techniques that should help you accomplish this, and later in the chapter I'll show you how to capture the test cases in a SharePoint list.

Glossary

There are several terms that I'll use throughout this section that have been used in different ways, so I'd like to provide a working definition for the remainder of this book.

- *Test case*: Specifies the expected outcome based on a specific input and defined preconditions.

- *Test coverage:* Specifies how much of the system has been exercised to verify that it functions as expected in all scenarios.

- *Test plan*: Describes a summary of the testing activities, including an estimated schedule. In a large project, especially one with multiple deliverables, the test plan provides the high-level coordination of resources and activities. A test plan will describe the types of testing that are included in the project, such as unit and integration tests.

- *Test scenario*: Refers to a set of related test cases that are typically performed in a specified sequence. A scenario performs a function and the test cases represent the individual steps. Test scenarios are often linked to a user story (see Chapter 6).

- *Test strategy*: Refers to the overall approach to ensuring the quality of the project. The strategy will specify the methodology and the resources that will be used. It will also define the high-level goals and philosophy of the testing process. The strategy should describe any special test harnesses that will be used and how automated testing will be employed.

- *Variations*: Refers to test cases that differ only by the input/output combinations. Often multiple test cases are used to verify the same function with a different set of inputs. In this case it might be more efficient to use a single test case and list the expected output based on each set of inputs.

Defining Test Cases

At this point in the project, the test strategy should be written and an initial test plan developed. The next step in the overall test plan is to define test cases that will verify that the end product fulfills the specified requirements.

Breadth First, Then Depth

Test cases are very detailed and specific. You could easily end up with hundreds, even thousands, of test cases. I have seen people make the mistake of just starting to write test cases without planning first. I have done this myself as well. I think one of the reasons for this is because it's easy to think of test cases. The problem is, however, that you need to define *all* the test cases. Starting at a high level and gradually drilling down is the approach that is most likely to produce good test coverage.

Another advantage of this approach is that you can still test without detailed test cases. For example, suppose you only had time to write 90 percent of the test cases. With the high-level approach, you would know which areas were missing detailed test cases. You could perform ad hoc testing in these areas and hopefully still achieve adequate coverage.

With this in mind, you should start the process by listing the test scenarios. As I explained in the glossary, a test scenario is a set of test cases that cover a particular function. Scenarios are described in general terms. For example, "Verify the login page." You can address specific areas that need to be addressed by listing additional scenarios such as "Handle expired passwords." Later you will address each scenario, writing the specific test cases that are needed.

Nonfunctional Testing

We tend to focus our attention on providing and then verifying functionality. Does the system deliver the required features and do they work as expected? However, there are often many nonfunctional requirements that need to be addressed as well. Areas such as performance, security, vulnerability, and scalability are often key factors to a successful project.

When defining the test scenarios, make sure you also include these areas. At this point, you don't have to figure out how you're going to test for vulnerability, for example. But you should identify risk areas and scenarios that must be considered. Again, you will later determine the specific tests that should be performed, but adding these to the list of test scenarios will keep these more intangible qualities on your testing radar.

Traceability

One approach to ensuring good test coverage is to link each test scenario with one or more requirements. Mapping each requirement to a set of test scenarios, and eventually to test cases, will help you see how well each requirement is *covered*. If you have a good set of detailed requirements, this will help you identify most of the test scenarios.

■**Caution**   Be careful about exclusively relying on the requirements to identify your test scenarios. Sometimes assumptions are made when the requirements are written and not explicitly stated. The requirements are still a good starting point; however, just look for implied requirements that should be covered as well.

If the agile methodology is used for development, traceability becomes even more important. The user stories that are included in an iteration must be tested before the iteration is complete. By linking each test scenario to a user story, you will be able to determine the scenarios (and eventually test cases) that must be tested during each iteration.

Operation Grid

One technique that may help you identify test scenarios is to create a spreadsheet that maps common operations to similar objects. For example, if your project is implementing several web pages, you may be able to factor out some common operations. Suppose each page needs to display a list of items, and allow one to be selected and displayed with details. The item can then be modified and saved. The page also allows the user to create a new item. You could create the grid shown in Figure 11-1. Each cell in the grid represents a test scenario.

Operation/Object Grid	Product	Vendor	Customer	Order
Operation				
Display list of items				
Provide search capability				
Display a single item w/details				
Modify item				
Create new item				

Figure 11-1. *A sample operation grid*

This approach works well if there are several items that have similar operations. It may not help in all situations. Use this technique if it helps you. Also, if you create a grid to identify common scenarios, keep in mind that there will often be additional test scenarios for the other features that are not common.

Organizing Test Scenarios

As you start collecting test scenarios, it will be helpful to divide them into groups. This will allow you to group together similar items, which generally improves your overall efficiency. You might want to prioritize these groups or assign different resources to each group. These groups could be based on functional areas (Operations, Sales, Inventory, etc.) or technology layers such as UI or business rules.

Your choice of groups will depend on how the test activities are planned and assigned. I suggest that you allow the end user to define these groups so they can tailor the solution to their needs.

Also, you might want to distinguish between functional and nonfunctional test scenarios. Nonfunctional test scenarios often require more effort to design test cases for and usually require a different test approach from functional tests.

Building a SharePoint Solution

Now you'll implement lists in SharePoint that will allow you to capture the results of this process. You will first build a Test Areas list, which is a simple list of group descriptions. By putting these in a list, the users can define their own groups of test scenarios. You will then create a list of test scenarios that can be linked to requirements and/or user stories. Finally, you will provide a facility for expanding these into specific test cases. In the next chapter you'll provide a way to record the test results based on these test cases.

Creating a Test Areas List

Because the Test Areas list contains only the Title column, you can create the list in SharePoint using the Custom List template without defining a new content type. Open the SharePoint site. From the Site Actions menu, click the *More Options* link, as shown in Figure 11-2.

Figure 11-2. *Selecting the More Options link*

In the Create dialog box, select the Custom List template and enter the name **Test Areas**. Click the More Options button. This list will be used to define the groups used for organizing the test scenarios. Once these have been set up, the users will not need to view or edit this list. Select the No option in the Navigation section, as shown in Figure 11-3.

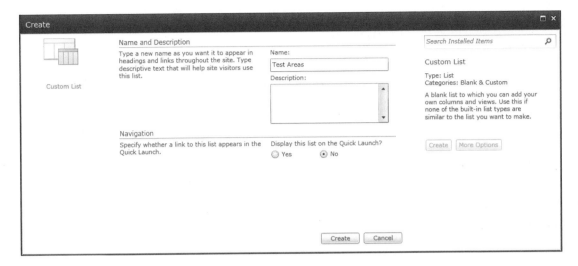

Figure 11-3. *Turning off the Quick Launch option*

This will exclude this list from the Quick Launch menu. Click the Create button to add the list. The empty list will be displayed. Use the *Add new item* link to add a few areas. When you're done, the list should look like Figure 11-4.

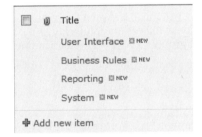

Figure 11-4. *The Test Areas list*

Building a Test Scenarios List

Now you'll create the Test Scenarios list, which you'll do in SharePoint Designer. From the Site Actions menu, click the *Edit in SharePoint Designer* link.

Adding Site Columns

You'll need to create a couple of site columns that this list will use. The first is a Lookup column for the Test Areas list that you just created. In SharePoint Designer, click the *Site Columns* link on the Navigation pane. Then click the New Column button in the ribbon and select the Lookup column type. Enter the name **Test Area** and select the Project Management group. In the Column Editor, select the Test

Areas list and the `Title` column, and select the "Allow blank values?" check box, as shown in Figure 11-5. Click the OK button to add the site column.

Figure 11-5. *Configuring the Test Area column*

The other column you'll need is a Boolean field that you can use to distinguish between functional and nonfunctional test scenarios. Click the New Column button and choose the Yes/No column type. Enter the name **Functional Scenario** and select the `Project Management` group. Click the Save icon at the top of the application to save your changes.

Creating a Content Type

Click the *Content Type* link in the Navigation pane and then click the Content Type button in the ribbon. In the Create a Content Type dialog box, enter the name **Test Scenario**, select `Item` as the parent content type, and select the `Project Management` group, as shown in Figure 11-6.

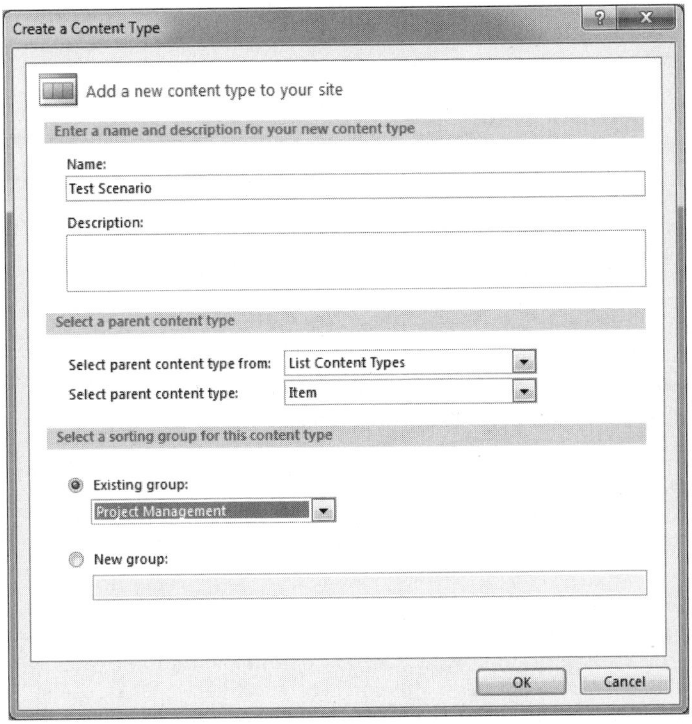

Figure 11-6. *Creating a new content type*

Click the *Test Scenario* link to edit this content type. In the Customization section, click the *Edit content type columns* link. The Title column will already be included, as it was inherited from the Item content type. Using the Add Existing Site Column button in the ribbon, add the following site columns to this content type:

- Functional Scenario
- Test Area
- % Complete
- User Story
- Story Requirements

■Tip In the Site Columns Picker dialog box, you can start typing the name of the site column, and the list will be automatically filtered based on what you enter. This is a quick way to find the column you're looking for.

When you have finished, the content type should look like Figure 11-7.

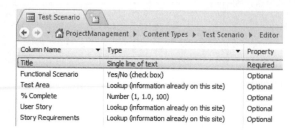

Figure 11-7. *The Test Scenario content type*

■**Note** The Test Scenario content type allows each scenario to be linked to a user story and one or more requirements. My intent is that you would use one or the other. If the agile methodology is used during development, test scenarios should be linked to user stories to support the intra-iteration testing. There is no need to also link scenarios to requirements in this case.

Creating the List

Click the *Lists and Libraries* link in the Navigation pane and then click the Custom List button in the ribbon. Enter the name **Test Scenarios** and click the OK button. This will create the Test Scenarios list and add it to the collection of lists. Click the *Test Scenarios* link to configure this list.

In the Settings section, unselect the "Allow attachments" check box and select the "Allow management of content types" check box. The Settings section will look like Figure 11-8.

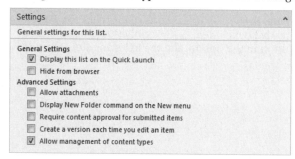

Figure 11-8. *The modified Settings section*

Click the Add button in the Content Types section and add the Test Scenario content type. Remove the Folder and Item content types. Click the Save icon to save your changes.

Go to the SharePoint site and select the Test Scenarios list. You may have to refresh the page if this list is not included in the Quick Launch area. The list will be empty and the default view will only include the Title column. From the List ribbon, click the Modify View button. Add the following columns and set the Position value so they will be displayed in this order:

- Functional Scenario

- Test Area

- % Complete

- User Story

- Story Requirements

The Columns section of the view definition should look like Figure 11-9. Click the OK button to the save the updated view.

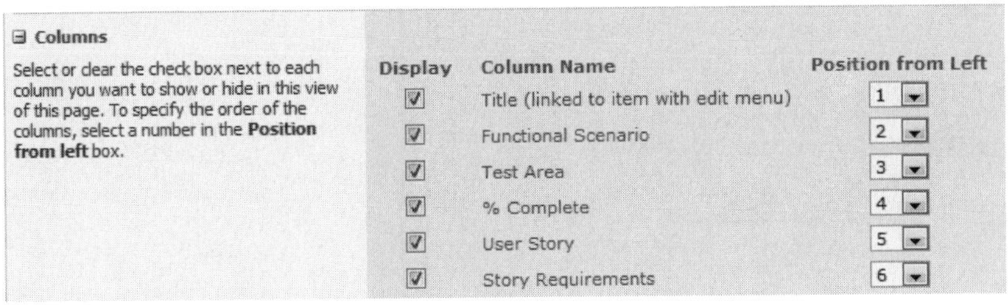

Figure 11-9. *Selecting the view columns*

Adding Test Scenarios

Now you're ready to add some scenarios to your list. Click the *Add new item* link and enter a test scenario, as shown in Figure 11-10.

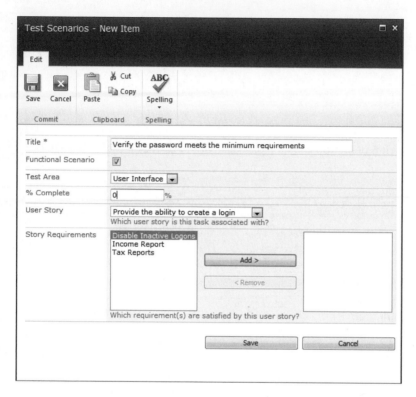

Figure 11-10. *Adding a test scenario*

Notice that the User Story can be selected from the drop-down but is not required. The Story Requirements column was configured to allow multiple values. To assign this test scenario to a requirement, select the requirement(s) and click the Add button. The % Complete column is used to indicate if all the test cases for this scenario have been entered. Initially these should be set to **0** or left blank.

Add several more scenarios so you'll have some data to test with. The view will be similar to Figure 11-11.

☐ Title	Functional Scenario	Test Area	% Complete	User Story
Verify the password meets the minimum requirements ☒ NEW	Yes	User Interface	0 %	Provide the ability to create a login
Handle duplicate logins ☒ NEW	Yes	User Interface	0 %	Provide the ability to create a login
Verify new login's initial access ☒ NEW	Yes	Business Rules	0 %	Provide the ability to create a login
Detect and disable inactive logins ☒ NEW	Yes	Business Rules	0 %	Provide the ability to create a login
Check on login response time ☒ NEW	No	System	0 %	Provide the ability to create a login

Figure 11-11. *The Test Scenario default view*

Using a Datasheet View

If you need to enter a lot of scenarios, which you probably will, you might find it more efficient to use a datasheet view. You can easily display the current view using a datasheet by clicking the Datasheet View button in the List ribbon. In datasheet mode, the default view will look like Figure 11-12.

Title	Functional Scenario ▼	Test Area ▼	% Complete ▼	User Story ▼	Story Requirements ▼
Verify the password meets the minimum requirements	☑	User Interface	0%	Provide the ability to create a login	
Handle duplicate logins	☑	User Interface	0%	Provide the ability to create a login	
Verify new login's initial access	☑	Business Rules	0%	Provide the ability to create a login	
Detect and disable inactive logins	☑	Business Rules	0%	Provide the ability to create a login	
Check on login response time	☐	System	0%	Provide the ability to create a login	
	☐				

Figure 11-12. *The default view in datasheet mode*

Notice that even in datasheet mode, you can still select the Test Area and User Story column from a drop-down list. Because the Story Requirements column allows multiple values, it works a little differently. When you click the drop-down icon, the available list is displayed with check boxes, as shown in Figure 11-13. You can click the check box on the appropriate requirement(s).

Figure 11-13. *Selecting a multivalued column*

Building a Test Cases List

Next, you'll create the Test Cases list. Just like with the Test Scenarios list, you first create the necessary site columns and then define the content type. Finally, you'll create the list and add the content type to it.

Creating the Site Columns

Test cases will be assigned to a test scenario, so you'll need a Lookup column for the Test Scenarios list. You will also need several columns for the test case details.

If SharePoint Designer is not already open, click the *Edit in SharePoint Designer* link in the Site Actions menu. Click the *Site Columns* link in the Navigation pane, and then click the New Column button in the ribbon and select the Lookup column type. Enter the name **Test Scenario** and select the Project Management group. In the column editor, select the Test Scenarios list and the Title column. Also, unselect the "Allow blank values?" check box, as shown in Figure 11-14. All test cases should be assigned to a scenario.

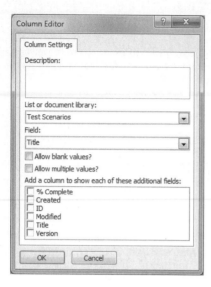

Figure 11-14. *Configuring the Test Scenario site column*

In the same way, create the following site columns:

- **Sequence**: Number (set to whole numbers only, don't allow blanks)

- **Test Preconditions**: Multi Lines of Text

- **Test Inputs**: Multi Lines of Text

- **Test Outputs**: Multi Lines of Text

Make sure you put all of these in the Project Management group. Click the Save icon to save your changes.

Creating the Content Type

Click the *Content Type* link in the Navigation pane and then click the Content Type button in the ribbon. Enter the name **Test Case**, select the Item content type as the parent, and select the Project Management group, as shown in Figure 11-15.

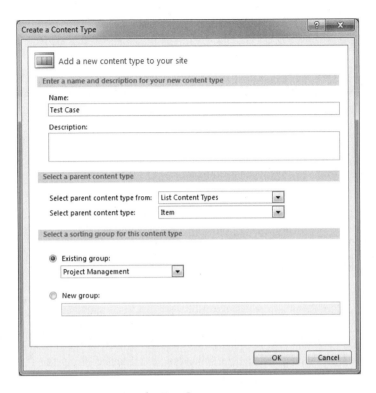

Figure 11-15. *Creating the Test Case content type*

Click the OK button, which will create the content type and include it in the list. Click the *Test Case* link to edit this content type. In the Customization section, click the *Edit content type columns* link. The Title column will already be included. Using the Add Existing Site Column button in the ribbon, add the following additional site columns:

- Test Scenario
- Sequence
- Test Preconditions
- Test Inputs
- Test Outputs
- % Complete

The content type should look like Figure 11-16 when you have finished. Make sure you save your changes.

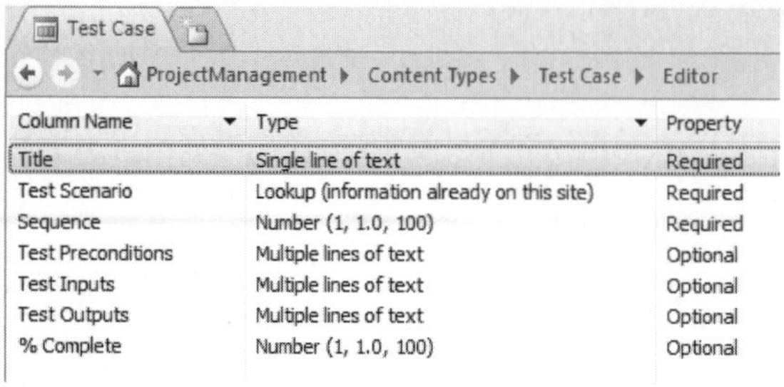

Column Name	Type	Property
Title	Single line of text	Required
Test Scenario	Lookup (information already on this site)	Required
Sequence	Number (1, 1.0, 100)	Required
Test Preconditions	Multiple lines of text	Optional
Test Inputs	Multiple lines of text	Optional
Test Outputs	Multiple lines of text	Optional
% Complete	Number (1, 1.0, 100)	Optional

Figure 11-16. *The Test Case content type columns*

Creating the Test Cases List

Click the *Lists and Libraries* link in the Navigation pane, and then click the Custom List button in the ribbon. Enter the name **Test Cases** and click the OK button. Then click the *Test Cases* link to configure this list. In the Settings section, select the “Allow management of content types” check box, which will allow you to add and remove content types from this list.

■ **Note** In the `Test Scenarios` list, you removed the “Allow Attachments” option. Test scenarios are simply a collection of test cases that verify a particular feature or function. Scenarios are basically a mechanism for grouping test cases—they don’t, in themselves, provide any testing details. However, a test case does define specific input, output, and preconditions. It is conceivable that attachments could be used to supply these details. So, the `Test Cases` list will allow attachments.

Click the Add button in the Content Types section, and select the `Test Case` content type. Then remove the `Folder` and `Item` content types. Go to the SharePoint site and display the `Test Cases` list. In the List ribbon, click the Modify View button. In the Columns section, remove the `Attachments` column and add the following columns:

- `Title` (should already be in the view)
- `Test Scenario`
- `Sequence`
- `% Complete`

Modify the Position property so these will be displayed in this order. The Columns section should look like Figure 11-17.

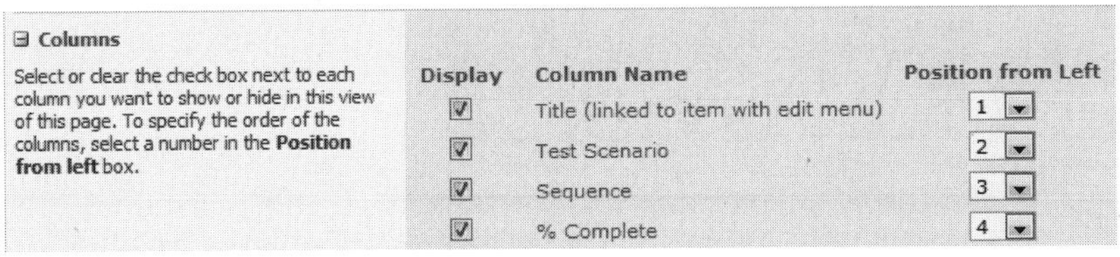

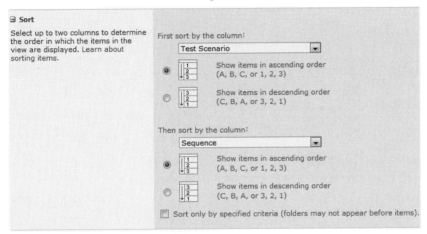

Figure 11-17. *The modified Columns section*

In the Sort section, sort by the Test Scenario and then by the Sequence columns, both in ascending order. The Sort section will look like Figure 11-18.

Figure 11-18. *The Sort section of the default view*

Click the OK button to save the changes to the view.

Adding Test Cases

Click the *Add new item* link and enter a test case, as shown in Figure 11-19.

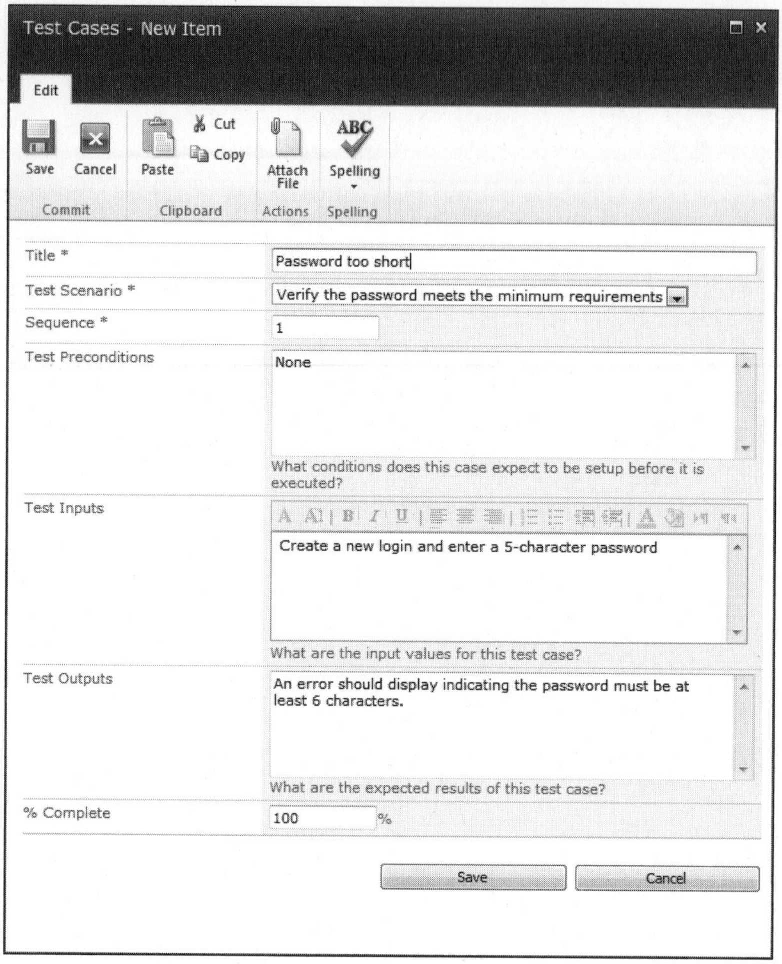

Figure 11-19. *Adding a test case*

Because this test case has been completely specified, the % Complete was set at 100. Sometimes you might just create the test case and fill in the details later. This is a good idea when you're trying to capture all the test cases—in a group session, for example. You can identify the need and come back to it later with the specifics. In this case, you'll set % Complete to something less that 100 (or just leave it blank). Also, you can use the Attach File button to add a separate document with supporting details.

Creating a Data Entry View

As with test scenarios, you will probably find it more efficient to enter test cases using a datasheet view. The current view, however, does not include all the columns that you'll need to enter. To accommodate data entry via a datasheet, you'll now create a new view for that purpose.

From the List ribbon, click the Create View button. Then click the *Datasheet View* link. Enter the name **Data Entry** and select the following columns:

- Title

- Test Scenario

- Sequence

- % Complete

- Test Preconditions

- Test Inputs

- Test Outputs

Set the Position value so these columns will be in this order. Also, in the Sort section, sort by the Test Scenario and Sequence columns, just like you did with the default view. Enter a few more test cases so you'll have some data to test with. The Data Entry view should look like Figure 11-20.

Title	Test Scenario	Sequ	% Cor	Test Preconditions	Test Inputs	Test Outputs
Password too short	Verify the password meets the minimum requirements	1	100%	None	Create a new login and enter a 5-character password	An error should display indicating the password must be at least 6 characters.
No numeric characters	Verify the password meets the minimum requirements	2	100%	None	Create a new login and enter a password with all lower-case characters and no numerics	An error should display indicating that at least one character must be numeric or upercase.
Valid password	Verify the password meets the minimum requirements	3	100%	None	Create a new login with a 8-character password that contains one uppercase and one numeric	The login should be created successfully
Time for successful login	Check on login response time	1	100%	Create a login before starting the test	Login 100 times	Average login is less than 1 second. No login takes loger than 5 seconds
Time for unsuccessful login	Check on login response time	2	0%			

Figure 11-20. *The Data Entry view*

Creating a Test Scenarios Page

You'll now create a web page that will list the test scenarios and also show the specific test cases for the selected scenario. This will allow you to easily browse the scenarios, view the existing test cases, and add more test cases if needed. You will use the same web part page used in previous chapters.

From the Site Actions menu, select the *More Options* link. In the Filter By section, select Page. Then select the Web Part Page template, as shown in Figure 11-21.

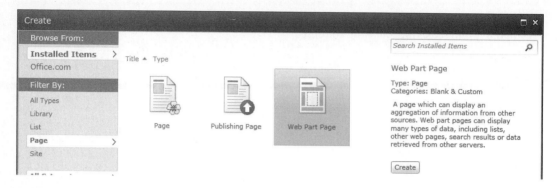

Figure 11-21. *Selecting the Web Part Page template*

Click the Create button. Enter the name **Test Scenarios** and select the Header, Footer, 3 Columns layout. Select the Site Pages library, as shown in Figure 11-22.

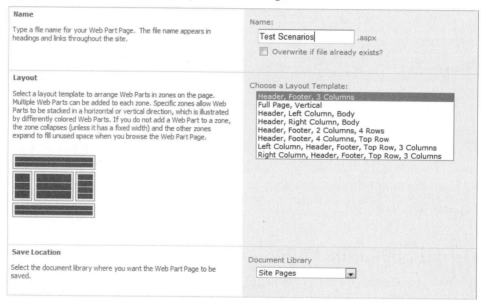

Figure 11-22. *Configuring the Test Scenarios page*

Click the *Add a Web Part* link in the Header section. From the Lists and Libraries category, select the Test Scenarios list and click the Add button. In the same way, add the Test Cases list to the Footer section.

Set up a connection between the web parts so the Test Cases list is filtered based on the selected test scenario. Click the drop-down icon on the Test Cases web part, and click the *Connections, Get Filter Values From,* and *Test Scenarios* links, as shown in Figure 11-23.

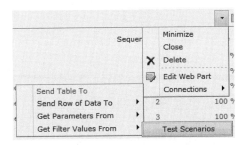

Figure 11-23. *Adding a connection*

In the dialog box, select the ID column for the provider and the Test Scenario column for the consumer, as shown in Figure 11-24.

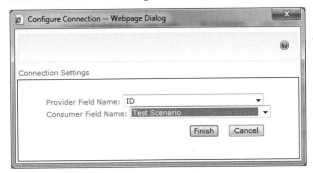

Figure 11-24. *Configuring the web part connection*

Click the Stop Editing button to display the Test Scenarios page. As you select a test scenario, the associated test cases will be displayed, as demonstrated in Figure 11-25.

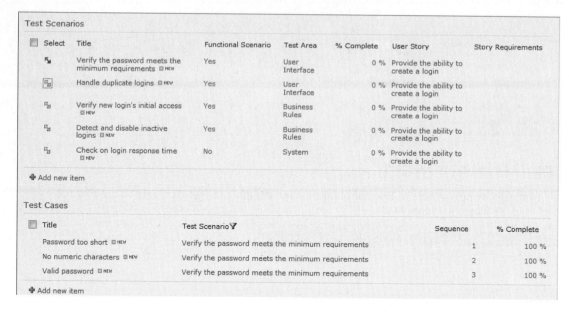

Figure 11-25. *The completed Test Scenarios page*

From this page you can add new test cases, as well as edit existing test cases and scenarios.

Summary

In this chapter you implemented a facility for defining test scenarios, which can then be expanded into detailed test cases. The scenarios are linked to either user stories or requirements, as appropriate, and are also categorized by user-defined test areas. You also provided some usability features to make data entry and analysis more efficient, including

- A datasheet view for capturing test scenarios

- A datasheet view for defining test cases

- The ability to enter partial information and fill in details later

- A web page to browse the scenarios, which also lists the associated test cases

These facilities support the test-planning activities. In the next chapter you'll use the test scenarios and test cases as the primary input into the actual testing process.

CHAPTER 12

■■■

Reporting Defects

In this chapter you'll provide a facility for defining a test cycle, which is a set of test cases that are to be performed against a specific release. You will then use this to record the test results.

Review

In the previous chapter you defined the test cases that will be used to verify your project. This process started by defining test scenarios. Each test scenario covers a particular topic or set of interactions, without the detailed input/output specifications. A scenario is usually a short description, often just a phrase or two. By keeping these brief and at a high level, you can more easily cover the entire scope that must be tested, without getting bogged down with the details. Scenarios can be used for both functional and nonfunctional requirements.

You provided for scenarios to be grouped into testing areas to help organize them. Test scenarios can also be assigned to either a user story or one or more requirements. This allows you to trace each test scenario back to the requirement that is being verified. This provides two advantages:

- The originating requirement is readily available when writing the detailed test cases.

- You can see at a glance the scenarios defined for each requirement and determine how well it has been covered.

Once the scenarios were defined, you then provided a means for entering the specific test cases. Each test case defines the specific input and expected output, as well as any assumed preconditions. Because of the volume of test cases, you created a datasheet view for easier data entry. You also provided a web page for viewing the test scenarios and the test cases associated with each.

When the test planning is complete, you will have a set of test cases that have been organized into scenarios. Each scenario, in turn, is associated with a user story or requirement. Now it's time to start testing and recording the results.

Test Cycles

As you probably know, tests are often repeated. For example, the system is released and the specified test cases are performed. Defects are reported and addressed and an update is then released. At this point, the tests are performed again. This cycle is repeated as often as necessary.

Test Items

A test cycle is simply the set of test cases that are to be executed against a specific release. It is a collection of test items, each of which references a test case. The test case specifies the test to be performed, including input and output details. The test item, however, records the results. When the test is repeated, in a subsequent test cycle, a separate test item will record those results. This is illustrated in Figure 12-1.

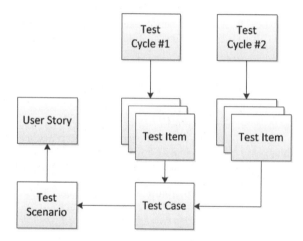

Figure 12-1. *The relationship between test cases and test items*

The same test case is used for both tests, which also references a test scenario. The scenario can be associated with a user story (or one or more requirements). These objects define the test that should be performed. The test item records a single execution of that test, including the results. The test cycle provides the context of the test execution—for example, the specific release that the test is performed against.

■Tip The target for each test cycle should remain static. In other words, you should not make any changes during the test. Changes can invalidate previous test results and leave you with an inaccurate assessment of the quality of the current release. If there are significant issues with the current release and it is difficult or impractical to complete the remaining tests, the test cycle should be cancelled. When the issues are addressed, a new release will be retested with a new test cycle.

At the beginning of each test cycle, the specific test cases are chosen to be included in that cycle. You don't necessarily have to execute every test case in every cycle. Part of the test planning is to determine the appropriate tests for each test cycle. In any case, a test item is created for each test case that should be performed. The test cycle, along with its set of test items, defines the work to be done. They also serve as the place to record the test results.

Agile Testing

This approach fits very well with the agile development methodology. The test cases associated with each iteration must be performed before the iteration is finished. So there will be at least one test cycle per iteration. Additional test cycles may be necessary as well.

If you're using the agile methodology for development, the definition of each test cycle becomes fairly straightforward. Each iteration is responsible for delivering a set of user stories. Each user story has a set of test scenarios that have been defined, which are then expanded into test cases. This is illustrated in Figure 12-2. Iterations and user stories are a very convenient (and effective) way to define your test cycles.

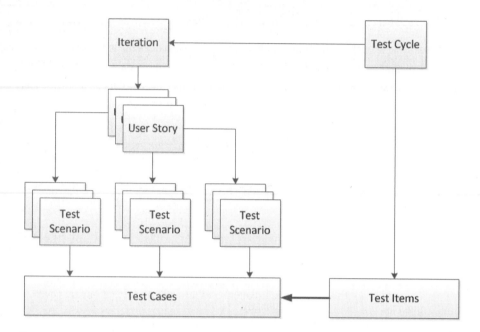

Figure 12-2. *Determining test cases for an iteration*

■**Note** The solution described in the remainder of this chapter is based on using the agile methodology. It uses the definition of the iteration and user stories to automate the creation of the test items for each test cycle. If you are not using agile, the concepts described here are still very much applicable. The only difference is that you will either need to populate the test cycle manually or provide some other criteria for automating this process.

Test Results

A test item captures a single execution of a test case. In addition to referencing a test case (that defines the test), a test item will record whether the test has been executed or not and a pass/fail indicator. For failed tests, a comment should be included to describe the defect.

Failed tests can be fed into whatever defect-reporting mechanism you may have in place. In Chapter 8, you implemented a defect list as part of the iteration backlog. The solution presented here will feed failed tests directly into the iteration backlog. You can modify this process to populate a separate bug list if you're not using the iteration backlog.

Implementing Test Cycles

The remainder of this chapter will show you how to build a solution that follows this approach. You will first create a Test Cycles list and a Test Items list. These will be created using SharePoint Designer, just like you created the previous lists. To automatically populate the Test Items list, you'll create a workflow using Visual Studio 2010. The workflow will be associated with the Test Cycles list. After creating a new test cycle, you'll execute the workflow, which will create the necessary test items.

You will then enhance this workflow to also copy the defects to the iteration backlog for any failed tests. To support this, you will modify the Iteration Defect content type to support a reference to a Test Items list. The test item provides the reference to the test case, which defines the test, as well as a description of the defect.

Defining Test Cycles

Open the SharePoint site. From the Site Actions menu, click the *Edit in SharePoint Designer* link, which will launch SharePoint Designer and open this site.

Creating the Test Status Site Column

Click the *Site Columns* link in the Navigation pane. Then click the New Column button in the ribbon and select the Choice column type. Enter the name **Test Status** and select the Project Management group. Define the following choices:

- **Initial**
- **Planned**
- **InProgress**
- **Completed**
- **Cancelled**

Enter **Initial** for the default value and unselect the "Allow blank values?" check box. The Column Editor dialog box will look like Figure 12-3. Click the OK button. Then click the Save icon to save the changes.

Figure 12-3. *Defining the Test Status column*

Creating the Test Cycle Content Type

Click the *Content Type* link in the Navigation pane and then click the Content Type button in the ribbon. Enter the name **Test Cycle** and select Item as the parent type. Also, select the Project Management group, as shown in Figure 12-4.

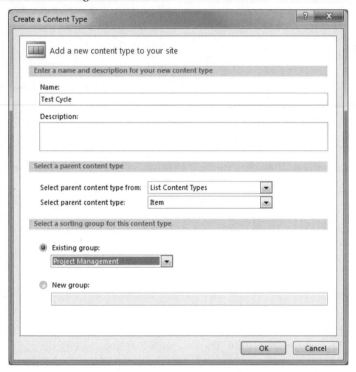

Figure 12-4. *Adding the Test Cycle content type*

Click the *Test Cycle* link in the list of content types, which will display the content type editor. Click the *Edit content type columns* link in the Customization section. Using the Add Existing Site Column button in the ribbon, add the following site columns to this content type:

- Iteration

- Test Status

- Start Date

- End Date

The list of columns should look like Figure 12-5.

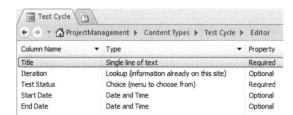

Figure 12-5. *The site columns included in the Test Cycle content type*

Creating the Test Cycles List

Click the *Lists and Libraries* link in the Navigation pane. Click the Custom List button in the ribbon, enter the name **Test Cycles**, and click the OK button. Click the *Test Cycles* link to configure this list. In the settings section, unselect the "Allow attachments" check box and select the "Allow management of content types" check box. The Settings section should look like Figure 12-6.

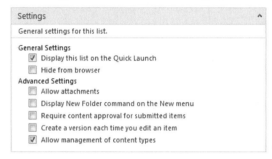

Figure 12-6. *Configuring the Settings section*

In the Content Type section, click the Add button and select the Test Cycle content type. Remove the Folder and Item content types. Click the Save icon to save your changes.

Modifying the Test Cycles Views

Go back to the SharePoint site and refresh the page so the Test Cycles list will be included in the Quick Launch area. Go to the Test Cycles list. The default view only includes the Title column. From the List ribbon, click the Modify View button. Add the following columns and change the position so they are displayed in this order:

- Test Status
- Iteration
- Start Date
- End Date

Now you'll add a view that only includes test cycles that are in progress. You are usually most interested in the current test cycle, and this view will make it easier to find it. From the List ribbon, click the Create View button and then click the *Standard View* link. Enter the name **Current**. The list of columns should be the same as the default view. Go to the Filter section, select the Test Status column, and enter **InProgress** for the criteria. The Filter section should look like Figure 12-7. Click the OK button to save this view.

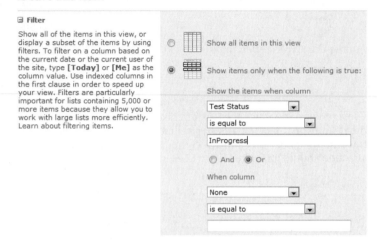

Figure 12-7. *Defining the filter for the Current view*

Adding a Test Cycle

Click the *Add new item* link to create a test cycle. Enter the Title as **Iteration 1 - 1st Pass** and select Iteration 1, as shown in Figure 12-8.

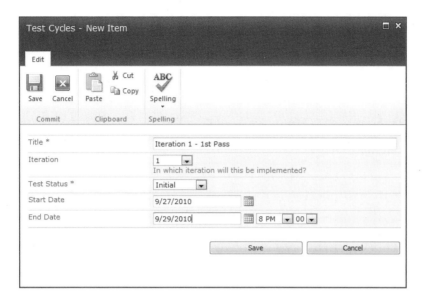

Figure 12-8. *Adding a test cycle*

■Tip You will need to select the All Items view to be able to see this test cycle, since it is in the Initial status and the Current view only shows InProgress test cycles.

Defining Test Items

Now you will create the Test Items list using the same approach. Each test item must reference the test cycle that it is included in, as well as the test case that it will execute. It will also record the test results.

Creating Additional Site Columns

You'll start by creating several site columns. Go back to SharePoint Designer and click the *Site Columns* link in the Navigation pane. Click the New Column button in the ribbon and select the Lookup column type. Enter the name **Test Cycle** and select the Project Management group. In the Column Editor dialog box, select the Test Cycles list and the Title column. Unselect the "Allow blank values?" check box, as shown in Figure 12-9.

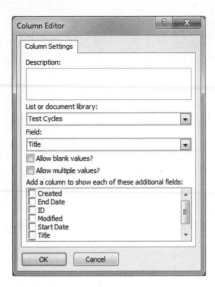

Figure 12-9. *Defining the Test Cycle column*

In the same way, create a site column named **Test Case** that references the Test Cases list, as shown in Figure 12-10.

Figure 12-10. *Defining the Test Case column*

In addition, create the following site columns, putting them in the Project Management group and using the default settings for each:

- *Test Pass/Fail*: Yes/No

- *Test Comment*: Multi Lines of Text

Make sure you save your changes.

Creating the Test Item Content Type

Click the *Content Type* link in the Navigation pane. Click the Content Type button in the ribbon. Enter the name **Test Item** and select Item as the parent type. Also, select the Project Management group. Click the OK button to create the content type. Then click the *Test Item* link in the list of content types, and click the *Edit content type columns* link in the Customization section. Using the Add Existing Site Column button in the ribbon, add the following site columns to this content type:

- Test Cycle

- Test Case

- Test Status

- Start Date

- End Date

- Test Pass/Fail

- Test Comment

Click the Save icon to save the changes. The list of columns should look like Figure 12-11.

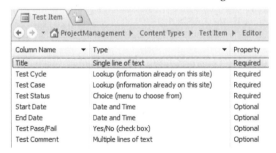

Figure 12-11. *The site columns of the Test Item content type*

Creating the Test Items List

Click the *Lists and Libraries* link in the Navigation pane and then click the Custom List button in the ribbon. Enter the name **Test Items** and click the OK button to create the list. Then click the *Test Items* link to configure this list. In the Settings section, unselect the "Display this list on the Quick Launch" and "Allow attachments" check boxes. Also, select the "Allow management of content types" check box, as shown in Figure 12-12.

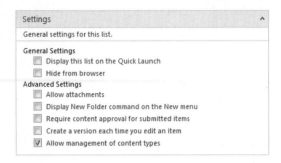

Figure 12-12. *Configuring the Test Items list*

■**Note** The Test Items list will not be in the Quick Launch area because you won't need to access it directly. Instead, you will be creating a site page that will allow you to view a test cycle and all of its test items.

In the Content Types section, add the Test Item content type and remove the Folder and Item content types. Click the Save icon to save the changes.

Implementing the Test Cycle Workflow

As I described earlier, the Test Items list can be populated automatically for a given test cycle. Each test cycle references an iteration. The iteration specifies a collection of user stories, each of which specifies a collection of test scenarios. Scenarios, in turn, contain a list of test cases. By traversing the Iterations, User Stories, Test Scenarios, and Test Cases lists, you can generate the set of test cases associated with a test cycle. To implement this logic, you'll create a workflow in Visual Studio.

■**Tip** The workflow that you'll create is not the typical workflow that generates tasks and has multiple steps in a process. Rather, as you'll see, it is simply some code that you can execute on demand.

Creating a Visual Studio Project

Start Visual Studio 2010 with administrator privileges. You can do this by right-clicking the Visual Studio shortcut and selecting the *Run as administrator* option, as shown in Figure 12-13.

Figure 12-13. *Running Visual Studio 2010 as administrator*

From the Start Page, click the *New Project* link. In the New Project dialog box, select the Sequential Workflow template from the SharePoint 2010 category, as shown in Figure 12-14. Select an appropriate folder to create the project in and click the OK button.

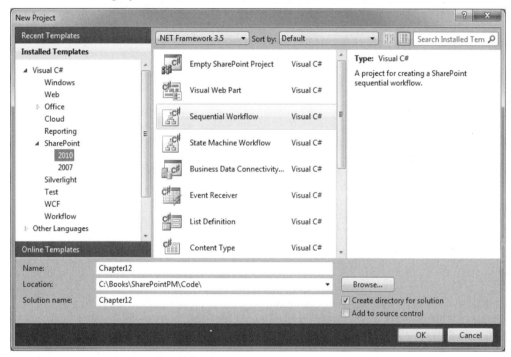

Figure 12-14. *Selecting the Sequential Workflow project template*

This will start the SharePoint Customization Wizard, which will present a series of dialogs to help configure the project. In the first dialog box, shown in Figure 12-15, enter the URL of the SharePoint site. The URL for your site will be different from the one shown here.

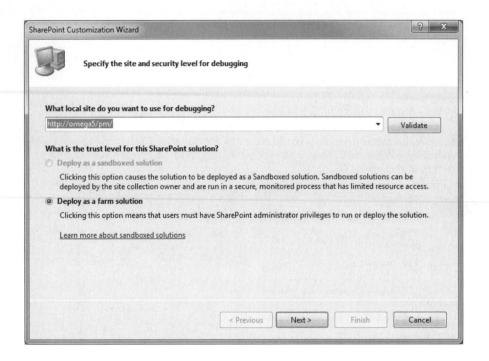

Figure 12-15. *Specifying the SharePoint site*

■**Note**   The sandbox solution is not available because workflows must be deployed as a farm solution.

In the second dialog box, you'll provide information about the workflow that you are creating. Enter the name **TestCycle** and select the List Workflow option, as shown in Figure 12-16. Workflows are typically associated with a specific list. SharePoint 2010 introduced the ability to define site workflows, which are not tied to a list or library. For this workflow, however, you'll want to associate this with the Test Cycle list.

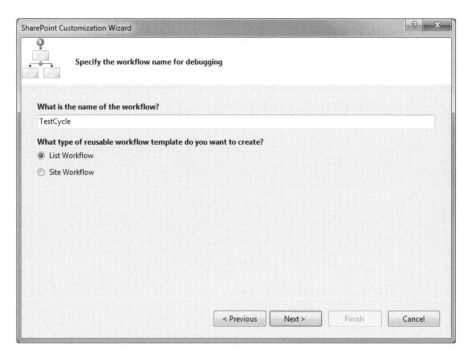

Figure 12-16. *Selecting the workflow type*

In the third dialog box, select the Test Cycles list as the one that the workflow should be associated with. You can leave the default options for the history and task lists. The dialog box should look like Figure 12-17.

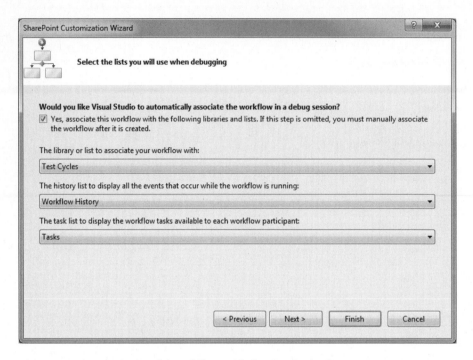

Figure 12-17. *Associating the workflow with the Test Cycles list*

The history list is an internal list used by the workflow engine to record when a workflow is executed. It can also be used to log information and error messages from the workflow. The tasks list is used to store tasks that may be generated by the workflow. (This workflow will not generate any tasks, however.)

The final dialog box allows you to specify when the workflow should be started. You can configure the workflow to start automatically when a new item is added to a list or when an item is changed. For your purposes, however, you only want the workflow to be executed manually. Unselect the other two options, as shown in Figure 12-18.

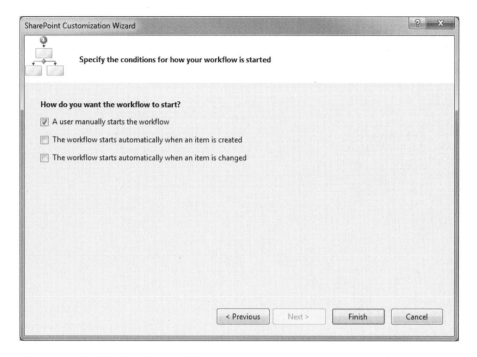

Figure 12-18. *Selecting the workflow start options*

Defining the Workflow

Now that the project wizard has configured the workflow, you're ready to implement the processing logic. The workflow diagram should be displayed with a single activity, as shown in Figure 12-19.

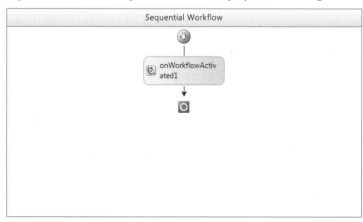

Figure 12-19. *The initial workflow design*

227

The onWorkflowActivated1 activity is executed when the workflow is started. The Toolbox window contains other activities that you can include in your workflow. Find the CodeActivity in the Toolbox and drag it to the workflow diagram, just below the onWorkflowActivated1 activity. The diagram should look like Figure 12-20.

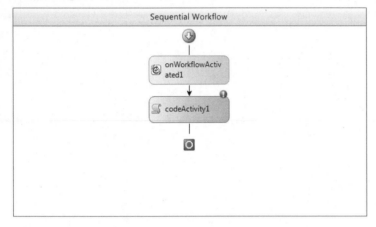

Figure 12-20. *The modified workflow design*

Notice the red circle with an exclamation point inside. This is letting your know that there is an error with your workflow. You can click this icon to view the error message. In this case, it is because the event handler has not been created for this activity. Double-click the codeActivity1 activity, which will generate the event handler and open the code-behind file where you will implement this handler.

Implementing the Workflow Logic

In the code-behind file, Workflow1.cs, add the following namespace just after the existing using statements:

```
using System.Collections.Generic;
```

For the codeActivity1_ExecuteCode event handler, enter the code shown in Listing 12-1.

Listing 12-1. *Implementation of the codeActivity1 Event Handler*

```
private void codeActivity1_ExecuteCode(object sender, EventArgs e)
{
    using (SPWeb web = SPContext.Current.Web)
    {
        // Get the test cycle that we're working on
        SPListItem cycle = workflowProperties.Item;

        // Get the status of the test cycle
        string cycleStatus = cycle["Test Status"] as string;
```

```
// Get the referenced iteration
SPFieldLookupValue value =
    new SPFieldLookupValue(cycle["Iteration"].ToString());
SPList iterations = web.Lists["Iterations"];
SPListItem iteration = iterations.GetItemById(value.LookupId);

// Get the lists that we will need later
SPList testScenarios = web.Lists["Test Scenarios"];
SPList testCases = web.Lists["Test Cases"];
SPList testItems = web.Lists["Test Items"];

// If the status is Initial, populate the Test Items list
if (cycleStatus == "Initial")
{

    // Iterate through all of the user stories
    List<int> userStoryIDs = new List<int>();
    SPList userStories = web.Lists["User Stories"];
    foreach (SPListItem userStory in userStories.Items)
    {
        if (userStory["Iteration"] != null &&
            userStory["Iteration"].ToString() ==
                cycle["Iteration"].ToString())
            userStoryIDs.Add(userStory.ID);
    }

    // Iterate through all of the test scenarios
    List<int> testScenarioIDs = new List<int>();
    foreach (SPListItem testScenario in testScenarios.Items)
    {
        if (testScenario["User Story"] != null)
        {
            SPFieldLookupValue userStoryFieldValue =
             new SPFieldLookupValue(testScenario["User Story"].ToString());

            if (userStoryIDs.Contains<int>(userStoryFieldValue.LookupId))
                testScenarioIDs.Add(testScenario.ID);
        }
    }

    // Iteration through all of the test cases
    foreach (SPListItem testCase in testCases.Items)
    {
        SPFieldLookupValue testScenarioFieldValue =
            new SPFieldLookupValue(testCase["Test Scenario"].ToString());

        if (testScenarioIDs.Contains<int>(testScenarioFieldValue.LookupId))
        {
            // Add this test case to the test cycle
            SPListItem testItem = testItems.Items.Add();
            testItem["Title"] = testCase.Title;
```

```
                      testItem["Test Status"] = "Planned";
                      testItem["Test Cycle"] =
                         cycle.ID.ToString() + ";#" + cycle.Title;
                      testItem["Test Case"] =
                         testCase.ID.ToString() + ";#" + testCase.Title;
                      testItem.Update();
                  }
              }

              // Mark the test cycle as Planned
              cycle["Test Status"] = "Planned";
              cycle.Update();
          }
      }
}
```

Most of this code should be self-explanatory, but I will explain some of the more salient points. The SPWeb class represents the SharePoint site and is used to access the lists within this site. This is obtained by using the static SPContext class and retrieving the Current.Web property. You should always access this within a using statement so it is automatically disposed of when it goes out of scope.

The SPList class represents a SharePoint list such as the Iterations or Test Cases lists. The SPListItem class represents a list item—a specific record within a list.

The workflowProperties variable is an instance of the SPWorkflowActivationProperties class. This was set up for you by the project template and provides information about the current workflow instance, such as any parameters that are being passed in. The Item property specifies the list item that the workflow was executed on. Since the workflow is associated with the Test Cycles list, this will be an item from this list. This tells us the specific test cycle that the workflow is supposed to process.

Navigating through a Lookup column is a little more complicated than you might expect. The actual value that is returned when accessing a Lookup column is a string that includes both the ID of the referenced object and the display column. This is typically the Title of the referenced record, but could be a different column depending on how the site column was defined. The two parts are delimited by the ;# characters. To obtain the ID from this value, you can parse the string yourself. However, SharePoint provides the SPFieldLookupValue class to do this for you. To use this, you create an instance of the SPFieldLookupValue class passing in the column value to the constructor. You can then use the LookupId property to obtain the ID portion. Once you have the ID, you can call the GetItemById() method of the SPList object to obtain the referenced object. This is demonstrated in the following code:

```
// Get the referenced iteration
SPFieldLookupValue value = new SPFieldLookupValue(cycle["Iteration"].ToString());
SPList iterations = web.Lists["Iterations"];
SPListItem iteration = iterations.GetItemById(value.LookupId);
```

The cycle variable is the SPListItem object associated with the test cycle that the workflow is being executed on. Its Iteration column is retrieved and passed to the SPFieldLookupValue class constructor. The LookupId property is then passed to the GetItemById() method of the Iterations list. This returns an SPListItem object that represents the specific iteration associated with this test cycle.

The workflow logic first checks the status of the test cycle. If it is set to Initial, the workflow then obtains all the relevant test cases and populates the Test Items list. If the status is not Initial, nothing more is done. This prevents duplicates from being created should the workflow be executed multiple times. The workflow logic traverses the User Stories, Test Scenarios, and Test Cases lists.

For each test case, a test item is created and added to the Test Items list. A reference to the test cycle and test case record is made by populating the associated Lookup columns. Notice that the value is computed by concatenating the ID with the Title property, separated by the same ;# delimiter. Finally, the test cycle is also updated, changing its status to Planned.

Deploying and Running the Workflow

Press F6 to build the project and fix any compiler errors that may occur. To deploy this solution to the SharePoint site, right-click the solution in Solution Explorer and choose the *Deploy Solution* link, as shown in Figure 12-21.

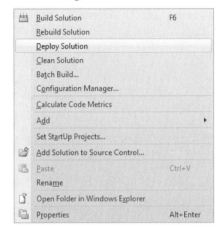

Figure 12-21. *Deploying the workflow*

■**Tip**   If you want to debug the workflow, set a breakpoint in your event handler code. Then, instead of deploying the workflow, simply press F5. This will deploy the workflow to the SharePoint site and start the Visual Studio debugger. The SharePoint site will be displayed in a new browser window and the Test Cycles list will be selected. Start the workflow from here as you would normally, and the execution will stop at your breakpoint. From there you can step through the code to verify the logic.

Go to the SharePoint site and select the Test Cycles list. Click the Title column of the existing test cycle record that you created earlier to display the View form. Click the Workflows button near the top of the form. This will display the available workflows, as shown in Figure 12-22.

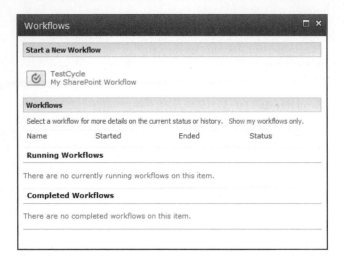

Figure 12-22. *Displaying the available workflows*

Click the *TestCycle* link to start this workflow. After a few seconds the workflow should finish, and you'll see the form shown in Figure 12-23. This is the All Items view (the default view), with a column added to display the workflow status.

Figure 12-23. *Displaying the list with the workflow status*

To verify the results of the workflow, you can display the contents of the Test Items list.

■**Tip** This list was not added to the Quick Launch area. Click the *Lists* link in the Quick Launch to display all of the lists. You can then select the Test Items list from there.

The default view of the Test Items list only includes the Title column. From the List ribbon, click the Modify View button. Add the following columns to the view:

- Test Cycle

- Test Status

- Test Case

- Test Pass/Fail

- Test Comment

The view should look like Figure 12-24.

	Title	Test Cycle	Test Status	Test Case	Test Pass/Fail	Test Comment
	Password too short ☑ NEW	Iteration 1 - 1st Pass	Planned	Password too short		
	No numeric characters ☑ NEW	Iteration 1 - 1st Pass	Planned	No numeric characters		
	Valid password ☑ NEW	Iteration 1 - 1st Pass	Planned	Valid password		
	Time for successful login ☑ NEW	Iteration 1 - 1st Pass	Planned	Time for successful login		
	Time for unsuccessful login ☑ NEW	Iteration 1 - 1st Pass	Planned	Time for unsuccessful login		

Figure 12-24. *The Test Items list populated by the workflow*

Recording the Test Results

At this point you have planned a test cycle and populated it with a test item for each test case. This would be assigned to the test team to perform the specified tests. Go to the Test Cycles list, edit the test cycle, and change the Test Status to InProgress.

To make this easier for the test team, you'll provide a web page that lists the test cycles that are in progress and displays all the test items associated with the selected test cycle. This will use the same web part page that you have used before.

Adding a Web Part Page

From the Site Actions menu, click the *More Options* link. Filter the template list to Page types only, select the Web Part Page template, and then click the Create button. Enter the name **Test Cycle**, select the Header, Footer, 3 Columns layout, and select the Site Pages library, as shown in Figure 12-25.

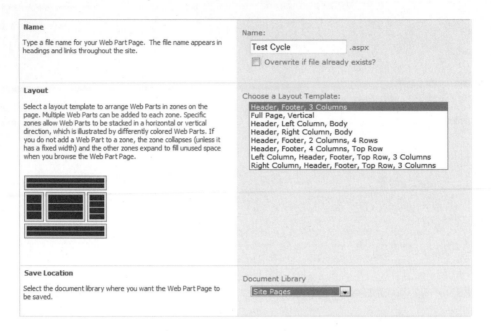

Figure 12-25. *Configuring the Test Cycle page*

Click the *Add a Web Part* link in the Header section. From the Lists and Libraries category, select the Test Cycles list and click the Add button. Edit the web part to select the Current view. This will filter the list to only test cycles that are in progress. Also change the toolbar type to No Toolbar.

In the same way, add the Test Items list to the Footer section. Set up a connection between these web parts so the Test Items list is filtered by the selected test cycle. From the drop-down icon next to the Test Items web part, click the *Connections, Get Filter Values From,* and *Test Cycles* links, as shown in Figure 12-26.

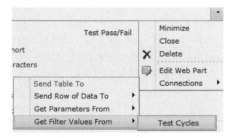

Figure 12-26. *Adding a web part connection*

In the dialog box that is displayed, select the ID column for the provider and the Test Cycle column for the consumer, as shown in Figure 12-27. Click the Stop Editing button in the ribbon.

Configure Connection -- Webpage Dialog
Connection Settings
Provider Field Name: ID
Consumer Field Name: Test Cycle
Finish
Cancel

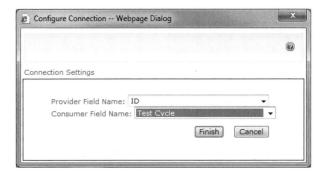

Figure 12-27. *Configuring the web part connection*

The page should look like Figure 12-28.

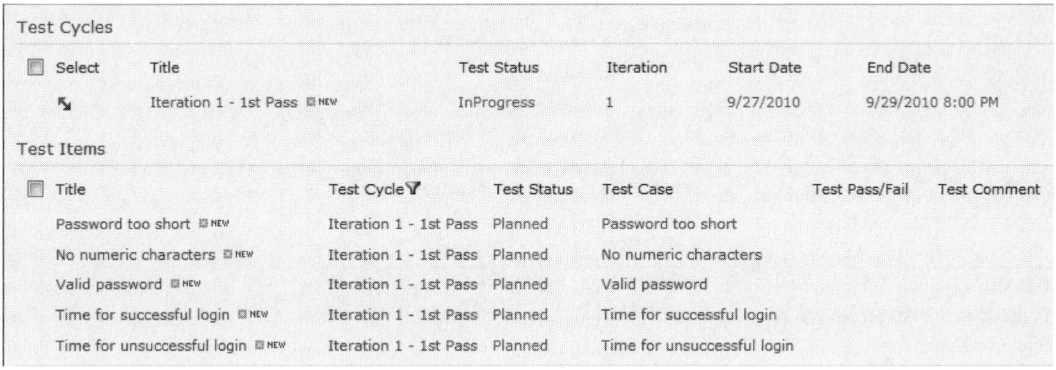

Test Cycles
Select Title Test Status Iteration Start Date End Date
Iteration 1 - 1st Pass NEW InProgress 1 9/27/2010 9/29/2010 8:00 PM
Test Items
Title Test Cycle Test Status Test Case Test Pass/Fail Test Comment
Password too short NEW Iteration 1 - 1st Pass Planned Password too short
No numeric characters NEW Iteration 1 - 1st Pass Planned No numeric characters
Valid password NEW Iteration 1 - 1st Pass Planned Valid password
Time for successful login NEW Iteration 1 - 1st Pass Planned Time for successful login
Time for unsuccessful login NEW Iteration 1 - 1st Pass Planned Time for unsuccessful login

Figure 12-28. *The Test Cycle page*

Performing the Tests

The `Test Cycle` page lists the cycles that are active, which is normally only one, and displays all the test items for the associated test cycle. The `Test Case` column is a link to the test case, which has all the details needed to execute the test. The drop-down menu next to the `Title` column can be used to edit the test item and report the test results.

Edit one of the test items and update the status, as shown in Figure 12-29.

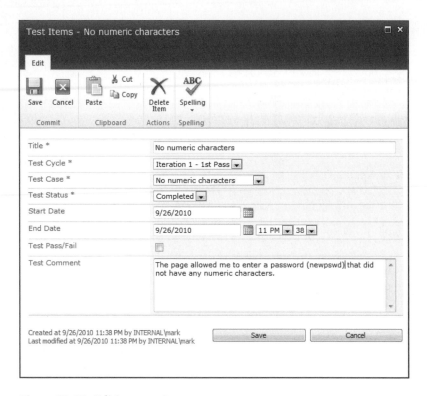

Figure 12-29. *Editing a test item*

Edit several more of the existing test items, making sure to change the status to Completed. On some, leave the Test Pass/Fail check box unselected, which indicates that the test failed. For failed tests, enter a Test Comment as well.

Generating Defects in the Iteration Backlog

For the final step in this chapter, you'll now enhance the workflow to also copy failed test items to the iteration backlog.

Modifying the Iteration Defect Content Type

To support this feature, you'll need to modify the Iteration Defect content type to include an optional reference to the Test Items list. When displaying the defect, the test item can then be viewed, which provides details of the test as well as a description of the defect. Because this is an existing content type, you'll use the SharePoint Site Settings page instead of SharePoint Designer. This will propagate the change to the Iteration Items list as well.

From the Site Actions menu, click the *Site Settings* link. Then click the *Site columns* link in the Galleries section. Click the *Create* link. In the New Site Column page, enter the name **Test Item**, select the Lookup column type, and select the Project Management group. In the Additional Column Settings section, select the `Test Items` list and the `Title` column. You can leave the remaining options with their default values. The sections should look like Figure 12-30.

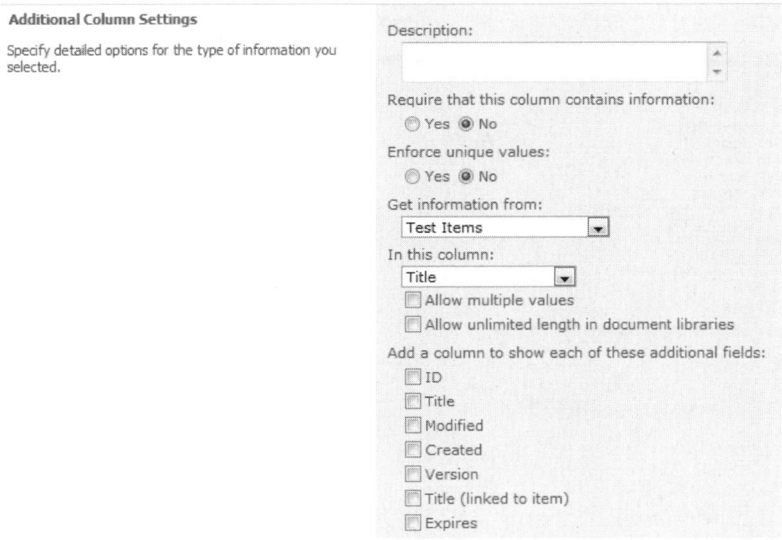

Additional Column Settings

Specify detailed options for the type of information you selected.

Description:

Require that this column contains information:
○ Yes ● No

Enforce unique values:
○ Yes ● No

Get information from:
Test Items

In this column:
Title
☐ Allow multiple values
☐ Allow unlimited length in document libraries

Add a column to show each of these additional fields:
☐ ID
☐ Title
☐ Modified
☐ Created
☐ Version
☐ Title (linked to item)
☐ Expires

Figure 12-30. *Configuring the Test Item site column*

Go back to the `Site Settings` page and click the *Site content types* link. Select the `Project Management` group to filter the list, and then click the *Iteration Defect* link to edit this content type. Click the *Add from existing site columns* link. Select the `Project Management` group to filter the list of site columns. Select the `Test Item` site column and click the Add button. Make sure to set the "Update all content types inheriting from this type?" option to Yes. The page should look like Figure 12-31.

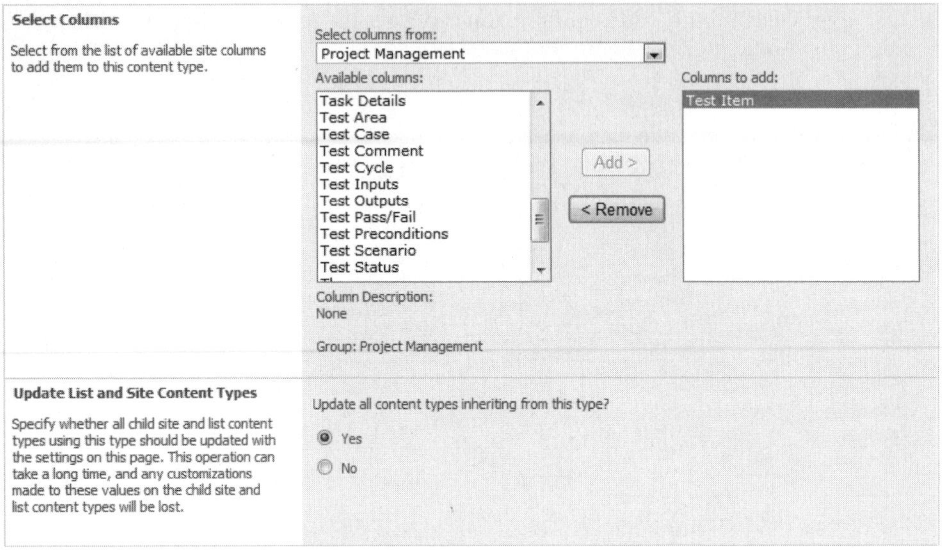

Figure 12-31. *Adding the Test Item site column*

Click the OK button to add the site column.

Adding the Workflow Logic

Go back to the Visual Studio project and add the code from Listing 12-2 to the event handler. The existing code includes logic inside an `if` statement to be executed only when the status is `Initial`. This code will add another `if` statement for when the status is `InProgress`.

Listing 12-2. *Logic for the InProgress Status*

```
if (cycleStatus == "InProgress")
{
    // Retrieve the failed items
    SPQuery query = new SPQuery();
    query.Query =
        "<Where>" +
            "<And>" +
                "<Eq>" +
                    "<FieldRef Name='Test_x0020_Cycle' LookupId='TRUE' />" +
                    "<Value Type='Lookup'>" + cycle.ID.ToString() + "</Value>" +
                "</Eq>" +
                "<And>" +
                    "<Eq>" +
                        "<FieldRef Name='Test_x0020_Status' />" +
                        "<Value Type='Choice'>Completed</Value>" +
                    "</Eq>" +
                    "<Eq>" +
```

```
                    "<FieldRef Name='Test_x0020_Pass_x002f_Fail' />" +
                    "<Value Type='Boolean'>No</Value>" +
                "</Eq>" +
            "</And>" +
        "</And>" +
    "</Where>";

SPListItemCollection failedItems = testItems.GetItems(query);

// If there are any that failed...
if (failedItems.Count > 0)
{
    SPContentType defectContent = web.ContentTypes["Iteration Defect"];
    SPList iterationItems = web.Lists["Iteration Items"];

    foreach (SPListItem failed in failedItems)
    {
        // See if this failure has already been reported
        SPQuery itemQuery = new SPQuery();
        itemQuery.Query =
            "<Where>" +
                "<And>" +
                    "<And>" +
                        "<And>" +
                            "<Eq>" +
                                "<FieldRef Name='Iteration' LookupId='TRUE' />" +
                                "<Value Type='Lookup'>" +
                                    iteration.ID.ToString() + "</Value>" +
                            "</Eq>" +
                            "<Eq>" +
                                "<FieldRef Name='ContentType' />" +
                                "<Value Type='Text'>Iteration Defect</Value>" +
                            "</Eq>" +
                        "</And>" +
                        "<Eq>" +
                            "<FieldRef Name='Test_x0020_Item' LookupId='TRUE' />" +
                            "<Value Type='Lookup'>" +
                                failed.ID.ToString() + "</Value>" +
                        "</Eq>" +
                    "</And>" +
                    "<Or>" +
                        "<Eq>" +
                            "<FieldRef Name='Item_x0020_Status' />" +
                            "<Value Type='Choice'>Pending</Value>" +
                        "</Eq>" +
                        "<Eq>" +
                            "<FieldRef Name='Item_x0020_Status' />" +
                            "<Value Type='Choice'>InProgress</Value>" +
                        "</Eq>" +
                    "</Or>" +
                "</And>" +
            "</Where>";
```

```
SPListItemCollection matches = iterationItems.GetItems(itemQuery);

// If this failure has not been reported...
if (matches.Count == 0)
{
    // ...add this failure to the defect list
    SPListItem defect = iterationItems.Items.Add();
    defect["ContentTypeId"] = defectContent.Id;
    defect["Title"] = failed.Title;
    defect["Item Status"] = "Pending";
    defect["Iteration"] = iteration.ID.ToString() + ";#" +
        iteration.Title;
    defect["Test Item"] = failed.ID.ToString() + ";#" + failed.Title;

    // Determine the user story
    SPFieldLookupValue testCaseFieldValue =
        new SPFieldLookupValue(failed["Test Case"].ToString());
    SPListItem testCase =
        testCases.GetItemById(testCaseFieldValue.LookupId);
    if (testCase != null)
    {
        SPFieldLookupValue testScenarioFieldValue =
            new SPFieldLookupValue(testCase["Test Scenario"].ToString());
        SPListItem testScenario =
            testScenarios.GetItemById(testScenarioFieldValue.LookupId);
        if (testScenario != null)
        {
            defect["User Story"] = testScenario["User Story"];
        }
    }

    defect.Update();
}
        }
    }
}
```

This logic uses the query support of SharePoint. Queries are performed by creating an SPQuery object and passing this to the GetItems() method of the SPList class. The actual query is specified in the Query property of the SPQuery class using Collaborative Application Markup Language (CAML), which is an XML-like syntax.

■**Tip** CAML is somewhat difficult to use but quite powerful. If you want more information about using CAML, I suggest you start with this site: http://msdn.microsoft.com/en-us/library/ms462365.aspx.

The first query returns all the failed test items for the current test cycle. It returns all items that are in this test cycle where the `Test Status` is `Completed` and the `Test Pass/Fail` column is `No`. Notice that the column names must be specified using their internal name, which doesn't allow spaces or special characters.

For each failed item, a second query is executed to see if there is already a defect linked to this test item. The query ignores completed defects. The intention here is that if the defect was marked complete and a subsequent test reported a failure, a new defect needs to be reported. If the defect is still open, then there's no need to create a duplicate record.

If no existing (incomplete) defect is found, a new item is added to the `Iteration Items` list.

Deploying and Running the Workflow

Press F6 to build the solution and fix any compiler errors. Then right-click the solution in Solution Explorer and choose the *Deploy Solution* link just like you did before. This will update the existing workflow with the revised logic.

Go to the SharePoint site and select the `Test Cycles` list. View the current test cycle and click the Workflow button near the top of the form. Then click the *TestCycle* link to start the workflow. After a few seconds the display should show that the workflow completed. Go to the `Iteration Items` list and you should see some additional defects.

Modifying the Iteration Backlog

Because the description of the defect is in the test item, you'll need to modify the Iteration Backlog view to include the new `Test Item` column. From the List ribbon, select the `Iteration Backlog` view. Then click the Modify View button. Select the `Test Item` column to be included in the view. Click the OK button to save the change.

The iteration backlog should now look like Figure 12-32.

	Content Type	Item Status	Blocking	Title	Hours Left	User Story	Test Item
					Sum= 145		
	Iteration Defect	Pending	Yes	There is no password field on the login page	2	Provide the ability to create a login	
	Iteration Issue	Pending	Yes	The password required are not defined	6	Allow the use to change their password	
	Iteration Defect	Pending	No	Pleese is spelled wrong on the login page	1	Provide the ability to create a login	
	Iteration Defect	Pending	No	No numeric characters ⊠ NEW	0	Provide the ability to create a login	No numeric characters
	Iteration Defect	Pending	No	Time for unsuccessful login ⊠ NEW	0	Provide the ability to create a login	Time for unsuccessful login
	Iteration Task	Pending		Design the database schema to support web logons	4	Provide the ability to create a login	
	Iteration Task	Pending		Implement the business rules to support web accounts	12	Provide the ability to create a login	
	Iteration Task	Pending		Implement the Logon page	16	Provide the ability to create a login	
	Iteration Task	Pending		Do a lot of other stuff	101	Provide the ability to create a login	
	Iteration Task	In Progress		Mockup the UI for the Logon page	3	Provide the ability to create a login	

Figure 12-32. *The modified Iteration Backlog view*

Notice that the two new defects have a link to the associated test item. The defects that were manually entered do not. In this case, the Title is a description of the test case and not necessarily a description of the defect. You'll need to click the link for the test item to see the defect description. If you prefer, you could modify the workflow to use the Test Comment column for the defect title.

Summary

In this chapter you implemented a Test Cycles list. A test cycle is used to define a set of test items that are to be performed against a specific release. You also created the Test Items list, which is used to contain these test items. Each test item references a specific test case.

You implemented a workflow in Visual Studio 2010. A workflow is a convenient place to write logic that should be executed as a background process. This workflow determines the appropriate set of test cases based on the iteration assigned to the test cycle. For each test case, a test item was added to the Test Items list. This process allows the users to automatically generate the items for a test cycle. You then created a web page for viewing the test items associated with the current test cycle. After several test items were updated, including some failed tests, you enhanced this workflow to automatically populate the iteration backlog.

The test team now has the tools it needs to plan and execute the specified test cases. In the next chapter you will analyze the test results to get some insight into the testing progress as well as the project's overall quality.

■■■

CHAPTER 13

Testing Metrics

In this chapter I'll present several metrics that will help communicate the testing progress and provide some indications as to the overall quality of the project. Then I'll show you how to add these to your SharePoint site.

Review

In Chapter 11 you developed the test cases to be used in verifying your project. You started this process by identifying test scenarios, which are a fairly brief description of a specific area that needs to be tested. I referred to this as defining breadth first, and then depth. By keeping scenarios brief, you can quickly list them as they come to mind, much like you would in a brainstorming session. I also suggested some other techniques, such a creating a matrix of objects against a set of common operations.

Scenarios can be assigned to a user story or one or more requirements. This *traceability* allows you to look at each requirement to see if it has been *covered* adequately. If you have a good set of user stories, these can be a great source of test scenarios. In fact, in a test-first approach to agile development, the acceptance tests are developed as part of the requirements definition. Scenarios should be used to identify nonfunctional areas as well.

The next step in the test-planning process is to refine each of the scenarios into a set of detailed test cases. Each test case defines a set of inputs and expected outputs. Specifying test cases at this level of detail will provide consistency in test results and remove ambiguity later. It will also allow you to use less-experienced testers.

In Chapter 12 you then provided the infrastructure for performing these tests. Testing is performed in a test cycle. Each test cycle includes a subset of test cases. At the beginning of the cycle you decide which test cases should be performed. You then execute these tests and report the defects that were found. Typically, these will be corrected and the tests can be repeated in a subsequent test cycle.

A test cycle contains a collection of test items, and each item references a single test case. The test case defines the test that should be performed, and the test item plans (and records) a particular execution of that test. The test-planning activity develops the test scenarios and test cases, whereas the test execution activity revolves around planning test cycles and the test cases that should be included.

In Chapter 12 you also implemented a workflow to populate a test cycle based on the hierarchy of iteration, user stories, test scenarios, and test cases. In agile development, each of the user stories in an iteration needs to be tested before the iteration is finished. So you'll need at least one test cycle for each iteration. Subsequent cycles will probably be needed as well. You enhanced this workflow to also copy the failed tests to the iteration backlog as defects.

■**Note**   In this chapter you will continue with the agile pattern. This provides a convenient platform for demonstrating the concepts of this chapter. These concepts work equally well when working with test cycles that are based on some other criteria. You will need to adjust the process to work with your particular structure.

Using Testing Metrics

The purpose of using metrics is to provide an objective assessment of your project. Testing metrics generally fall into two categories: *progress* and *quality*. Progress metrics indicate how much work has been done and how much is left. Quality metrics try to answer the question "How good is the end result." This can be somewhat subjective.

Progress Metrics

Measuring progress is fairly straightforward. For the current test cycle, you will have assigned a certain number of test cases. The number of test cases that have been completed is compared to the number planned, as follows:

```
test progress (CTC/TTC) = # of completed test cases / # of planned test cases x 100%
```

The metric only considers test cases that are actually completed (whether passed or failed is irrelevant). In a given test cycle you may not be able to complete all the test cases. For example, a defect could prevent you from exercising related test cases. Therefore, you could show that you are only 90 percent complete, but there are no more test cases available. For completeness, you may want to also report cancelled test cases or remove these from the total number. This metric should be updated on a daily basis, as this should reflect the progress of the current cycle in near real time.

Another useful metric is the total test cases performed for each iteration. This is really more a measure of effort than progress. This is computed by adding the total *completed* test cases for all test cycles in an iteration. For the current iteration, this may not be complete, so you should be careful about comparing it with previous iterations. You may want this available for prior iterations only.

Quality Metrics

There are many ways to measure quality. My intent in this chapter is not to provide you with an exhaustive study of testing, but rather to give you some useful techniques for capturing and reporting metrics.

■**Note**　In this chapter, I will focus on metrics that can be fairly easily gleaned from data that you're already capturing. This will give you a very good starting point. There are other techniques, such as surveys, that are also useful, but require more work to gather the data. If you want to add more metrics, start by deciding what information will help you improve the process, and then determine how best to collect the information. You should be able to incorporate additional metrics into your SharePoint site using an approach similar to the ones shown here.

The theory of testing is that a given project has a fixed number of defects, and the goal is to find all of them before the product is released. The main problem is that we don't know what that number is, so we're never quite sure when we have found the last one. This is kind of like an Easter egg hunt, where you hide eggs all over the yard and then watch the children try to find them. If you don't count the eggs before hiding them, then you don't know if they have all been found. I have come across some stragglers months, even years, later. That's what delivered defects are; they're the ones you didn't know about that often show up down the road.

Coverage

The term *coverage* describes how thoroughly the project was tested (e.g., was every line of code executed?). A *white box* approach looks at the detailed design and tries to ensure that every decision path has been verified. In contrast, a *black box* approach tries to test every possible combination of inputs. These are both excellent ways to ensure coverage. However, I suggest an easier and more practical approach.

You can measure relative coverage by comparing the number of test cases for each story point. Recall from Chapter 6 that a story point is an arbitrary but consistent scale applied to each user story. More complex user stories will be assigned more story points. For a given iteration you know how many story points are included. Once all the test cases have been written, you can compute the total number of test cases for that iteration. The formula is expressed as follows:

```
test coverage (TC/SP) = # of test cases / # of story points
```

This does not give you an insurance policy that every branch has been tested. Rather, it gives you a relative measurement. Twenty TC/SP is better than ten, but not as good as thirty. You can then adjust this ratio based on experience. If you're noticing that too many defects are not being caught, try increasing this ratio.

Initial Quality

This is a measure of the quality of the system before it enters the testing phase, and is determined based on the number of defects that were found. There are many factors that influence quality, such as clear requirements, good design, skilled implementers, and effective tools. Some would argue that these things—as opposed to effective testing—are what produce a quality product. Well, we need both, but measuring the initial quality is an important metric.

Initial quality is computed as follows:

```
quality ratio (D/SP) = # of defects / # of story points
```

You might want to provide a weight factor for each defect. A major failure that keeps the system from working may be given more weight that a cosmetic issue. Keep it simple, however. For example, just use a simple scale of 1 to 5, or perhaps just a blocking vs. nonblocking flag.

Defect Removal Effectiveness

While the initial quality metric is a reflection on the development activities, defect removal measures the ability to fix the reported defects. There are two metrics that are helpful here. The first is the ratio of repeated defects. A defect is considered to be repeated if it is reported in one test cycle and still exists in a subsequent test cycle. This metric is computed as follows:

```
repeated defect ratio (RD/CSP) = (# of repeated defects × 100) / # of story points
```

This is the number of repeated defects per 100 story points. The factor of 100 is added because this number will be fairly small and most people like whole numbers between 0 and 100. If a defect is still reported in a third test cycle, it will be counted, again, as a repeated defect.

With each subsequent test cycle, the number of defects should be decreasing. This is graphed as the quality indicator (D/SP) shown for each test cycle. The slope of the curve is a good indication of how many defects still exist. This metric can be calculated as follows:

```
defect removal rate (DRR) = # of weighted defects × (# of test cycles - 1) / (# of initial
weighted defects - # of weighted defects)
```

This formula calculates the average number of defects removed in each test cycle, and then estimates the number of test cycles left to remove the remaining defects. This metric estimates the number of additional test cycles that you will need before all the defects are removed, based on past experience.

■**Tip** It often happens that the initial defects are removed only to find new defects appear. This could be the fault of the testers for not finding all the defects in the first test cycle. To be fair, this sometimes happens because the initial defects prevent adequate testing of all the features. This can also be caused by fixes introducing new defects. Whatever the cause, however, this metric still presents an accurate picture of when the defects will be removed.

Analyzing Defect Source

In addition to the metrics just described, you should capture the source of each defect. Was this defect caused by unclear requirements or a flawed design, or was it just something that was overlooked in implementation? Was this introduced with a fix to a previous defect? This information should be captured for each defect and then later analyzed.

You should choose the categories that you can assign based on your situation. You'll implement this as a dynamic list so you can add new categories later. This data will be helpful when performing a postmortem of the project. Along the same lines, you might want to include some other data points that may provide some useful analysis. You can add these to the appropriate list and analyze them using the approach that will be described later in this chapter.

Supporting Testing Metrics

In the remainder of this chapter I'll show you how to capture and report the metrics I just described. You'll start by adding the necessary columns to the existing lists. Some of these values will be manually entered in the associated form. The rest will be generated by the system using data that already exists in your site. To do that, you'll implement a workflow just like you did in Chapter 12.

Creating Additional Site Columns

You will need several new site columns to store the data that will be used to compute the testing metrics. I will explain how to create these using the SharePoint UI.

■**Tip**   If you prefer, you can create these site columns using SharePoint Designer just like you've done in the previous chapters. The end result is the same either way.

Adding the Defect Properties

Open the SharePoint site. From the Site Actions menu, click the *Site Settings* link. Click the *Site columns* link, which is in the Galleries section. This will display the Site Settings page, which lists all of the existing site columns. Click the *Create* link to create a new column. Enter the name **Repeated Defect** and select the Yes/No column type. Select the Project Management group and set the default value to No, as shown in Figure 13-1. Click the OK button to create the column.

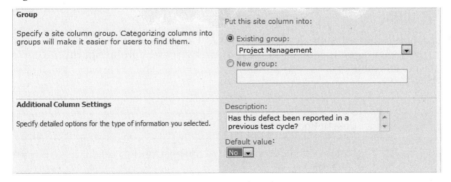

Figure 13-1. *Creating the Repeated Defect site column*

Click the *Create* link again to create a second column named **Defect Severity**. Select the Number column type and select the Project Management group. Configure the column to require a value, with a default value of **1**. Specify a minimum value of **1** and a maximum value of **3**, as shown in Figure 13-2.

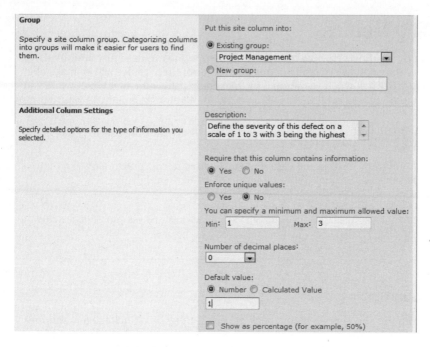

Figure 13-2. *Configuring the Defect Severity column*

Adding the Totals Columns

Now you'll create several columns that will store accumulated totals. Create a site column for each of the entries in Table 13-1. Use the Number column type, select the Project Management group, specify **0** decimal places, and set the default value to **0**.

Table 13-1. *Totals Columns*

Column Name	Description
Weighted Defects	Number of defects, weighted by severity
Initial Weighted Defects	Number of defects, weighted by severity, in the initial test cycle
Repeated Defects	Number of repeated defects
Test Cycle Count	Number of completed test cycles

Column Name	Description
Test Cases Planned	Number of planned test cases
Test Cases Completed	Number of completed test cases
Test Cases Cancelled	Number of cancelled test cases
Test Cases Failed	Number of failed test cases

The Additional Column Settings section should look like Figure 13-3.

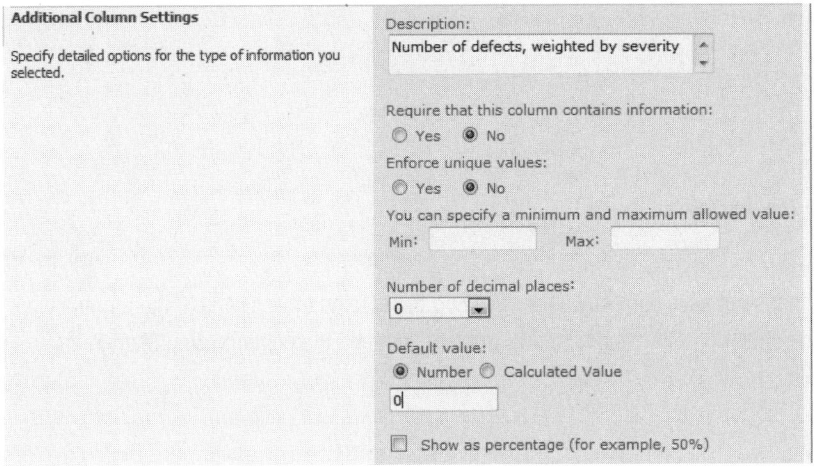

Figure 13-3. *The Additional Column Settings section for the totals columns*

Adding the Calculated Columns

Now you'll create the columns that will compute the actual metric value. These will be Calculated columns that will execute the appropriate formula using the data from the other columns. Click the *Create* button to create a new column. Enter the name **Test Progress**, select the Calculated column type, and select the Project Management group.

Next to the Formula field, there is a list of the existing site columns. Double-click the Test Cases Completed and Test Cases Planned columns to add these to the formula. Enter a / character between these to indicate that the value of the Test Cases Completed column should be divided by the value of the Test Cases Planned column. Select Number for the data type as and select the "Show as percentage" check box. The Additional Column Settings section should look like Figure 13-4.

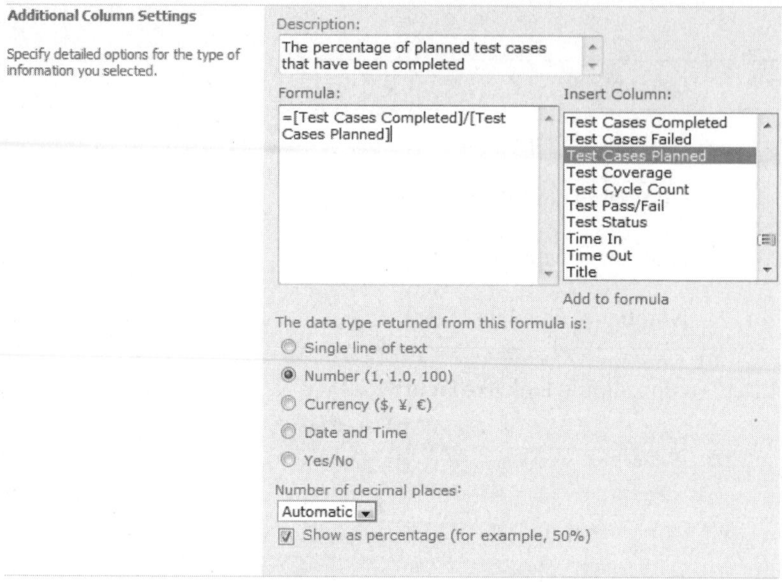

Additional Column Settings

Specify detailed options for the type of information you selected.

Description:

The percentage of planned test cases that have been completed

Formula:

=[Test Cases Completed]/[Test Cases Planned]|

Insert Column:

Test Cases Completed
Test Cases Failed
Test Cases Planned
Test Coverage
Test Cycle Count
Test Pass/Fail
Test Status
Time In
Time Out
Title

Add to formula

The data type returned from this formula is:

○ Single line of text

◉ Number (1, 1.0, 100)

○ Currency ($, ¥, €)

○ Date and Time

○ Yes/No

Number of decimal places:

Automatic ▾

☑ Show as percentage (for example, 50%)

Figure 13-4. *Configuring the Test Progress column*

▓**Caution**   I had a couple columns not save correctly. When viewing the column after saving it, the formula was blank. This appeared to be a SharePoint bug. If you notice this problem, just edit the column using SharePoint Designer and reenter the formula.

Likewise, create another calculated column named **Test Coverage**. The formula should be

=[Test Cases Planned]/[Story Points]

Configure the returned data type as a Number. This time, however, this is not a percentage, so leave the "Show as percentage" check box unselected. Set the number of decimal places to **1** as shown in Figure 13-5.

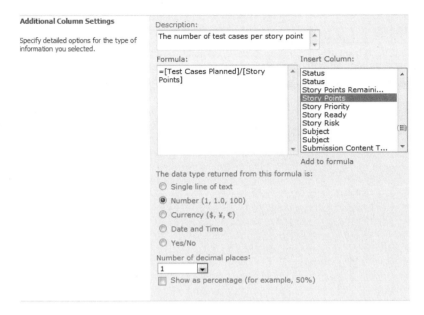

Figure 13-5. *Configuring the Test Coverage column*

The formula for each of the calculated columns is listed in Table 13-2. Create a column for the remaining items using the same settings as the Test Coverage column.

Table 13-2. *Calculated Columns*

Column Name	Formula
Test Progress	=[Test Cases Completed]/[Test Cases Planned]
Test Coverage	=[Test Cases Planned]/[Story Points]
Quality Ratio	=[Weighted Defects]/[Story Points]
Repeated Defect Ratio	=100*[Repeated Defects]/[Story Points]
Defect Removal Rate	=[Weighted Defects]*([Test Cycle Count]-1)/([Initial Weighted Defects]-[Weighted Defects])

Modifying the Lists

You have defined new site columns to store the metrics and the intermediate values that are used to compute the metrics. Now you will modify the existing lists by adding the appropriate columns.

Modifying the Test Items List

Click the *Lists* link in the Quick Launch area and then click the *Test Items* link. From the List ribbon, click the List Settings button. The Columns section will list the existing columns included in the `Test Items` list. There are links at the bottom of the list that are used to modify the columns, as shown in Figure 13-6.

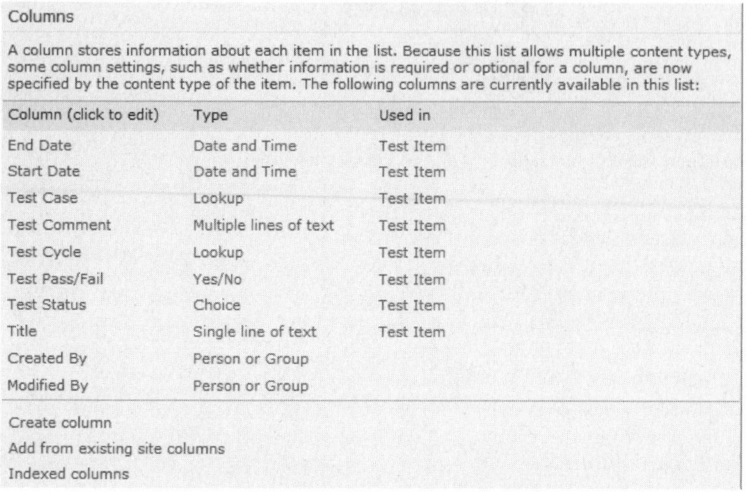
Columns
A column stores information about each item in the list. Because this list allows multiple content types, some column settings, such as whether information is required or optional for a column, are now specified by the content type of the item. The following columns are currently available in this list:
Column (click to edit)
Type
Used in
End Date
Date and Time
Test Item
Start Date
Date and Time
Test Item
Test Case
Lookup
Test Item
Test Comment
Multiple lines of text
Test Item
Test Cycle
Lookup
Test Item
Test Pass/Fail
Yes/No
Test Item
Test Status
Choice
Test Item
Title
Single line of text
Test Item
Created By
Person or Group
Modified By
Person or Group
Create column
Add from existing site columns
Indexed columns

Figure 13-6. *The Columns section of the List Settings page*

Click the *Add from existing site columns* link. Select the `Project Management` group to filter the list of columns. Select the `Defect Severity` and `Repeated Defect` columns and click the Add button. Leave the "Add to all content types" and "Add to default view" check boxes selected, as shown in Figure 13-7. Click the OK button to update the list.

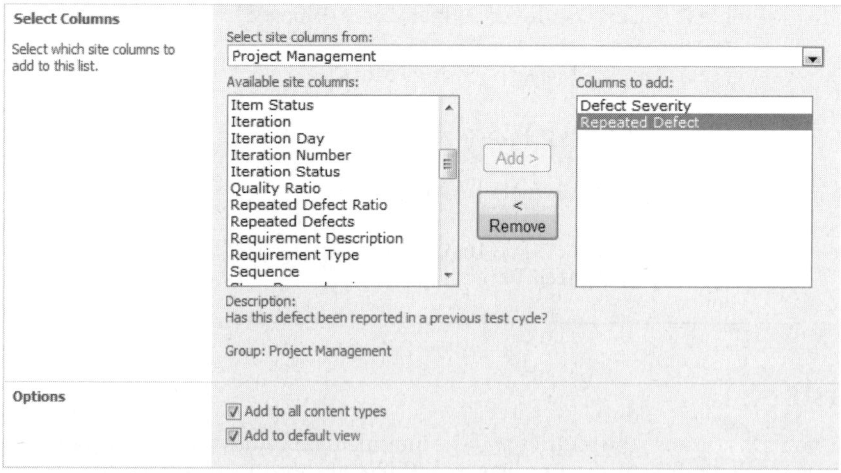
Select Columns
Select which site columns to add to this list.
Select site columns from:
Project Management
Available site columns:
Item Status
Iteration
Iteration Day
Iteration Number
Iteration Status
Quality Ratio
Repeated Defect Ratio
Repeated Defects
Requirement Description
Requirement Type
Sequence
Add >
< Remove
Columns to add:
Defect Severity
Repeated Defect
Description:
Has this defect been reported in a previous test cycle?
Group: Project Management
Options
Add to all content types
Add to default view

Figure 13-7. *Adding columns to the Test Items list*

Display the Test Items list and notice that the additional columns have been added to the view. However, they are currently empty. Edit each of the existing items (you only need to update the failed items) and enter a severity, and set the Repeated Defect column to No. The view will look like Figure 13-8.

☐ Title		Test Cycle	Test Status	Test Case	Test Pass/Fail	Test Comment	Defect Severity	Repeated Defect
Password too short	▼	Iteration 1 - 1st Pass	Planned	Password too short				
No numeric characters		Iteration 1 - 1st Pass	Completed	No numeric characters	No	The page allowed me to enter a new password (newpswd) that did not have any numeric characters.	2	No
Valid password		Iteration 1 - 1st Pass	Completed	Valid password	Yes			
Time for successful login		Iteration 1 - 1st Pass	Planned	Time for successful login				
Time for unsuccessful login		Iteration 1 - 1st Pass	Completed	Time for unsuccessful login	No	It took more than 10 seconds for a failed login.	3	No

Figure 13-8. *The modified Test Items list*

Modifying the Test Cycles List

You'll now modify the Test Cycles list in a similar fashion. Go to the Test Cycles list and click the List Settings button in the List ribbon. Then click the *Add from existing site columns* link. Filter the list of columns by selecting the Project Management group. Then select the following columns and click the Add button:

- Repeated Defects
- Story Points
- Test Cases Cancelled
- Test Cases Completed
- Test Cases Failed
- Test Cases Planned
- Weighted Defects

Unselect the "Add to default view" check box, as shown in Figure 13-9. The columns will be added to the list as well as the content type, but they will not be displayed in the default view.

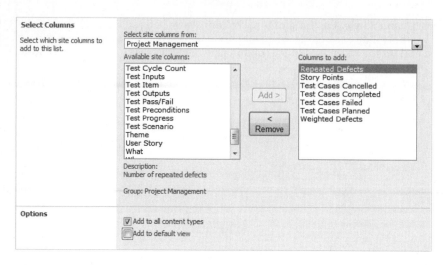

Figure 13-9. *Adding columns to the Test Cycles list*

Using the same procedure, add the following columns to the Test Cycles list. With these columns, however, leave the "Add to default view" check box selected. These calculated columns represent the final metrics, and you'll want to show these when viewing the list of test cycles.

- Quality Ratio

- Test Progress

The default view should look like Figure 13-10.

Figure 13-10. *The Test Cycles list with new metrics*

Notice that the value of the new columns is #DIV/0!. This is because the divisor is 0, since the data values have not been calculated yet.

Modifying the Iterations List

Go to the Iterations list and from the List Settings page, add the following site columns. For these columns, unselect the "Add to default view" check box but leave the "Add to all content types" check box selected.

- Initial Weighted Defects

- Repeated Defects

- Test Cases Completed

- Test Cases Planned
- Test Cycle Count
- Weighted Defects

Then add the following calculated columns, leaving both check boxes selected:

- Defect Removal Rate
- Quality Ratio
- Repeated Defect Ratio
- Test Coverage

The default view will now include the calculated columns, but the value will also be displayed as #DIV/0! because the data has not been calculated yet.

Computing the Metrics

Now that you have all the additional data elements defined, you're ready to compute the metric values. To gather the summary values from the existing data, you'll implement a workflow process just like you did in the previous chapter. In fact, you will reuse the same workflow project and add additional logic to it.

Reusing the Chapter12 Project

You will create a Chapter13 Visual Studio solution and copy the Chapter12 project into the new solution. That will leave the existing project/solution as is. By copying the project, however, you'll save some work. More importantly, the new solution will support the needs of both chapters. The workflow that you'll implement now will replace the existing workflow.

Start Visual Studio 2010 as an administrator. On the start page, select the Empty SharePoint Project template in the SharePoint 2010 category, as shown in Figure 13-11. Enter the solution name **Chapter13**.

Figure 13-11. *Creating the Chapter13 solution*

The SharePoint Customization Wizard will then run, but only present the initial dialog. Enter the URL for your SharePoint site and select the farm solution, as shown in Figure 13-12.

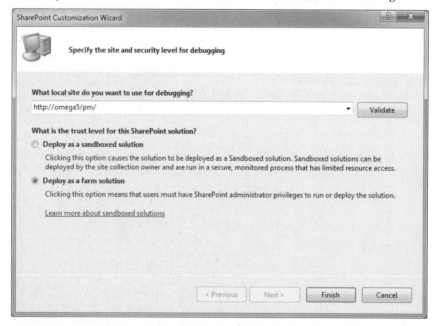

Figure 13-12. *Configuring the SharePoint solution*

■**Caution**   Some SharePoint features, such as workflows, are not supported in a sandboxed solution. This is why the sandboxed solution was not available when you created the solution for Chapter 12. However, since this is an empty solution, both options are available in the Customization Wizard. Make sure you select the farm solution option.

Open Windows Explorer and navigate to the Chapter12 solution folder. There will be a Chapter12 subfolder that contains the Chapter12 project. Copy this to the Chapter13 folder that was just created for this solution. The Chapter13 folder will now have both Chapter12 and Chapter13 subfolders, as shown in Figure 13-13.

Figure 13-13. *Copying the Chapter12 project folder*

Go back to Visual Studio. From Solution Explorer, right-click the Chapter13 project and click the *Remove* link. Then right-click the Chapter13 solution and click the *Add ➤ Existing Project* links. In the Add Existing Project dialog box, navigate to the Chapter13\Chapter12 folder and select the Chapter12.csproj file, as shown in Figure 13-14. Click the Open button to add this project.

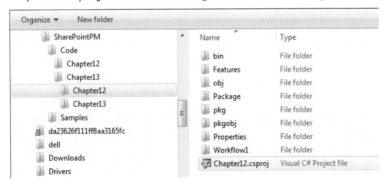

Figure 13-14. *Adding the Chapter12 project*

Solution Explorer should show a Chapter13 solution that contains a Chapter12 project, as shown in Figure 13-15.

Figure 13-15. *Solution Explorer with the Chapter12 project*

Implementing the Metric Logic

In Solution Explorer, expand the Workflow1 feature. Then double-click the Workflow1.cs file, which will open the workflow designer shown in Figure 13-16.

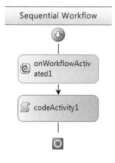

Figure 13-16. *The workflow designer*

Double-click the codeActivity1 activity, which will open the code-behind file and show the current implementation that you entered in Chapter 12. This code first checks the status of the test cycle and then performs different actions based on this status. For the Initial status, it populates the Test Items list based on the test cases defined for the associated iteration. If the test cycle is InProgress, it looks for failed test cases and creates an item in the Iteration Items list (iteration backlog).

Modifying the InProgress Block

You will now add code to accumulate the data values needed to compute the metrics. If the status is InProgress, this code will accumulate values within this test cycle. If the status is Completed, the code will roll up these values to the associated iteration. The code for the InProgress block is shown in Listing 13-1. The modified code is shown in bold.

Listing 13-1. *The Modified Implementation of the "InProgress" Block*

```
if (cycleStatus == "InProgress" || cycleStatus == "Completed")
{
    // Retrieve the failed items
    SPQuery query = new SPQuery();
    query.Query =
        "<Where>" +
            "<And>" +
                "<Eq>" +
                    "<FieldRef Name='Test_x0020_Cycle' LookupId='TRUE' />" +
                    "<Value Type='Lookup'>" + cycle.ID.ToString() + "</Value>" +
                "</Eq>" +
                "<And>" +
                    "<Eq>" +
                        "<FieldRef Name='Test_x0020_Status' />" +
                        "<Value Type='Choice'>Completed</Value>" +
                    "</Eq>" +
                    "<Eq>" +
                        "<FieldRef Name='Test_x0020_Pass_x002f_Fail' />" +
                        "<Value Type='Boolean'>No</Value>" +
                    "</Eq>" +
                "</And>" +
            "</And>" +
        "</Where>";

    SPListItemCollection failedItems = testItems.GetItems(query);

    // If there are any that failed...
    if (failedItems.Count > 0)
    {
        SPContentType defectContent = web.ContentTypes["Iteration Defect"];
        SPList iterationItems = web.Lists["Iteration Items"];

        foreach (SPListItem failed in failedItems)
        {
            // See if this failure has already been reported
            SPQuery itemQuery = new SPQuery();
            itemQuery.Query =
                "<Where>" +
                    "<And>" +
                        "<And>" +
                            "<And>" +
                                "<Eq>" +
                                    "<FieldRef Name='Iteration' LookupId='TRUE' />" +
                                    "<Value Type='Lookup'>" +
                                        iteration.ID.ToString() + "</Value>" +
                                "</Eq>" +
                                "<Eq>" +
                                    "<FieldRef Name='ContentType' />" +
                                    "<Value Type='Text'>Iteration Defect</Value>" +
```

```
                                "</Eq>" +
                            "</And>" +
                            "<Eq>" +
                                "<FieldRef Name='Test_x0020_Item' LookupId='TRUE' />" +
                                "<Value Type='Lookup'>" +
                                    failed.ID.ToString() + "</Value>" +
                            "</Eq>" +
                        "</And>" +
                        "<Or>" +
                            "<Eq>" +
                                "<FieldRef Name='Item_x0020_Status' />" +
                                "<Value Type='Choice'>Pending</Value>" +
                            "</Eq>" +
                            "<Eq>" +
                                "<FieldRef Name='Item_x0020_Status' />" +
                                "<Value Type='Choice'>InProgress</Value>" +
                            "</Eq>" +
                        "</Or>" +
                    "</And>" +
                "</Where>";

    SPListItemCollection matches = iterationItems.GetItems(itemQuery);

    // If this failure has not been reported...
    if (matches.Count == 0)
    {
        // ...add this failure to the defect list
        SPListItem defect = iterationItems.Items.Add();
        defect["ContentTypeId"] = defectContent.Id;
        defect["Title"] = failed.Title;
        defect["Item Status"] = "Pending";
        defect["Iteration"] = iteration.ID.ToString() + ";#" +
            iteration.Title;
        defect["Test Item"] = failed.ID.ToString() + ";#" + failed.Title;

        // Determine the user story
        SPFieldLookupValue testCaseFieldValue =
            new SPFieldLookupValue(failed["Test Case"].ToString());
        SPListItem testCase =
            testCases.GetItemById(testCaseFieldValue.LookupId);
        if (testCase != null)
        {
            SPFieldLookupValue testScenarioFieldValue =
                new SPFieldLookupValue(testCase["Test Scenario"].ToString());
            SPListItem testScenario =
                testScenarios.GetItemById(testScenarioFieldValue.LookupId);
            if (testScenario != null)
            {
                defect["User Story"] = testScenario["User Story"];
            }
        }
```

```
            defect.Update();
        }
    }
}

/*-----------------------------------*/
// Gather TestCycle metrics
/*-----------------------------------*/
// Walk through all the test items
int planned = 0;
int completed = 0;
int cancelled = 0;
int failedCount = 0;
int weightedDefect = 0;
int repeated = 0;

SPQuery testItemQuery = new SPQuery();
testItemQuery.Query =
    "<Where>" +
      "<Eq>" +
        "<FieldRef Name='Test_x0020_Cycle' LookupId='TRUE' />" +
        "<Value Type='Lookup'>" + cycle.ID.ToString() + "</Value>" +
      "</Eq>" +
    "</Where>";

SPListItemCollection items = testItems.GetItems(testItemQuery);
foreach (SPListItem item in items)
{
    planned++;
    string status = item["Test Status"].ToString();
    switch (status)
    {
        case "Completed":
            completed++;
            if (item["Test Pass/Fail"].ToString() == "False")
            {
                failedCount++;
                weightedDefect +=
                    int.Parse(item["Defect Severity"].ToString());

                if (item["Repeated Defect"].ToString() == "True")
                    repeated++;
            }
            break;

        case "Cancelled":
            cancelled++;
            break;
    }
}

// Compute the total story points
```

```
SPList userStories = web.Lists["User Stories"];
int storyPoints = 0;

SPQuery userStoryQuery = new SPQuery();
userStoryQuery.Query =
    "<Where>" +
        "<Eq>" +
            "<FieldRef Name='Iteration' LookupId='TRUE' />" +
            "<Value Type='Lookup'>" + iteration.ID.ToString() + "</Value>" +
        "</Eq>" +
    "</Where>";

SPListItemCollection stories = userStories.GetItems(userStoryQuery);
foreach (SPListItem story in stories)
    storyPoints += int.Parse(story["Story Points"].ToString());

// Store the accumulated totals
cycle["Repeated Defects"] = repeated;
cycle["Test Cases Cancelled"] = cancelled;
cycle["Test Cases Completed"] = completed;
cycle["Test Cases Failed"] = failedCount;
cycle["Test Cases Planned"] = planned;
cycle["Weighted Defects"] = weightedDefect;
cycle["Story Points"] = storyPoints;

cycle.Update();
}
```

■**Caution**   The If statement for this block was changed to include the Completed status as well as InProgress. This code is designed to be able to run multiple times without duplicating data, so there's no harm in running it again. The Completed status was added in case the user marks the test cycle as Completed before running the workflow.

This code queries the Test Items list for all items in the current test cycle. It walks through the items that are returned and computes the number of items planned, completed, failed, and so on. It then gets the list of user stories for the associated iteration and computes the total number of story points. The test cycle is then updated with the computed values.

Adding the Completed Block

If the test cycle has been completed, the statistics for the iteration is recomputed to include this test cycle. Add the Completed block using the code shown in Listing 13-2.

Listing 13-2. *Implementation of the Completed Block*

```
// If the status is Completed, accumulate the Iteration metrics
if (cycleStatus == "Completed")
{
    // Walk through all the test cycles for this iteration
    int initialWeightedDefects = 0;
    int currentWeightedDefects = 0;
    int totalCompleted = 0;
    int totalPlanned = 0;
    int totalRepeated = 0;
    int cycleCount = 0;
    int storyPoints = 0;

    SPList testCycles = web.Lists["Test Cycles"];

    SPQuery cycleQuery = new SPQuery();
    cycleQuery.Query =
        "<Where>" +
            "<And>" +
                "<Eq>" +
                    "<FieldRef Name='Iteration' LookupId='TRUE' />" +
                    "<Value Type='Lookup'>" + iteration.ID.ToString() + "</Value>" +
                "</Eq>" +
                "<Eq>" +
                    "<FieldRef Name='Test_x0020_Status' />" +
                    "<Value Type='Choice'>Completed</Value>" +
                "</Eq>" +
            "</And>" +
        "</Where>" +
        "<OrderBy>" +
            "<FieldRef Name='StartDate' />" +
        "</OrderBy>" ;

    SPListItem initialCycle = null;
    SPListItem currentCycle = null;

    SPListItemCollection items = testCycles.GetItems(cycleQuery);
    foreach (SPListItem item in items)
    {
        cycleCount++;

        // Since the test cycles are returned in chronological order,
        // the first one will be the initial cycle and the last one
        // will be the current (or most recent) test cycle
        if (initialCycle == null)
            initialCycle = item;
        currentCycle = item;

        totalCompleted += int.Parse(item["Test Cases Completed"].ToString());
        totalPlanned += int.Parse(item["Test Cases Planned"].ToString());
```

```
            totalRepeated += int.Parse(item["Repeated Defects"].ToString());

            // Accumulate
        }

        // Get the initial and current defect counts
        if (initialCycle != null)
            initialWeightedDefects =
                int.Parse(initialCycle["Weighted Defects"].ToString());

        if (currentCycle != null)
        {
            currentWeightedDefects =
                int.Parse(currentCycle["Weighted Defects"].ToString());
            storyPoints = int.Parse(currentCycle["Story Points"].ToString());
        }

        // Update the iteration
        iteration["Initial Weighted Defects"] = initialWeightedDefects;
        iteration["Weighted Defects"] = currentWeightedDefects;
        iteration["Repeated Defects"] = totalRepeated;
        iteration["Test Cases Planned"] = totalPlanned;
        iteration["Test Cases Completed"] = totalCompleted;
        iteration["Test Cycle Count"] = cycleCount;
        iteration["Story Points"] = storyPoints;

        iteration.Update();
    }
```

This code queries the Test Cycles list for all completed test cycles for the associated iteration.

■**Note**   InProgress or Cancelled test cycles are not included in the iteration metrics.

The results are returned in chronological order so the initial test cycle will be returned first and the most recent test cycle will be last. The code uses this to determine the initial and current defect counts. The other data values are simply accumulated. Finally, the iteration is updated to store the current metrics.

■**Note** This code sums the `Test Cases Completed` column for all test cycles. If there were 100 test cases defined and all of these were completed in each of three test cycles, the value would then be 300. This figure is used to compute the `Test Coverage`. So, with this logic, each time the same tests are reexecuted, the `Test Coverage` value is increased. Arguably, this may not be accurate. Does rerunning the same test cases actually provide better coverage? For scripted test cases, probably not, but if you're performing manual testing, rerunning the same test again can find defects not found the first time around. You may want to change this logic to use the largest number from each of the test cycles.

Running the Workflow

Press F6 to build the solution and fix any compiler errors. From Solution Explorer, right-click the `Chapter12` project and click the *Deploy* link. This will retract the current version of this workflow and deploy the current version. Go to the `Test Cycles` list and edit the current test cycle to set the status to `Completed`. Then view this test cycle and click the Workflow button, which will display the Workflows dialog shown in Figure 3-17.

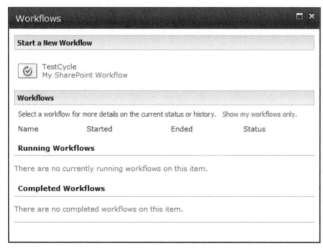

Figure 3-17. *Using the Workflows dialog to start the TestCycle workflow*

Click the *TestCycle* link to start the workflow. In a few seconds the workflow will finish. Close the dialog box and refresh the page. View the test cycle to see the computed values. The View form should look like Figure 3-18.

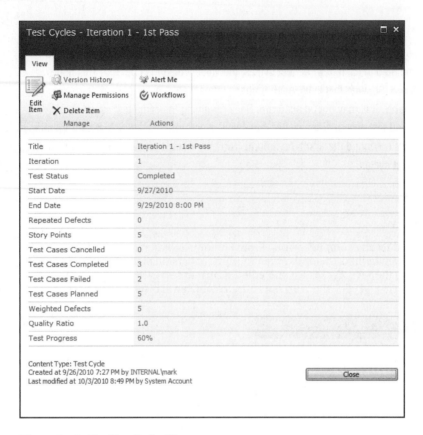

Figure 3-18. *The Test Cycles View page*

Notice that the intermediate values have been computed as well as the calculated columns. The `Quality Ratio`, for example, is set to 1.0 because the total weighted defects is five and there are five story points. Also, the `Test Progress` is set at 60 percent because three out of five test cases have been completed.

■**Note**   You will likely have different data points, so the metrics values may be different.

Go to the `Iterations` list and view the current iteration. You will probably have several additional web parts on the View form that you added in previous chapters. Scroll to the bottom of the form to see the computed metrics. The form should look similar to Figure 3-19.

Title	Iteration 1
Iteration Number	1
Iteration Status	Current
Start Date	9/6/2010
End Date	9/17/2010 4:00 PM
Story Points Remaining	100
Initial Weighted Defects	5
Repeated Defects	0
Test Cases Completed	3
Test Cases Planned	5
Test Cycle Count	1
Weighted Defects	5
Defect Removal Rate	#DIV/0!
Quality Ratio	1.0
Repeated Defect Ratio	0.0
Test Coverage	1.0

Figure 3-19. *The iteration metric values*

Because there is only a single test cycle, some of the values for the iteration will be the same as the test cycle. Notice that the `Initial Weighted Defects` column is equal to the `Weighted Defects` column, which is the current number of defects. Because of this, the `Defect Removal Rate` is shown as `#DIV/0!`. Because no defects have yet been removed, it is not able to compute the removal rate.

Creating Another Test Cycle

To finish testing the metrics, you'll need to generate another test cycle. Go to the `Test Cycles` list and click the *Add new item* link. Enter the name **Iteration 1 - 2nd Pass** and leave the status as `Initial`, as shown in Figure 3-20. Click the Save button to add the test cycle.

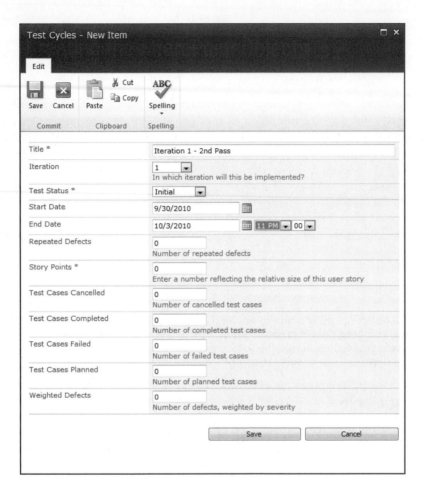

Figure 3-20. *Adding a new test cycle*

Now view this test cycle and click the Workflows button. Click the TestCycles link to run this workflow. The workflow will change the status to Planned. Edit this test cycle and change the status to InProgress. Click the *Site Pages* link in the Quick Launch area and select the Test Cycle page, which is shown in Figure 3-21.

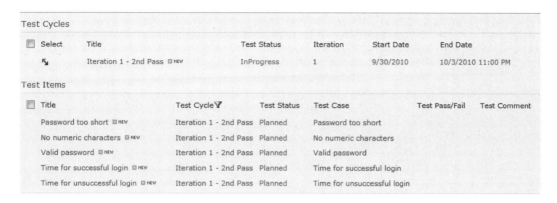

Figure 3-21. *The Test Cycles page showing the second test cycle*

Edit each of these test items, marking them complete. Mark one of them as failed and select the Repeated Defect check box, as shown in Figure 3-22.

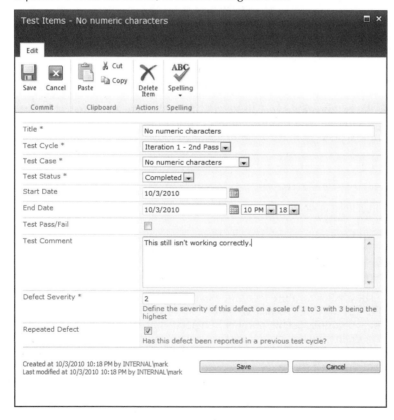

Figure 3-22. *Marking a test item as failed*

Go to the Test Cycles list and edit the second test cycle, and set the status to Completed. Then view this test cycle and run the TestCycle workflow. After it has finished, view the test cycle. Notice the Test Progress is at 100 percent because all of the test cases have been completed. Go to the Iterations list and view the current iteration. You should see different metrics, as demonstrated in Figure 3-23.

Title	Iteration 1
Iteration Number	1
Iteration Status	Current
Start Date	9/6/2010
End Date	9/17/2010 4:00 PM
Story Points Remaining	100
Initial Weighted Defects	5
Repeated Defects	1
Test Cases Completed	8
Test Cases Planned	10
Test Cycle Count	2
Weighted Defects	2
Defect Removal Rate	0.7
Quality Ratio	0.4
Repeated Defect Ratio	20.0
Test Coverage	2.0

Figure 3-23. *The revised iteration metrics*

Notice that the Defect Removal Rate is showing 0.7. This means that it will take 0.7 more test cycles to remove all defects based on the current rate. The weighted defect count dropped from 5 to 2 in one cycle. Based on that rate, the remaining defects will take another 0.7 cycles. Also notice that the Quality Ratio has decreased from 1.0 to 0.4.

■**Note** Because of the limited data points in our test data, the metrics may seem odd. You can test the logic with more test cases and test cycles and verify it is working as expected.

Adding Defect Source Analysis

Before I finish this chapter I want to show you one more technique to help you analyze your test results. You will add a column to the Iteration Items list to record the source of the defect. This will give you some insight into your process to help you minimize the number of defects that are introduced.

First, you'll need to create a list to define the defect sources that can be chosen. You will then create a Lookup column for this list and add it to the Iteration Defect content type. Finally, you'll create a view that summarizes the number of defects for each source.

Creating the Defect Source List

From the Site Actions menu, click the *More Options* link. Select the Custom List template and enter the name **Defect Sources**, as shown in Figure 3-24. Click the Create button to add the list.

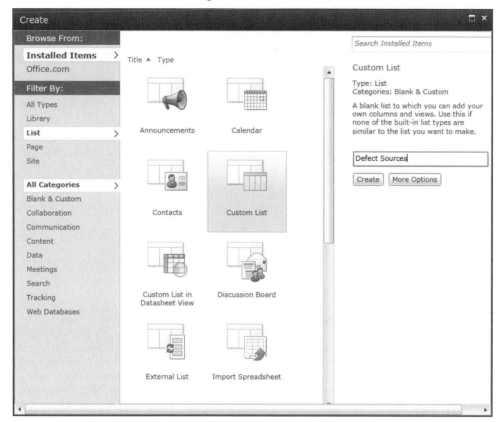

Figure 3-24. *Adding the Defect Sources list*

Using the *Add new item* link, create several sources of defects. The view will look like Figure 3-25.

Figure 3-25. *The Defect Sources list*

Creating a Lookup Column

From the Site Actions menu, click the *Site Settings* link. Then click the *Site columns* link in the Galleries section. Click the *Create* link to add a new site column. On the Create Column page, enter the name **Defect Source**, and select the Lookup column type and the Project Management group. In the Additional Column Settings section, select the Defect Sources list and the Title column, as shown in Figure 3-26.

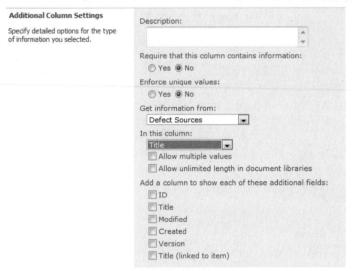

Figure 3-26. *Configuring the Defect Source site column*

From the Site Settings page, select the *Site content types* link. Select the Project Management group to filter the list of existing content types. Click the *Iteration Defect* link, and then click the *Add from existing site columns* link. Select the Project Management group, and then select the Defect Source column and click the Add button. Make sure the "Update all content types inheriting from this type?" option is set to Yes, as shown in Figure 3-27. Click the OK button to save the changes.

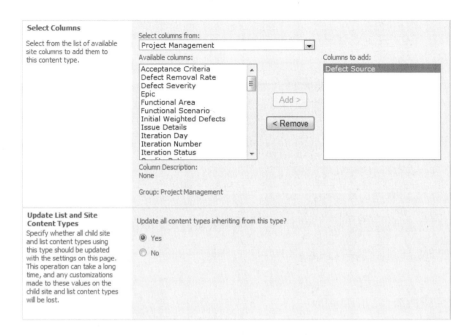

Figure 3-27. *Adding the Defect Source column*

Go to the Iteration Item list and edit each of the items that use the Iteration Defect content type. Specify a defect source for each of these.

Creating a Group By View

Go to the Iteration Items list and click the Create View button in the List ribbon, and then click the *Standard View* link. Enter the name **Defects** and add Defect Source to the column list. In the Filter section, select the Content Type column and enter **Iteration Defect**, as shown in Figure 3-28.

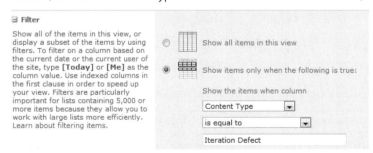

Figure 3-28. *Adding a filter to the Defects view*

Expand the Group By section and select the Defect Source column. Select the Collapsed display option, as shown in Figure 3-29.

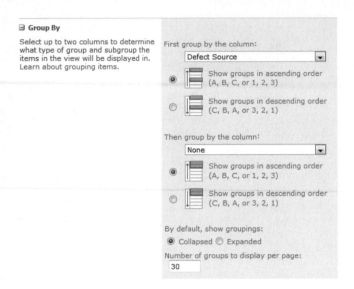

Figure 3-29. *Grouping by the Defect Source column*

Click the OK button to create the new view. The view will show a summary line for each defect source indicating how many defects are from that source. You can expand one of these to view the details for that source, as demonstrated in Figure 3-30.

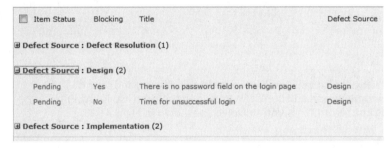

Figure 3-30. *Expanding the Defects view*

Summary

In this chapter you added columns to both the Test Cycles list and the Iterations list to record valuable statistics. You also added the following calculated columns to compute specific metrics:

- Test Progress
- Quality Ratio
- Repeated Defect Ratio

- `Defect Removal Rate`

You modified the workflow implemented in Chapter 12 to provide logic to accumulate the data necessary to compute the metrics. With this solution, you can simply rerun the workflow to recalculate either the test cycle or iteration metrics. You also modified the `Iteration Items` list to allow the source to be specified for each defect. The summary information was displayed in a new view using the Group By feature.

■ ■ ■

PART 4

Postproduction

You have completed your project and everyone is enjoying the benefits of it. However, your work is not finished yet. In this phase you'll need to provide ongoing support and maintenance. The nature of this phase will vary greatly depending on the type of product and your organizational structure. In this section you'll build a system to process and track issues that have been reported. These could be defects not caught in testing, enhancement requests, or support questions.

I worked on a project one time that had a ridiculously unrealistic deadline. For the last couple of months prior to launch our team literally worked around the clock. The day came and we went live, on schedule. Feeling a sense of accomplishment and sheer exhaustion we were thankful to have that project behind us. Little did we realize, however, that the next few months would be far worse than the last. Once live, we were dealing with bugs reported by real customers and the pressure to resolve them was multiplied. Hopefully your projects will go much more smoothly than this, but postproduction issues are inevitable, so you need to plan for them . . . before they arrive.

To effectively handle these items, you will implement a custom workflow that will track each item as it is worked through various stages. In Chapter 14 I'll explain the workflow design, and you will create the lists and content types that are needed to support the workflow process. In Chapter 15 you'll create a state machine workflow using Visual Studio 2010. In Chapter 16 you'll use InfoPath 2010 to create custom task forms.

Workflow Tasks

In this chapter you'll begin building a workflow to handle the postproduction requests. These could be defects that need to be corrected, support questions, or enhancements that should be considered for future releases. The basic concepts introduced here can be used in other types of requests as well.

Understanding Workflows

A workflow is a process that performs steps in a predefined order. Using conditional logic, some steps can be skipped if not required, and other steps can be repeated as needed. The workflow design consists of both the steps and the logic for determining the particular steps to be executed for each instance.

Human-Centric Workflows

When most of the steps in a workflow are implemented by people, it is considered a *human-centric* workflow. The steps in this case are called *tasks*. Even human-centric workflows can have automated steps, such as computing a value, generating a file, or sending an e-mail. However, the focus is typically on the tasks that require a person to do something. An example of a human-centric workflow is shown in Figure 14-1.

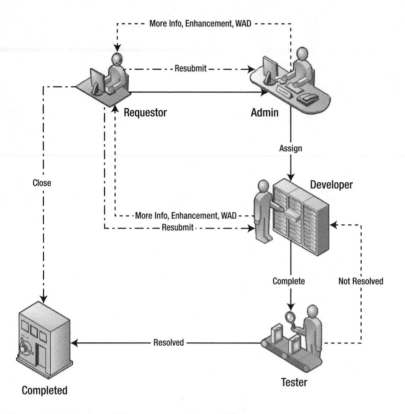

Figure 14-1. *A sample human-centric workflow*

The requestor submits a request, which is then reviewed by an administrator and assigned to a developer. When the developer has completed the work, a tester then verifies that it is working as expected and the issue is closed. That is the normal, expected path. The dotted lines represent some of the alternate paths. The administrator may send it back to the requestor for clarification, for example. The requestor could close the request or resubmit it. Likewise, the tester may find a problem and send it back to the developer for correction. A good workflow design anticipates the various alternate paths that should be allowed.

State Machine Workflows

SharePoint 2010 supports two types of workflows:

- Sequential
- State machine

You have already implemented a sequential workflow, which completes each task in sequential order. Sequential workflows are good for simple processes. A state machine workflow, however, is better suited for implementing human-centric workflows.

Defining the States

As its name suggests, a state machine workflow is designed by specifying the possible states. A *state* represents a stable condition of the workflow. Often a workflow will be idle, waiting for something to happen. That idle condition is represented by a state. When that something occurs, there is some activity, and the result is that the workflow becomes idle again, usually in a different state. That something is represented by an *event*, which is usually triggered when a task is updated.

For example, in the scenario described in Figure 14-1, when an issue is entered, it goes in to a New state and waits. When the admin reviews the issue and assigns it, the issue then goes into an Assigned state. Once again, the issue becomes idle waiting for the developer to work on it. The first step in designing a state machine workflow is to define these idle points.

■**Tip**   The first step in designing a state machine workflow is to determine the idle points of the process. These will be modeled as states.

The states that correspond to the workflow shown in Figure 14-1 include the following:

- New: Waiting to be reviewed by the administrator

- Assigned: Waiting for a developer to work on it

- Resolved: Completed and waiting to be verified by a tester

- Waiting: Waiting on input from the requestor

These are illustrated in Figure 14-2.

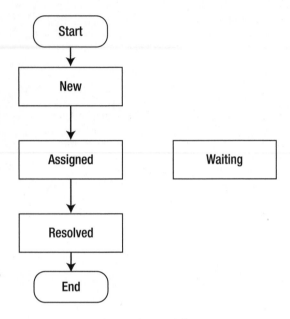

Figure 14-2. *Defining the workflow states*

Only the primary paths are included in this diagram, and there are no paths to the Waiting state since this is not part of the normal path.

Defining the Workflow Tasks

Each state also represents a task that needs to be completed. In the New state, for example, the workflow is waiting for the administrator to assign the issue to a developer (or return it to the requestor). Typically, when a workflow enters a state, a task is created, which represents the work that is required. The workflow then waits for that task to be updated, and the workflow executes some action based on the result of that task.

States can also be used to wait for some nonhuman input. You could create a state, for example, that waits for a database value to be updated or a message to be received. We do *not* use tasks for these states. Tasks are reserved for human actions only.

■**Tip** Using a consistent naming convention will help avoid confusion. The state names are usually based on what has just happened. For example, a *new* issue was reported (it's in the New state) or an issue was just *assigned* (it's in the Assigned state). The task being performed in that state is often associated with the next state. For example, in the New state, the issue is assigned, which moves it to the Assigned state. I will use the state name as the name of the associated task even though it may not describe the action performed by that task. One of the reasons for doing this is because there can be multiple actions in a given state. In the New state, for example, the administrator could also send it back to the requestor, which will move it to the Waiting state. So the name of the task will be New to indicate that this task is to review all new requests.

Tasks in SharePoint

A workflow is basically a sequence of tasks. The workflow will define these tasks and their proper sequencing. As the workflow executes, tasks are generated. From a user's perspective, however, the user simply works on the tasks that are assigned to them. There are often many issues being worked on simultaneously, so each person can have numerous tasks assigned to them at any point in time.

Using the Tasks List

SharePoint provides a standard Tasks list, which you already have in your SharePoint site. This was created for you because the site was created using the Team Site template. The tasks that are generated by the workflow are placed in this Tasks list. You can create a view of this list that only includes active tasks assigned to you. This can then be used as your to-do list. If you're a developer, your task list will include the issues that have been assigned to you that are not yet resolved. It will also include the resolved issues that the tester found a problem with.

The Tasks list is not specific to this workflow; it is used for the entire SharePoint site. You can create several workflows that all feed into the same Tasks list. You can also manually add tasks to this list. This provides a consolidated view of all the work items that are assigned to you. However, each task could require different information. For example, tasks in the New state need a place for the administrator to assign a developer. In contrast, tasks in the Resolved state need a place to indicate whether the resolution worked.

■**Note** You can create additional task lists, and when you configure the workflow you can specify which list to use. However, it is generally best to have a single list so each person only needs to check one place to see their work items.

To deal with this, each type of task can use a custom content type. This will allow you to define the fields that are applicable for each type of task. All items in the Tasks list should use the Task content type or a content type derived from it. All tasks generated by a workflow must use the Workflow Task content type (which is derived from the Task content type) or a custom content type derived from Workflow Task.

■**Tip**   Creating a custom content type for each type of task will also allow you to create custom task forms. You will do this in Chapter 16. All the tasks will be in a single list, but when you open each one, a custom form will be used that will include only the applicable fields.

Understanding the Payload

Tasks are generated to perform a specific action on behalf of the related issue. As an issue is processed, tasks are generated to assign it, to resolve it, to test it, and so on. Tasks represent the work that is done, but the issue is the *payload* that the tasks are attached to. As the issue works its way through the various states of the workflow, the tasks that are generated are attached to the issue.

This relationship is very important from both perspectives. First, each the task references the associated issue. The information in the task item includes only task-specific details such as who it is assigned to and the status of the task. When working on a particular task, the issue contains all the details of the issue, not the task. Secondly, when reviewing an issue, you'll be able to see all the tasks that were generated for that issue. So you'll know who assigned it and when and who tested it.

The workflow can automate the copying of data between a task and its related issue. For example, the title of each task should include the title of the related issue. Also, when a task is generated, the issue can be updated to reflect what state it is in. When the developer completes their task and enters a description of the resolution in the task form, this can be copied to the issue.

Keep in mind that the issue that is created will be stored in an Issues list. The tasks that are generated go into the Tasks list. So you'll have two different lists to use. The Tasks list defines the work items and is generally the primary list that is used by the people participating in the workflow process. You can also view the Issues list to see which ones are still open and check their current status. The requestor, for example, may use the Issues list to see what is happening to their requests.

Designing an Issue-Tracking System

The issue-tracking system that you will build in the next three chapters is similar to the sample workflow described previously in this chapter. There are two "improvements" that are useful and will also help to demonstrate some interesting "twists" that workflows often require you to deal with.

Adding an Active State

The first improvement is that there will be an Active state. This indicates that the developer has started working on it. The other tasks are fairly short lived, but the developer's tasks could take some time to complete. It will be helpful to know that this is actively being worked on. In this case, when moving from the Assigned state to the Active state, no new task is needed.

The states that you'll use for this project are

- New: Waiting to be reviewed by the administrator

- Assigned: Waiting for a developer to work on it

- Active: Currently in progress

- Resolved: Completed and waiting to be verified by a tester

- Waiting: Waiting on input from the requestor

Defining Resolution Types

The second improvement is that there are multiple reasons for an item to be in the Waiting state. These are

- *More info*: As previously discussed, this indicates that some clarification is needed

- *Working as designed*: The issue that was reported is actually working correctly. This may indicate that documentation or training needs to be improved, but in any case, no system change is required.

- *Enhancement*: The request is an enhancement to the current system. This will not be acted upon in the support system but will be recorded and used when planning the next release.

Both the administrator (in the New state) and the developer (in the Assigned and Active states) can move the issue to the Waiting state by indicating one of these three reasons. To allow for different task forms, a separate content type will be used for each reason. However, they will all go into a single Waiting state.

For the More Info task, the requestor is asked to provide some details for the request. For the other tasks (Working as Designed and Enhancement), the requestor is being informed as to the resolution of this issue. They can appeal this decision by resubmitting the request, with additional information, if appropriate. Otherwise, they can simply close the issue.

The issue will have a resolution type, which will be one of the following values:

- Working as Designed: The reported issue is working correctly.

- Enhancement: The request will be treated as an enhancement and considered for a future release.

- Closed: The user closed the issue.

- Resolved: The issue was resolved and verified by the tester.

■**Note**   Notice that the issue can only be closed by the requestor or by the tester.

The resolution type will allow you to find all the issues that were considered an enhancement, for example. When planning the next release, these issues can be part of the requirement-gathering process.

Creating the SharePoint Objects

For the rest of this chapter, you will create the site columns, content types, and lists that will be needed for the implementation of this workflow. You'll start by creating the Issues list, which will serve as the payload for the workflow, and then define the custom content types used for each of the tasks. In Chapter 15, you will create the workflow logic that will require these objects.

Designing the Issues List

You'll now create the list that will record the issues that are entered and, eventually, the resolution of those issues. You will first create the additional site columns that are needed and then define a content type. The Issues list can then be created using the new content type.

Adding Site Columns

You will need several new site columns. Open the SharePoint site, and from the Site Actions menu, click the *Edit in SharePoint Designer* link. Click the *Site Columns* link in the Navigation pane, and then click the New Column button in the ribbon and select the Choice column type. Enter the name **PM Issue Status** and select the Project Management group, as shown in Figure 14-3.

Figure 14-3. *Creating the PM Issue Status column*

Enter the following values for the allowed choices (each of these values is associated with a state in the workflow):

- **New**
- **Assigned**
- **Active**
- **Resolved**
- **Pending**
- **Closed**

Enter **New** for the default value and unselect the "Allow blank values?" check box, as shown in Figure 14-4.

Figure 14-4. *Configuring the PM Issue Status column*

In the same way, create a site column named **Resolution Type** with the following choices:

- **Resolved**
- **Working as Designed**
- **Enhancement**
- **Closed**

In this case, however, don't enter a default value, and leave the "Allow blank values?" check box selected. This column will not be set until the issue has been processed through the workflow. The column settings should look like Figure 14-5.

Figure 14-5. *Configuring the Resolution Type column*

Add the following additional site columns using the `Multi Lines of Text` column type. Put these in the `Project Management` group, and use the default values for all of the other properties:

- **Resolution**
- **Issue Feedback**

Click the Save icon to save the changes.

Creating the PM Issue Content Type

Next you'll create a content type to store the properties of each issue. Click the *Content Types* link in the Navigation pane and then click the Content Type button in the ribbon. Enter the name **PM Issue**, select `Item` as the parent content type, and select the `Project Management` group, as shown in Figure 14-6. Click the OK button to create the content type.

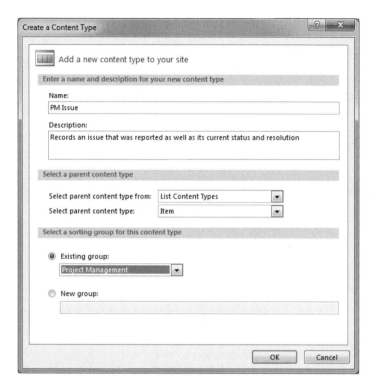

Figure 14-6. *Creating the PM Issue content type*

Then select this content type from the list to configure it. Click the *Edit content type columns* link in the Customization section. Using the Add Existing Site Column button in the ribbon, add the following columns:

- Date Created
- PM Issue Status
- Description
- Priority
- Assigned To
- Date Completed
- Resolution Type
- Resolution
- Issue Feedback

Click the Save icon to save these changes. The column list should look like Figure 14-7.

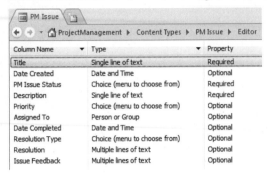

Figure 14-7. *Adding the site columns*

■**Caution**   The SharePoint site already has an Issue content type, so you named your content type PM Issue. Likewise, there is also an existing Issue Status column, so you named the new column PM Issue Status.

Creating the Issues List

Now click the *List and Libraries* link in the Navigation pane and click the Custom List button in the ribbon. Enter the name **Issues**, as shown in Figure 14-8.

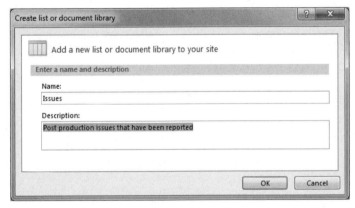

Figure 14-8. *Creating the Issues list*

Then click the *Issues* link in the list to configure it. In the Settings section, select the "Allow management of content types" check box and click the Save icon. Then click the Add button in the

Content Types section and select the PM Issue content type. Remove the Folder and Item content types from this list.

Go back to SharePoint and open the Issues list. You may need to refresh the page for this list to be included in the Quick Launch area. From the List ribbon, click the Modify View button and add the following columns to the default view:

- PM Issue Status

- Priority

- Assigned To

- Resolution Type

Click the OK button to save the changes. The default view should look like Figure 14-9.

Figure 14-9. *The empty default view*

Creating the Task Content Types

The last step in this chapter is to create a content type for each task that could be generated by the workflow. You will first create the additional site columns that will be needed.

Creating the Site Columns

In each of the workflow tasks, the user will need to take some kind of action. For example, the administrator will need to either assign the issue to a developer or send it back to the requestor. The tester will need to either indicate that the issue has been resolved or send it back to the developer. On each task form, you'll include an action column where the user will indicate the action being taken. The choices available, however, will be different for each workflow state. To accomplish this, you'll create a site column for each state using the Choice column type and enter the appropriate actions on each.

Go back to SharePoint Designer and click the *Site Columns* link in the Navigation pane. For each of the columns listed in Table 14-1, click the New Column button, select the Choice column type, and select the Project Management group. Then enter the choices shown in the table. The default choice for each column should be **None**. Unselect the "Allow blank values?" check box for each column.

Table 14-1. *Defining the Action Columns*

Name	Allowed Choices
Issue New Action	None, Assign, More Info, Working as Designed, Enhancement
Issue Assigned Action	None, Completed, More Info, Working as Designed, Enhancement
Issue Resolved Action	None, Resolved, Not Resolved
Issue Waiting Action	None, Close, Resubmit

The configuration of the Issue New Action column will look like Figure 14-10. The others will be identical, except they will have a different set of allowed choices.

Figure 14-10. *Configuring the Issue New Action column*

You will also need an additional column that will be on the developer's task so they can indicate that they are starting work on this issue. Click the New Column button and select the Yes/No column type. Enter the name **Issue Started**, select the Project Management group, and click the OK button. Then click the Column Settings button in the ribbon and change the default value to No, as shown in Figure 14-11.

Figure 14-11. *Configuring the Issue Started column*

In the New state, the administrator will need to assign a developer and set the priority of the issue, so you'll need a column to store these values. The Task content type already has an Assigned To column and a Priority column. However, these apply to the task, and you'll need additional columns that will be used to update the issue.

Click the New Column button in the ribbon and select the Person or Group column type. Enter the name **Issue Assigned To**, and select the Project Management group. Click the OK button to create the column. Then click the Column Settings button and change the option to allow all users, as shown in Figure 14-12.

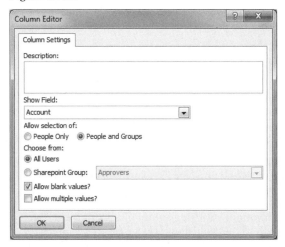

Figure 14-12. *Configuring the Issue Assigned To column*

Click the New Column button again and select the Choice column type. Enter the name **Issue Priority**, select the Project Management group, and click the OK button. In the Column Editor dialog box enter the following choices:

- **(1) High**

- **(2) Normal**

- **(3) Low**

Leave "Allow blank values?" checked and clear the default value, as shown in Figure 14-13.

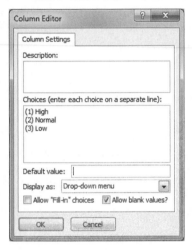

Figure 14-13. *Configuring the Issue Priority column*

Click the Save icon to save the changes.

Modifying the Workflow Task Content Type

The custom content types that will be used by the workflow must be derived from the `Workflow Task` content type. Unfortunately, this is defined as a hidden type, and you cannot select it from the Create a Content Type dialog box. To work around this issue, you'll need to modify this content type so that it is selectable.

Because this content type is hidden, you can't view or modify it using SharePoint Designer or the normal SharePoint UI. However, there is a backdoor method that will allow you access to it. Start Internet Explorer and enter the following URL (you'll need to insert the server name for your SharePoint site):

```
http://<your SharePoint server>/_layouts/ManageContentType.aspx?ctype=0x010801
```

By entering the `ctype=0x010801` parameter, you can navigate directly to a specific content type (`0x010801` is the ID for the `Workflow Task` content type). This bypasses the logic that hides the content type.

■**Note**   This content site is defined at the home site, not in your ProjectManagement site. The URL specifies the server name but does not include the path of your particular site. This change will affect all sites on that server.

This URL should display the page shown in Figure 14-14.

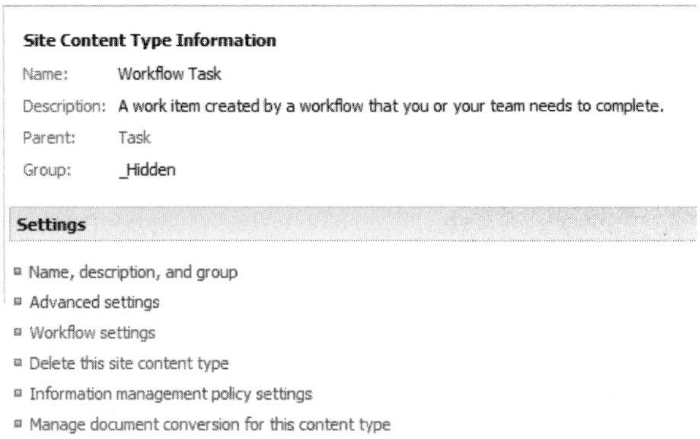

Site Content Type Information

Name: Workflow Task

Description: A work item created by a workflow that you or your team needs to complete.

Parent: Task

Group: _Hidden

Settings

▫ Name, description, and group

▫ Advanced settings

▫ Workflow settings

▫ Delete this site content type

▫ Information management policy settings

▫ Manage document conversion for this content type

Figure 14-14. *Displaying the Workflow Task content type*

Notice that the group is _Hidden; this is what makes this content type unavailable. Click the *Name, description, and group* link, which will allow you to change the group. Select the List Content Types group, as shown in Figure 14-15.

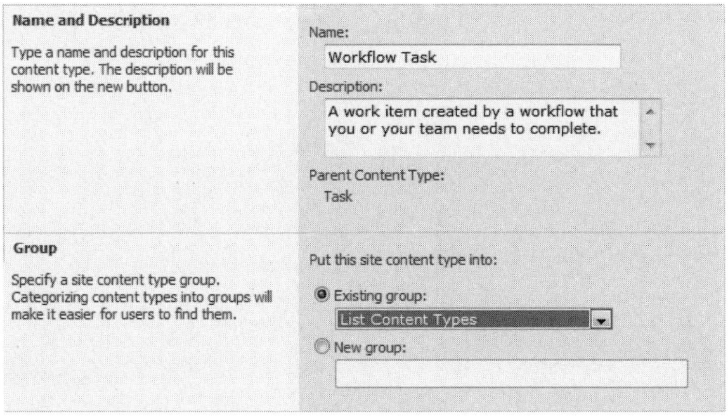

Name and Description

Type a name and description for this content type. The description will be shown on the new button.

Name:

Workflow Task

Description:

A work item created by a workflow that you or your team needs to complete.

Parent Content Type:

Task

Group

Specify a site content type group. Categorizing content types into groups will make it easier for users to find them.

Put this site content type into:

◉ Existing group:

List Content Types

○ New group:

Figure 14-15. *Changing the group*

■**Tip** If you want, after creating your custom content types, you can edit the `WorkflowTask` content type and put it back in the `_Hidden` group. The `_Hidden` group is not included in the list of groups. Instead, you can select the "New group" radio button and enter **_Hidden** for the group name.

Creating the Content Types

Go back to SharePoint Designer and click the *Content Types* link in the Navigation pane. Click the Content Type button in the ribbon. In the Create a Content Type dialog box, enter the name **Issue New** and select `Workflow Task` from the `List Content Types` group as the parent type, as shown in Figure 14-16.

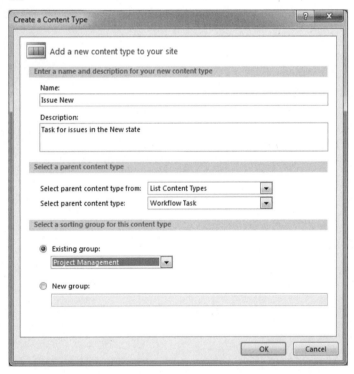

Figure 14-16. *Creating the Issue New content type*

Then select the `Issue New` content type from the list and click the *Edit content type columns* link in the Customization section. Notice that it already has quite a few columns, which were inherited from the `Task` or `Workflow Task` content types. Using the Add Existing Site Column button in the ribbon, add the following columns:

- Issue New Action
- Issue Assigned To
- Issue Priority

Click the Save icon to save the changes. The complete list of columns should look like Figure 14-17.

Figure 14-17. *The Issue New columns*

In the same way, create the content types listed in Table 14-2. These content types are identical to the Issue New content type, except the list of additional columns will be different.

Table 14-2. *Creating the Remaining Task Content Types*

Content Type	Additional Columns
Issue Assigned	Issue Assigned Action, Issue Started, Resolution
Issue Resolved	Issue Resolved Action, Issue Feedback
Issue WAD	Issue Waiting Action, Issue Feedback
Issue Enhancement	Issue Waiting Action, Issue Feedback
Issue Info	Issue Waiting Action, Issue Feedback

Adding the Content Types to the Tasks List

Finally, you'll need to modify the Tasks list to allow the new content types. Click the *Lists and Libraries* link in the Navigation pane and then select the Tasks list. Using the Add button in the Content Types section, add the following content types:

- Issue New
- Issue Assigned
- Issue Resolved
- Issue Info
- Issue Enhancement
- Issue WAD

If you click the *Content Types* link (this is also the label for the Content Types section), the list of allowed content types should look like Figure 14-18.

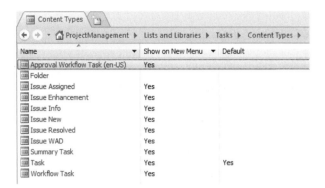

Figure 14-18. *The supported content types for the Tasks list*

Summary

In this chapter I explained the overall design of the issue-tracking system that you will implement. This is based on a state machine model that uses the following states:

- New: Waiting to be reviewed by the administrator

- Assigned: Waiting for a developer to work on it

- Active: Currently in progress

- Resolved: Completed and waiting to be verified by a tester

- Waiting: Waiting on input from the requestor

At each of these states, the workflow will create a task for a person to complete. When the task has been completed, the workflow will progress to the appropriate state and generate a new task.

You then implemented the Issues list and the underlying content type. Each item in this list specifies the details of the issue being reported and will contain the eventual resolution once the workflow has completed. The Issues list is the payload that workflow tasks are associated with.

Finally, you defined a content type for each of the tasks that will be generated by the workflow. These content types were derived from the Workflow Task content type. To do that, you had to first change this content so it was not in the _Hidden group.

■ ■ ■

CHAPTER 15

State Machine Workflows

In the previous chapter I presented the design of an issue-tracking system and you created the lists and content types that will be used. In this chapter you will implement the workflow logic using a state machine workflow.

■**Note**   Creating a state machine workflow in Visual Studio requires more technical expertise than the previous exercises. This kind of project is typically assigned to a developer rather than a power user. I will explain, step by step, how to use the toolset to create the workflow. You might prefer to download the complete solution from www.apress.com. If you do, there are a few things that you'll need to change to work with your specific SharePoint site. I'll point these out throughout this chapter.

Creating the Workflow Project

Start Visual Studio with administrator privileges. From the start page, click the *New Project* link. Select the State Machine Workflow template from the SharePoint 2010 category. Enter the name **Chapter15** and choose a suitable location, as shown in Figure 15-1.

Figure 15-1. *Creating a state machine workflow project*

Configuring the Workflow Project

The SharePoint Customization wizard will then display a series of dialog boxes. In the first dialog box, the site should default to the pm site (the site you used for the first Visual Studio project in Chapter 12); use this default value. In the second dialog box, enter the workflow name **IssueTracking**, and select the List Workflow type, as shown in Figure 15-2.

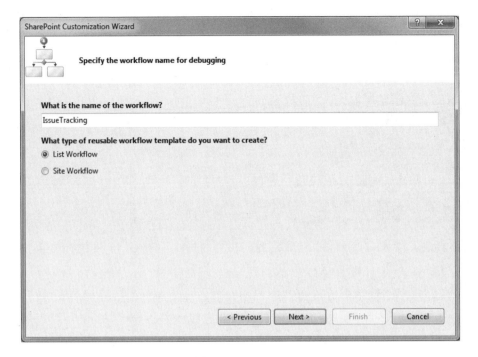

Figure 15-2. *Configuring the workflow settings*

In the third dialog box, select the Issues list to associate this workflow with, as shown in Figure 15-3.

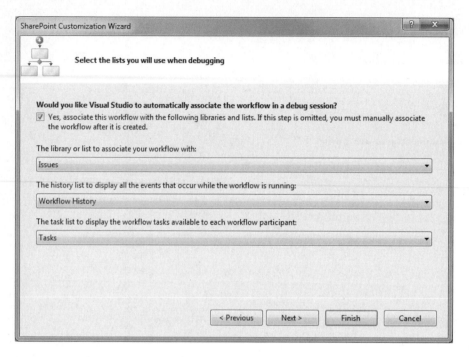

Figure 15-3. *Associating the workflow with the Issues list*

In the final dialog box, set the start options so the workflow is started when an item is added to the list. You should have only the middle check box checked, as shown in Figure 15-4.

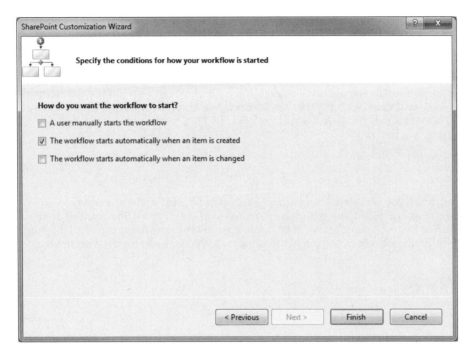

Figure 15-4. *Selecting the start options*

Understanding Workflow States

Visual Studio should display the workflow designer with a single activity named `Workflow1InitialState`. This is a `StateActivity`, and it contains a single activity called `eventDrivenActivity1`. If you double-click the `eventDrivenActivity1`, you'll see what looks like a miniworkflow, similar to the one shown in Figure 15-5.

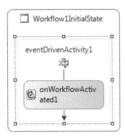

Figure 15-5. *EventDrivenActivity sequence*

This sequence contains the same `OnWorkflowActivated` activity that you've used on your previous workflow in Chapter 12. This event handler is executed when a workflow instance is first started. The `EventDrivenActivity` is a special type of sequence; in fact, its parent class is `SequenceActivity`. So, like

SequenceActivity, it can contain any number of child activities, but it has some unique rules. Essentially, the sequence can contain only one activity that handles events, and that must be the first child activity.

Activities that handle events include the HandleExternalEventActivity and activities that are derived from it. Workflow event activities, such as OnWorkflowActivated and OnTaskChanged, are derived from HandleExternalEventActivity. So, the workflow generated by the template satisfies that rule.

A state can have multiple EventDrivenActivity objects, but each one must respond to a different event. You could have one EventDrivenActivity that has OnWorkflowActivated for its first child activity, and the second EventDrivenActivity could use OnWorkflowModified. Which sequence is executed is determined by which event was raised.

Navigation

As you probably noticed, when you double-click a sequence to expand it, only that sequence is displayed. The rest of the workflow is hidden. With state machine workflows, you'll find yourself doing that a lot since all of the real "work" is done on sequences that are not visible from the top-level diagram. To help find your way within the workflow, the top of the workflow designer includes a navigation bar, which is shown in Figure 15-6.

Figure 15-6. *The workflow navigation bar*

The main (or top-level) diagram is Workflow1. The state is called Workflow1InitialState; this is the second level. You are currently on the third level, which is the eventDriveActivity1 sequence. The top-level diagram displays both the first and second levels. That is, it displays the main workflow (level 1), which includes the states (level 2). If you click either link on the navigation bar, the top-level diagram will be displayed.

Initialization and Finalization

The StateActivity is also a special sequence activity. It can contain only four types of activities. The first you've already seen, which is the EventDrivenActivity. Navigate back to the top-level diagram, and right-click the Workflow1InitialState activity. Figure 15-7 displays the content menu.

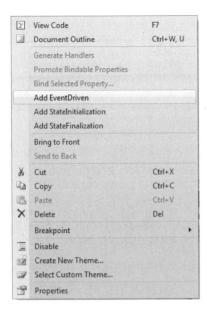

Figure 15-7. *Context menu for a StateActivity*

Two of your other choices of activities are included in this menu. In addition to the EventDrivenActivity, you can also add a StateInitializationActivity and a StateFinalizationActivity. These are also derived from SequenceActivity, and can have multiple child activities. The StateInitializationActivity contains activities that you want executed whenever the workflow enters that state. Similarly, the StateFinalizationActivity contains activities that are executed when the workflow leaves that state.

Both of these are optional, and you can have one without the other. But you cannot have more than one of each. You should not put any event handlers in these sequences; the workflow should never become idle during these activities. Their purpose is to perform initialization or cleanup activities for this state.

Substates

The fourth type of activity that can be included on a StateActivity is another StateActivity. These are known as substates. In a complex workflow, you may want to model a mini–state machine for a particular state.

In our issue-tracking system, for example, when an issue is in the New state, it is reviewed and assigned to a developer. Suppose the review process requires several steps to complete, such as multiple reviewers or developer feedback. You could model that review process as its own state machine. That would keep the overall state machine more manageable.

To use substates, drag the StateActivity objects onto the top-level state. Then define the events just like you would for top-level states.

SetState

You will use the SetStateActivity to transition to another state. The SetStateActivity is normally used in an EventDrivenActivity. For example, when an issue is reviewed and assigned, this will trigger an OnTaskChanged event. The event handler will then use the SetStateActivity to move the workflow to the Assigned state.

■**Caution**   In the toolbox there are two activities labeled SetState. The one in the "Windows Workflow 3.0" section is the one I'm referring to here and is the one you will use throughout this chapter. The SetState activity in the "SharePoint Workflow" section is completely different and is used for setting workflow properties. Do not use this one.

You can also use the SetStateActivity in a StateInitializationActivity. You may want to do this if the initialization activities determine that this state is not required. The initialization sequence can immediately move the workflow to the next state, essentially skipping this state.

■**Caution**   You cannot use a SetStateActivity in a StateFinalizationActivity.

Setting Up the Workflow

There's some initial configuration work you'll need to do before you start implementing the state logic. Select the Workflow1InitialState activity, and in the Properties window, change the name to **stateInitial**. Then select the eventDrivenActivity1 activity and rename it to **eventInitial**. Double-click the eventInitial activity to display the sequence for this event. The sequence contains only the onWorkflowActivated1 activity. Double-click this activity to generate the event handler, and open the Workflow1.cs code-behind file. Add the following namespaces:

```
using System.Collections.Generic;
using System.Xml.Linq;
```

Add the class members shown in Listing 15-1 (these should go just after the workflowProperties member and before the onWorkflowActivated1_Invoked() event handler):

Listing 15-1. *Specifying Additional Class Members*

```
private string _admin = "internal\\test1";
private string _test = "internal\\test2";

// Issue data
private string _title;
private string _description;

// Task data
private string _action = "";
private string _priority = "(2) Normal";
private string _assign = "";
```

```
private string _resolution;
private string _feedback;

// Task IDs
private Guid _taskId = Guid.Empty;
private Guid _workTaskId = Guid.Empty;
```

The _admin and _test members will store the logon names of the users that the tasks will be assigned to. For now, just hard-code these to whatever values you want to use. You'll add an association form later to allow these to be specified by the end users. The _title and _description members will store these values that are obtained from the Issues item. These will be used in setting the properties of the tasks that will be generated.

The section labeled "Task data" contains properties that you will extract from the tasks as they are processed by the workflow. The _taskId and _workTaskId members are used to store the IDs of the tasks. I will explain how these are used later.

For the implementation of the onWorkflowActivated1_Invoked() event handler, add the following code:

```
// Get the details from the Issue item that we'll need later
_title = workflowProperties.Item.Title;
_description = workflowProperties.Item["Description"].ToString();

// Set the Date Created
SPListItem item = workflowProperties.Item;
item["_DCDateCreated"] = DateTime.UtcNow;
item.Update();
```

This code first gets the Title and Description columns from the Issues list item and stores them in the class members. Recall from Chapter 12 that the workflowProperties.Item property represents the list item that the workflow is being executed for. The event handler then sets the Date Created column to the current date/time.

■**Tip** Workflow stores dates using Coordinated Universal Time (UTC). The workflow client translates this based on the localization configuration. Since you are setting the date in code, you should use the UtcNow property.

Defining the States

As I indicated in the previous chapter, the first step in designing a state machine workflow is to identify the states, which are the idle points in a workflow process. In a human-centric workflow, such as this one, states will usually have a user task associated with them.

Initial and Final States

There are two special states that all workflows will have: an initial state and a completed (or final) state. The initial state is where the workflow will start. The project template created the initial state for you, which you renamed stateInitial. Right-click the stateInitial activity, and click the *Set as Initial State* link. Notice that the icon in the activity changes to a green circle indicating this is the initial state.

The completed state represents a workflow that has finished. No activity may be performed on a completed state. It is simply a placeholder, indicating the end of the workflow. Drag a `StateActivity` to the workflow diagram and change its name to **stateFinal**. Right-click the `stateFinal` activity and click the *Set as Completed State* link. Notice that the icon changes to a red circle, and the helper text disappears.

The initial workflow design should look like Figure 15-8.

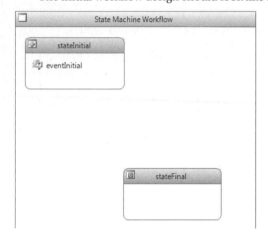

Figure 15-8. *The initial workflow design*

Adding the Remaining States

Your workflow will have the following additional states. For each state, drag an additional `StateActivity` object onto the workflow diagram and rename it as **state<State Name>** (e.g., **stateNew**, **stateAssigned**, etc.).

- `New`: Waiting to be reviewed by the administrator

- `Assigned`: Waiting for a developer to work on it

- `Active`: Currently in progress

- `Resolved`: Completed and waiting to be verified by a tester

- `Waiting`: Waiting on input from the requestor

The diagram should look like Figure 15-9.

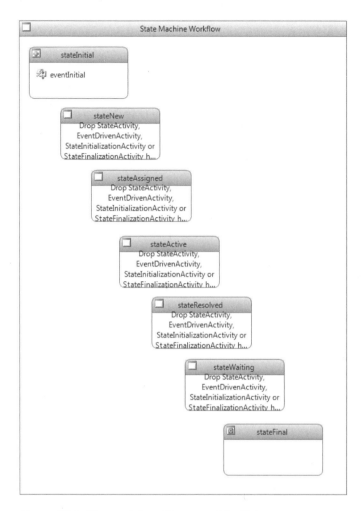

Figure 15-9. *The workflow diagram with all the states*

Notice the helper text that is displayed when you drag a StateActivity to the workflow. It is reminding you to include one of the four types of activities that are allowed on a StateActivity.

Implementing the Event Handlers

I have found it to be a little more efficient to write all the event handlers first, and then when configuring the activities, select them from the drop-down list.

CreateTask MethodInvoking Event

To generate a task, you will use the CreateTaskWithContentType activity. This works just like the CreateTask activity except it allows you to specify a custom content type. It raises a MethodInvoking event just before the activity creates the task. You will need to provide an event handler for this to specify the properties of the task that is to be created.

Add the code shown in Listing 15-2 to the Workflow1.cs class. There is a separate event handler for each type of task that can be generated.

Listing 15-2. *CreateTask MethodInvoking Event Handlers*

```
/*----------------------------------------------------------*/
/* Create task event handlers                               */
/*----------------------------------------------------------*/
// New
private void createNewTask_MethodInvoking(object sender, EventArgs e)
{
    CreateTaskWithContentType task = sender as CreateTaskWithContentType;
    task.TaskId = Guid.NewGuid();

    SPWorkflowTaskProperties wtp = new SPWorkflowTaskProperties();
    wtp.PercentComplete = (float)0.0;
    wtp.AssignedTo = _admin;
    wtp.TaskType = 0;
    wtp.DueDate = DateTime.UtcNow.AddDays(1);
    wtp.Title = "New: " + _title;
    wtp.Description = _description;

    task.TaskProperties = wtp;
}

// Assigned
private void createAssignedTask_MethodInvoking(object sender, EventArgs e)
{
    CreateTaskWithContentType task = sender as CreateTaskWithContentType;
    task.TaskId = Guid.NewGuid();
    _workTaskId = task.TaskId;

    SPWorkflowTaskProperties wtp = new SPWorkflowTaskProperties();
    wtp.PercentComplete = (float)0.0;
    wtp.AssignedTo = _assign;
    wtp.TaskType = 1;
    wtp.DueDate = DateTime.UtcNow.AddDays(1);
    wtp.Title = "Issue: " + _title;
    wtp.Description = _description;

    task.TaskProperties = wtp;

    // Update the item to show the assignee
    SPUser u = workflowProperties.Web.SiteUsers[_assign];
    SPListItem item = workflowProperties.Item;
```

```
    item["AssignedTo"] = u;
    item.Update();
}

// Resolved
private void createResolvedTask_MethodInvoking(object sender, EventArgs e)
{
    CreateTaskWithContentType task = sender as CreateTaskWithContentType;
    task.TaskId = Guid.NewGuid();

    SPWorkflowTaskProperties wtp = new SPWorkflowTaskProperties();
    wtp.PercentComplete = (float)0.0;
    wtp.AssignedTo = _test;
    wtp.TaskType = 2;
    wtp.DueDate = DateTime.UtcNow.AddDays(1);
    wtp.Title = "Resolved: " + _title;
    wtp.Description = _description;

    task.TaskProperties = wtp;
}

// Waiting - Working as Designed
private void createWADTask_MethodInvoking(object sender, EventArgs e)
{
    CreateTaskWithContentType task = sender as CreateTaskWithContentType;
    task.TaskId = Guid.NewGuid();

    SPWorkflowTaskProperties wtp = new SPWorkflowTaskProperties();
    wtp.PercentComplete = (float)0.0;
    wtp.AssignedTo = _admin;
    wtp.TaskType = 3;
    wtp.DueDate = DateTime.UtcNow.AddDays(1);
    wtp.Title = "Working as Designed: " + _title;
    wtp.Description = _resolution;

    task.TaskProperties = wtp;

    // Update the items's Resolution Type
    SPListItem item = workflowProperties.Item;
    item["Resolution Type"] = "Working as Designed";
    item.Update();
}

// Waiting - Enhancement
private void createEnhancementTask_MethodInvoking(object sender, EventArgs e)
{
    CreateTaskWithContentType task = sender as CreateTaskWithContentType;
    task.TaskId = Guid.NewGuid();

    SPWorkflowTaskProperties wtp = new SPWorkflowTaskProperties();
    wtp.PercentComplete = (float)0.0;
    wtp.AssignedTo = _admin;
```

```
        wtp.TaskType = 4;
        wtp.DueDate = DateTime.UtcNow.AddDays(1);
        wtp.Title = "Enhancement: " + _title;
        wtp.Description = _resolution;

        task.TaskProperties = wtp;

        // Update the items's Resolution Type
        SPListItem item = workflowProperties.Item;
        item["Resolution Type"] = "Enhancement";
        item.Update();
    }

// Waiting - More Info
private void createInfoTask_MethodInvoking(object sender, EventArgs e)
{
    CreateTaskWithContentType task = sender as CreateTaskWithContentType;
    task.TaskId = Guid.NewGuid();

    SPWorkflowTaskProperties wtp = new SPWorkflowTaskProperties();
    wtp.PercentComplete = (float)0.0;
    wtp.AssignedTo = _admin;
    wtp.TaskType = 5;
    wtp.DueDate = DateTime.UtcNow.AddDays(1);
    wtp.Title = "More info needed: " + _title;
    wtp.Description = _description;

    task.TaskProperties = wtp;

    // Update the items's Resolution Type
    SPListItem item = workflowProperties.Item;
    item["Resolution Type"] = "Closed";
    item.Update();
}
```

Each of these event handlers work basically the same way. First, the sender parameter is cast as a CreateTaskWithContentType activity. Then its TaskId property is set by generating a new Guid. An SPWorkflowTaskProperties object is then created, the appropriate properties are set, and this object is stored in the task's TaskProperties property.

In most cases, the associated Issues list item is also updated as appropriate.

OnTaskChanged Events

The OnTaskChanged event is raised whenever a task is updated. A copy of the before and after properties are passed to the event handler. The code can then determine what has changed and take the appropriate action.

Accessing Extended Properties

The properties that need to be retrieved are custom columns that are not included in the base Workflow Task content type. Consequently, these are not included in the SPWorkflowTaskProperties class. To access these, you'll need to use the ExtendedProperties collection. Unfortunately, to do that, you'll need to provide the field Id.

To obtain the Id of a particular field, you can use the following code:

```
workflowProperties.TaskList.Fields.GetField("Issue Priority").Id
```

The workflowProperties.TaskList property specifies an SPList object that represents the list used to store the workflow tasks. In this case, it's the standard Tasks list. Its Fields property is a collection of all the fields that are defined for that list. The GetField() method finds the specified field in the collection and returns an SPField object. You can then obtain its Id property.

Adding the Event Handlers

Add the code shown in Listing 15-3, which implements an OnTaskChanged event handler for each workflow state.

Listing 15-3. *OnTaskChanged Event Handlers*

```
/*----------------------------------------------------------*/
/* OnTaskChanged event handlers                             */
/*----------------------------------------------------------*/
// New
private void onNewChanged_Invoked(object sender, ExternalDataEventArgs e)
{
    CreateTaskWithContentType task = sender as CreateTaskWithContentType;
    SPTaskServiceEventArgs args = (SPTaskServiceEventArgs)e;

    _taskId = args.taskId;

    SPWorkflowTaskProperties after = args.afterProperties;
    if (after != null)
    {
        _action = after.ExtendedProperties[
            workflowProperties.TaskList.Fields
            .GetField("Issue New Action")
            .Id].ToString();

        _priority = after.ExtendedProperties[
            workflowProperties.TaskList.Fields
            .GetField("Issue Priority")
            .Id].ToString();

        _assign = after.ExtendedProperties[
            workflowProperties.TaskList.Fields
            .GetField("Issue Assigned To")
            .Id].ToString();
```

```
        // Store the item's priority
        if (_priority.Length > 0)
        {
            SPListItem item = workflowProperties.Item;

            if (_priority.Length > 0)
                item["Priority"] = _priority;

            item.Update();
        }
    }
}

// Assigned
private void onAssignedChanged_Invoked(object sender, ExternalDataEventArgs e)
{
    CreateTaskWithContentType task = sender as CreateTaskWithContentType;
    SPTaskServiceEventArgs args = (SPTaskServiceEventArgs)e;

    _taskId = args.taskId;

    SPWorkflowTaskProperties after = args.afterProperties;
    if (after != null)
    {
        _action = after.ExtendedProperties[
            workflowProperties.TaskList.Fields
            .GetField("Issue Assigned Action")
            .Id].ToString();

        bool started = bool.Parse(after.ExtendedProperties[
            workflowProperties.TaskList.Fields
            .GetField("Issue Started")
            .Id].ToString());

        if (started)
            _action = "Start";

        _resolution = after.ExtendedProperties[
            workflowProperties.TaskList.Fields
            .GetField("Resolution")
            .Id].ToString();

        if (_resolution.Length > 0)
        {
            SPListItem item = workflowProperties.Item;
            item["Resolution"] = _resolution;
            item.Update();
        }
    }
}

// Active
```

```csharp
private void onActiveChanged_Invoked(object sender, ExternalDataEventArgs e)
{
    CreateTaskWithContentType task = sender as CreateTaskWithContentType;
    SPTaskServiceEventArgs args = (SPTaskServiceEventArgs)e;

    _taskId = args.taskId;

    SPWorkflowTaskProperties after = args.afterProperties;
    if (after != null)
    {
        _action = after.ExtendedProperties[
            workflowProperties.TaskList.Fields
            .GetField("Issue Assigned Action")
            .Id].ToString();

        bool started = bool.Parse(after.ExtendedProperties[
            workflowProperties.TaskList.Fields
            .GetField("Issue Started")
            .Id].ToString());

        if (!started)
            _action = "Pause";

        _resolution = after.ExtendedProperties[
            workflowProperties.TaskList.Fields
            .GetField("Resolution")
            .Id].ToString();

        if (_resolution.Length > 0)
        {
            SPListItem item = workflowProperties.Item;
            item["Resolution"] = _resolution;
            item.Update();
        }
    }
}

// Resolved
private void onResolvedChanged_Invoked(object sender, ExternalDataEventArgs e)
{
    CreateTaskWithContentType task = sender as CreateTaskWithContentType;
    SPTaskServiceEventArgs args = (SPTaskServiceEventArgs)e;

    _taskId = args.taskId;

    SPWorkflowTaskProperties after = args.afterProperties;
    if (after != null)
    {
        _action = after.ExtendedProperties[
            workflowProperties.TaskList.Fields
            .GetField("Issue Resolved Action")
            .Id].ToString();
```

```
            _feedback = after.ExtendedProperties[
                workflowProperties.TaskList.Fields
                .GetField("Issue Feedback")
                .Id].ToString();

            if (_feedback.Length > 0 && _feedback != "<DIV></DIV>")
            {
                SPListItem item = workflowProperties.Item;
                if (item["Issue Feedback"] != null)
                    item["Issue Feedback"] += "\r\n";
                item["Issue Feedback"] += _feedback;
                item.Update();
            }
        }
    }
}

// Waiting
private void onWaitingChanged_Invoked(object sender, ExternalDataEventArgs e)
{
    CreateTaskWithContentType task = sender as CreateTaskWithContentType;
    SPTaskServiceEventArgs args = (SPTaskServiceEventArgs)e;

    _taskId = args.taskId;

    SPWorkflowTaskProperties after = args.afterProperties;
    if (after != null)
    {
        _action = after.ExtendedProperties[
            workflowProperties.TaskList.Fields
            .GetField ("Issue Waiting Action")
            .Id].ToString();

        _feedback = after.ExtendedProperties[
            workflowProperties.TaskList.Fields
            .GetField("Issue Feedback")
            .Id].ToString();

        if (_feedback.Length > 0 && _feedback != "<DIV></DIV>")
        {
            SPListItem item = workflowProperties.Item;
            if (item["Issue Feedback"] != null)
                item["Issue Feedback"] += "\r\n";
            item["Issue Feedback"] += _feedback;
            item.Update();
        }
    }
}
```

State Initializers

When entering a state, in addition to creating a task for that state, you will also want to update the associated issue to indicate the current state. To do that you'll use a CodeActivity. Enter the code shown in Listing 15-4, which implements a method for each state.

Listing 15-4. *State Initialization Code*

```
/*----------------------------------------------------------*/
/* State initializers                                       */
/*----------------------------------------------------------*/
private void codeInitNew_ExecuteCode(object sender, EventArgs e)
{
    SPListItem item = workflowProperties.Item;
    item["PM Issue Status"] = "New";
    item.Update();
}

private void codeInitAssigned_ExecuteCode(object sender, EventArgs e)
{
    SPListItem item = workflowProperties.Item;
    item["PM Issue Status"] = "Assigned";
    item.Update();
}

private void codeInitActive_ExecuteCode(object sender, EventArgs e)
{
    SPListItem item = workflowProperties.Item;
    item["PM Issue Status"] = "Active";
    item.Update();
}

private void codeInitResolved_ExecuteCode(object sender, EventArgs e)
{
    SPListItem item = workflowProperties.Item;
    item["PM Issue Status"] = "Resolved";
    item.Update();
}

private void codeInitWaiting_ExecuteCode(object sender, EventArgs e)
{
    SPListItem item = workflowProperties.Item;
    item["PM Issue Status"] = "Pending";
    item.Update();
}
```

By now you should be familiar with this code. It simply obtains the associated issue and sets its PM Issue Status column to the appropriate value based on the state being entered.

Remaining Events

There are a couple of additional event handlers that you'll need. Add the code shown in Listing 15-5 to implement these.

Listing 15-5. *Additional Event Handlers*

```
/*----------------------------------------------------------*/
/* Complete task event handlers                             */
/*----------------------------------------------------------*/
private void completeTask_MethodInvoking(object sender, EventArgs e)
{
    CompleteTask ct = (CompleteTask)sender;
    ct.TaskId = _taskId;
}

private void completeWorkTask_MethodInvoking(object sender, EventArgs e)
{
    CompleteTask ct = (CompleteTask)sender;
    ct.TaskId = _workTaskId;
}


/*----------------------------------------------------------*/
/* Misc code activity handlers                              */
/*----------------------------------------------------------*/
private void codeSetClosed_ExecuteCode(object sender, EventArgs e)
{
    // Now set the BugStatus and the completed date
    SPListItem item = workflowProperties.Item;
    item["DateCompleted"] = DateTime.UtcNow;
    item["PM Issue Status"] = "Closed";
    item.Update();
}

private void codeSetResolved_ExecuteCode(object sender, EventArgs e)
{
    // Now set the BugStatus and the completed date
    SPListItem item = workflowProperties.Item;
    item["DateCompleted"] = DateTime.UtcNow;
    item["PM Issue Status"] = "Closed";
    item["Resolution Type"] = "Resolved";
    item.Update();
}
```

The CompleteTask activity will be used to mark a particular task as complete. It will raise the MethodInvoking event just before the activity is executed. You will use this to specify the TaskId property. There are two versions of this event handler. The first one provides the Id property of the current task. The other provides the Id of the work task, which I'll explain later.

The other two methods are called to close the issue. They both set the DateCompleted and PM Issue Status columns. The second implementation also overrides the Resolution Type column, setting it to

Resolved. When an issue is put into the Waiting state because it is an enhancement or working as designed, the Resolution Type column is set accordingly. When the issue is then closed, the first version is used, which leaves the Resolution Type property as it is. However, when an issue is closed from the Resolved state, the second version is used to ensure the Resolution Type is set to Resolved.

Using a Work Task

When entering a state, a task is generated for working that state for the issue. If an issue reenters the same state again, a new task is generated. For example, when an issue is created, it enters the New state and a task is created. When the task is worked, it is marked completed. If the issue goes to the Waiting state and is then resubmitted, it will go to the New state again. In this case another task is generated.

The exception to this logic is the developer's task in the Assigned or Active states. Once it has been assigned to a developer, we want to reuse the same task. If the tester finds an issue with the resolution, it should go back to the same developer for them to finish the task. It's not a new task; rather, the developer is making an adjustment to the original task. I refer to the developer's task as the *work* task. It is the task where the principle work is being performed.

To support this design, the workflow records the TaskId property of the work task in the _workTaskId class member. The first time the workflow enters the Assigned state, a task is generated and its TaskId property is stored. When entering the Assigned or Active states, if this is populated, the task is reused instead of creating a new one.

■**Note**   I realize that this design is somewhat arbitrary. You could argue that the tester's task or the admin's task should be reused as well. I designed it this way to demonstrate both approaches. You can modify the logic if this design needs to be adjusted to suit your requirements.

Designing the State Initialization

Now you're ready to design the workflow logic. On each event you can add logic for

- State initialization
- Event handlers
- State finalization

For this design you'll only need the first two. The basic pattern that you'll use is to create a task in the state initialization and then wait for it to be updated in the event handler.

Initializing the New State

Drag a StateInitialization activity to each state except stateInitial and stateFinal. Change the activity name to **init<state name>** (e.g., **initNew**).

> **■Tip**   All of the activities in the workflow must have unique names. The workflow designer will automatically generate unique names for you by taking the name of activity type and adding a sequential number (such as `eventDrivenActivity1`). This is OK for simple workflows, but for complex workflows such as this one, more meaningful names will help you keep track better. As you start debugging, you may not remember which state `eventDrivenActivity6` was for.

Double-click the `initNew` activity (in the New state), which will display an empty sequence. Drag a `CreateTaskWithContent` type activity to the sequence and rename it **createNewTask**.

Correlation Tokens

Correlation tokens allow you to associate activities that need to be performed on the same object instance. For example, when you add an `OnTaskChanged` event handler, you'll want it to operate on the same task instance that you're creating here. You ensure this by assigning the same correlation token to both activities. You will have other `CreateTask`/`OnTaskChanged` activity pairs in your workflow, and you will assign a different correlation token to each.

There are generally two types of correlation tokens. You'll use one at the workflow level and one at the task level. The project template already set up a token at the workflow level called `workflowToken`. The Properties window for the `OnWorkflowActivated1` activity (on the `eventInitial` sequence) is shown in Figure 15-10.

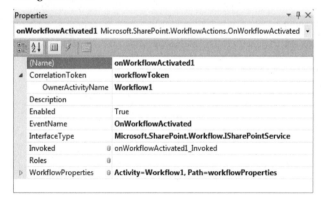

Figure 15-10. *OnWorkflowActivated Properties window*

If you expand the `CorrelationToken` property, you'll see the `OwnerActivityName` property, which is used to define the scope of the token. In this case, it is defined for `Workflow1`, which is the name of the workflow.

Select the `createNewTask` activity that you just created, and in the Properties window, enter the `CorrelationToken` as **newToken**. Then expand this property, and select `stateNew` for the `OwnerActivityName`. This will limit the scope of this token to the New state, since both the task creation and the handling of the `OnTaskChanged` event are contained in this state.

■**Caution**   Since the project template already generated a workflowToken for you, there is a temptation to use it everywhere that an activity requires a CorrelationToken. Be careful about doing that. When you have multiple tasks in your workflow, you need to correlate events with the correct task.

Specifying the Content Type

The CreateTaskWithContentType activity allows you to specify a custom content type to use for this task. You do this by specifying the Id of the content type in the Properties window. To determine the Id of the Issue New content type, you can use SharePoint Designer. Select this content type and the ID will be displayed, as shown in Figure 15-11. Enter the ID in the Properties window. Your ID will be different from the one shown here.

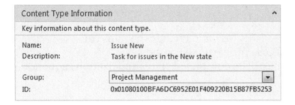

Figure 15-11. *Displaying the content type in SharePoint Designer*

■**Caution**   If you are using the Visual Studio solution from the Apress web site (www.apress.com), make sure you change the ContentTypeId property to use the one assigned on your site. There are several other places, later in this chapter, where you'll also need to change the ContentTypeId property.

You will also need to specify the MethodInvoking event handler. Select the createNewTask_MethodInvoking method from the drop-down list. This will set the TaskProperties and TaskId properties in code. The completed Properties window should look like Figure 15-12.

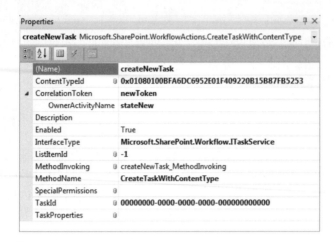

Figure 15-12. *The createNewTask Properties window*

Drag a `CodeActivity` to the sequence just below `createNewTask` and change the name to **codeInitNew**. In the Properties window, for the `ExecuteCode` property, select the `codeInitNew_ExecuteCode` method from the drop-down list. The completed state initialization sequence will look like Figure 15-13.

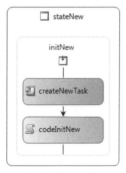

Figure 15-13. *The initialization sequence for the New state*

Initializing the Assigned State

Navigate back to the main workflow diagram then double-click the `initAssigned` activity. This sequence will create a task and execute a `CodeActivity` just like the first one. However, because this is the work task, we need to see if the task has already been created.

IfElseActivity

Drag an `IfElseActivity` onto the `initAssigned` sequence. The workflow diagram should look like Figure 15-14.

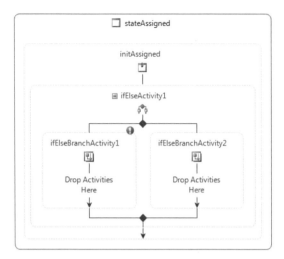

Figure 15-14. *An initial IfElseActivity*

An IfElseActivity can have any number of branches, and all except the last branch must specify a boolean condition. The processing goes from left to right until it finds a branch with a condition that is true. Each branch can contain a sequence of activities. The first branch with a true condition is then executed, and the activity is completed (no other branches are executed). If no true condition is found, the last branch is executed if it does *not* have a condition.

For a typical if-then-else scenario, use two branches. The left branch will have a condition and the right will not. If the left branch's condition is true, the left branch is executed; otherwise, the right branch is executed.

You can also use the IfElseActivtity like a switch statement. Specify the appropriate case condition on each branch. Leave the condition blank on the last branch if you want an else case.

■**Caution** If you specify a condition on all branches, then it is possible that none of the branches will be executed. In that case, the IfElseActivity is simply skipped, and processing will continue with the next activity.

There are two ways that you can specify a condition. You can use a code condition by implementing an event handler that returns true or false in the event arguments. The other method is to define a declarative rule condition, which you'll use here.

Defining Declarative Rule Conditions

In the workflow designer, select the left branch, and change the name to **ifNotCreated**. In the Properties window, for the Condition property, select Declarative Rule Condition, and then expand this property. Select the ConditionName, and click the ellipses. This will display the Select Condition dialog box shown in Figure 15-15.

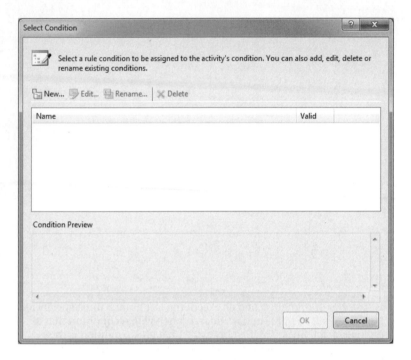

Figure 15-15. *An empty Select Condition dialog box*

This dialog box should be empty since you have not created any conditions yet. Click the *New* link to create one. In the Rule Condition Editor shown in Figure 15-16, enter **this._workTaskId == System.Guid.Empty**.

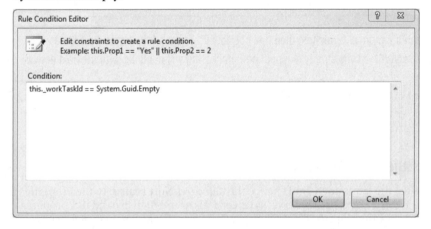

Figure 15-16. *The Rule Condition Editor*

■Tip   The `Condition` property uses standard C# syntax. You can access workflow members using the `this.` notation. You can also access static members such as `DateTime.Now`.

When you click the OK button, the condition will be created but will be given the name `Condition1`. Click the *Rename* link and change the name to **notCreated**. While the Select Condition dialog is displayed, go ahead and create all the other conditions that you will need. Create the conditions listed in Table 15-1.

Table 15-1. *Declarative Code Conditions*

Name	Condition
Assign	`this._action == "Assign" && this._assign > ""`
Assigned	`this._assign > ""`
Close	`this._action == "Close"`
Completed	`this._action == "Completed"`
Enhancement	`this._action == "Enhancement"`
MoreInfo	`this._action == "More Info"`
notCreated	`this._workTaskId == System.Guid.Empty`
notResolved	`this._action == "Not Resolved"`
Pause	`this._action == "Pause"`
Resolved	`this._action == "Resolved"`
Resubmit	`this._action == "Resubmit"`
Start	`this._action == "Start"`
Wad	`this._action == "Working as Designed"`
WorkTask	`this._workTaskId != System.Guid.Empty`

Select the `notCreated` condition and click the OK button to update the Properties window. The completed Properties window should look like Figure 15-17.

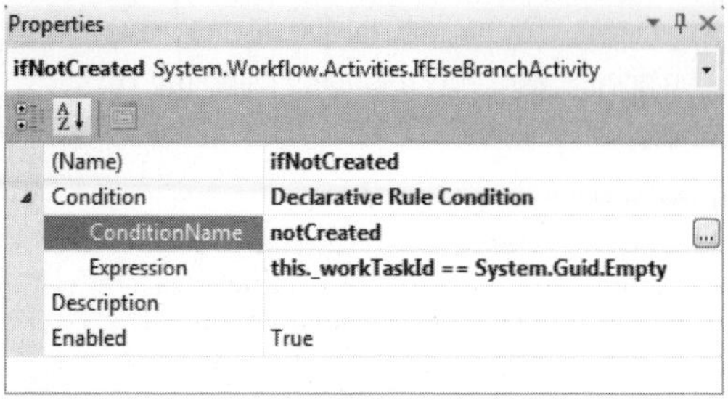
Properties
ifNotCreated System.Workflow.Activities.IfElseBranchActivity
(Name)
ifNotCreated
Condition
Declarative Rule Condition
ConditionName
notCreated
Expression
this._workTaskId == System.Guid.Empty
Description
Enabled
True

Figure 15-17. *The completed Properties window for the ifNotCreated branch*

Drag a `CreateTaskWithContentType` activity to the left branch of the `IfElseActivity` and change the name to **createAssignedTask**. In the Properties window, enter the `ContentTypeId` property using the ID of the `Issue Assigned` content type. For the `CorrelationToken`, enter **taskToken**, and then expand the property and select `Workflow1` for the `OwnerActivityName`. Select the `createAssignedTask_MethodInvoking` method for the `MethodInvoking` property. The completed Properties window should look like Figure 15-18.

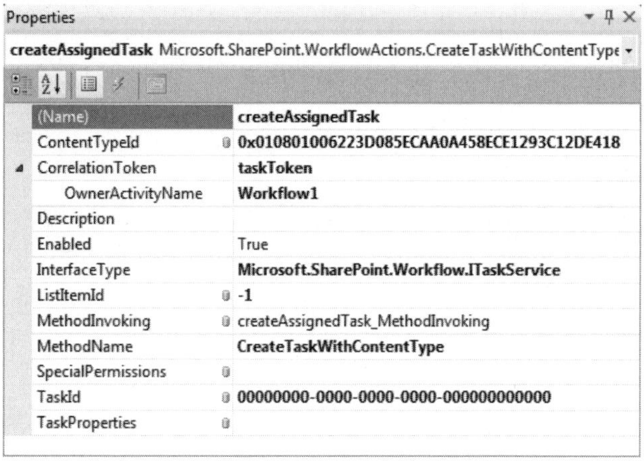
Properties
createAssignedTask Microsoft.SharePoint.WorkflowActions.CreateTaskWithContentType
(Name)
createAssignedTask
ContentTypeId
0x010801006223D085ECAA0A458ECE1293C12DE418
CorrelationToken
taskToken
OwnerActivityName
Workflow1
Description
Enabled
True
InterfaceType
Microsoft.SharePoint.Workflow.ITaskService
ListItemId
-1
MethodInvoking
createAssignedTask_MethodInvoking
MethodName
CreateTaskWithContentType
SpecialPermissions
TaskId
00000000-0000-0000-0000-000000000000
TaskProperties

Figure 15-18. *Configuring the createAssignedTask activity*

Drag a `CodeActivity` below the `IfElseActivity` and change its name to **codeInitAssigned**. For the `ExecuteCode` property select the `codeInitAssigned_ExecuteCode` method. The initialization sequence should look like Figure 15-19.

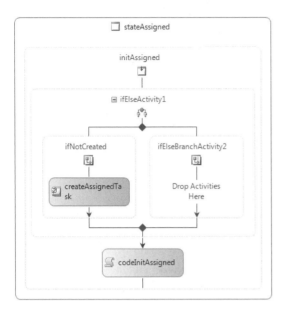

Figure 15-19. *The Assigned state initialization sequence*

Initializing the Active State

The Active state is a little different from the other states because you don't need to create a task. To get to the Active state, the workflow must have first been in the Assigned state so the work task will have already been created. Navigate back to the main workflow diagram and then double-click the initActive activity. Drag a CodeActivity to the sequence and rename it **codeInitActive**. In the Properties window, select the codeInitActive_ExecuteCode method.

Initializing the Resolved State

From the main workflow diagram, double-click the initResolved activity. Drag a CreateTaskWithContentTypeActivity and rename it **createResolvedTask**. In the Properties window, enter the ID of the Issue Resolved content type. Enter **resolvedToken** for the CorrelationToken. Expand the property and select stateResolved for the OwnerActivityName. Select the createResolvedTask_MethodInvoking method.

Drag a CodeActivity below the createResolvedTask activity. Change its name to **codeInitResolved** and select the codeInitResolved_ExecuteCode method. The initialization sequence should look like Figure 15-20.

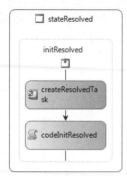

Figure 15-20. *The Resolved state initialization sequence*

Initializing the Waiting State

From the main workflow diagram, double-click the initWaiting activity on the Waiting state. The initialization sequence for the Waiting state will create a task using one of three content types depending on the action that moved the workflow to the Waiting state. You'll use an IfElseActivity to determine which content type to use.

Drag an IfElseActivity to the initWaiting sequence. Rename the left branch **ifWaitingWad** and the right branch **ifWaitingEnhancement**. Right-click the IfElseActivity and click the *Add Branch* link. Rename this branch **elseMoreInfo**. Select the first branch, select Declarative Rule Condition for the Condition property, and then expand this property. Select the ConditionName and click the ellipses. This will display the Select Condition dialog box. Select the Wad condition and click the OK button. In the same way, select the Enhancement condition for the second branch.

Drag a CreateTaskWithContentType activity to the ifWaitingWad branch. Rename it **createWaitingWadTask**. Enter the appropriate ContentTypeId. Enter **waitingToken** for the CorrelationToken property, expand this property, and select stateWaiting for the OwnerActivityName. Select the createWADTask_MethodInvoking method. The completed Properties window should look like Figure 15-21 (your ContentTypeId will be different from the one shown here).

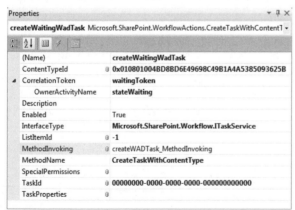

Figure 15-21. *The createWaitingWadTask Properties window*

Now you can copy this activity to the other two branches. Right-click the createWaitingWadTask and click the *Copy* link. Then right-click inside the second branch (where the text says "Drop Activities Here") and click the *Paste* link. Likewise right-click the third branch and click the *Paste* link. Rename these activities **createWaitingEnhancementTask** and **createWaitingMoreInfoTask**, respectively. You'll also need to change the ContentTypeId property and select the corresponding MethodInvoking event handlers (createEnhancementTask_MethodInvoking and createInfoTask_MethodInvoking, respectively).

Finally, drag a CodeActivity below the IfElseActivity and rename it **codeInitWaiting**. Select the codeInitWaiting_ExecuteCode method. The completed sequence should look like Figure 15-22.

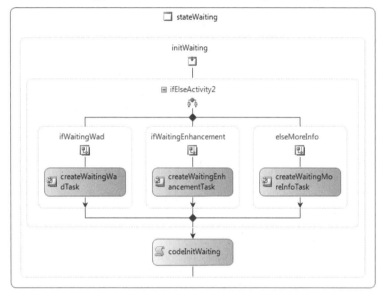

Figure 15-22. *The Waiting state initialization sequence*

Designing the Event Handlers

Now you'll design the activity sequences to respond to the OnTaskChanged events.

Designing the Initial State

The workflow always starts in the Initial state. As soon as the workflow is activated you'll want to move to the New state, which is where your custom logic starts. To do that, you'll use a SetState activity.

The stateInitial object already has an EventDrivenActivity object, eventInitial. Double-click it to display the activity sequence. So far it only has the onWorkflowActivated1 event handler. Drag a SetStateActivity below this and rename it **setInitialNew**. In the Properties window, select the stateNew state for the TargetStateName property. The completed sequence should look like Figure 15-23.

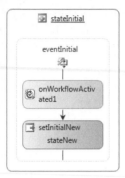

Figure 15-23. *The initial state event handler*

Navigate back to the main workflow diagram. Notice that there is now a connection between the eventInitial activity and the New state, as illustrated in Figure 15-24. This indicates that this event handler can cause the workflow to transition to the New state.

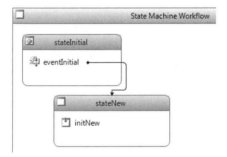

Figure 15-24. *The workflow diagram showing a state connection*

For the remainder of the states (except Final), drag an EventDrivenActivity to the state. Change the activity name to **event<State name>** (e.g., **eventNew**).

Designing the New State

As I mentioned earlier, the first activity in an EventDrivenActivity sequence must be an event handler. For all of these sequences, you will use the OnTaskChanged activity. This is executed whenever the associated task is modified.

Double-click the eventNew activity to display its sequence, which should be empty. Drag an OnTaskChanged activity to the sequence and rename it **onNewChanged**. In the Properties window, select newToken as the CorrelationToken and select the onNewChanged_Invoke method for the Invoked event handler. The completed Properties window should look like Figure 15-25.

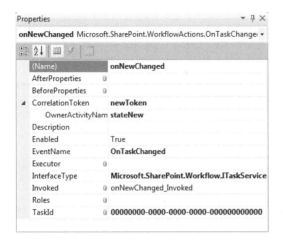

Figure 15-25. *The onNewChanged Properties window*

The Invoked event handler is called when the onTaskChanged event is raised. You implemented this code earlier. It simply extracts the pertinent properties from the task and stores them in class members. The primary class member that drives the workflow logic is the _action member. For each state, the corresponding content type provides an action field that contains the choices that are applicable. The remaining event handler logic will take the appropriate action based on the action that was selected.

■**Tip**　It is certainly possible that the task was modified but no action was taken. The None action is allowed for all content types, and is the default value. If the user does not select an action, no action is taken and the workflow leaves the issue in the current state.

In the New state, there are four possible actions (other than None):

- Assign
- More Info
- Working as Designed
- Enhancement

Drag an IfElseActivity below the onNewChanged activity. Add two more branches and rename all the branches as follows: **ifNewAssign**, **ifNewMoreInfo**, **ifNewWad**, and **ifNewEnhancement**. For each branch, use a declarative rule condition and select an existing condition, which you defined earlier. The conditions to use are Assign, MoreInfo, Wad, and Enhancement, respectively.

For each branch, you'll need to complete the New task since an action was taken. Drag a CompleteTask activity to each branch, and rename these **completeNewAssign**, **completeNewMoreInfo**, **completeNewWad**, and **completeNewEnhancement**, respectively. For each of these activities, select newToken for the CorrelationToken and select the completeTask_MethodInvoking method. The Properties window will look like Figure 15-26.

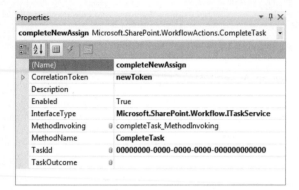

Figure 15-26. *The completeNewAssign Properties window*

Drag a SetStateActivity to each branch to cause a transition to the appropriate state. Name these activities **setNewAssign**, **setNewMoreInfo**, **setNewWad**, and **setNewEnhancement**, respectively. For the TargetStateName property, select stateAssigned for setNewAssign, and select stateWaiting for all the others. The completed sequence should look like Figure 15-27.

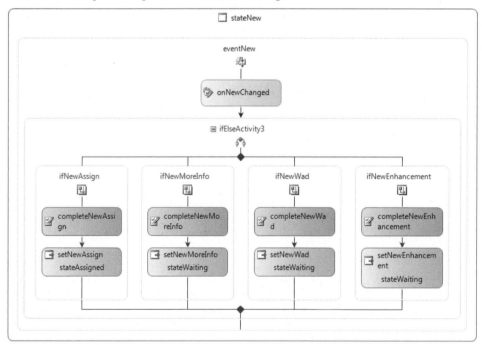

Figure 15-27. *The eventNew sequence*

Designing the Assigned State

This event handler will be very similar to the last one. It starts with an `OnTaskChanged` activity to capture the values from the modified task. It then uses an `IfElseActivity` to take appropriate action based on the action selected. In this case there will be five branches because there are five possible actions, as follows:

- `Start`
- `Completed`
- `More Info`
- `Working as Designed`
- `Enhancement`

Double-click the `eventAssigned` activity on the main workflow diagram. This will display the empty sequence. Drag an `OnTaskChanged` activity to the sequence and rename it **onAssignedChanged**. Select the `taskToken` and the `onAssignedChanged_Invoked` method.

Drag an `IfElseActivity` below this, set a total of five branches, and name them using the same naming convention you used in the previous sequence and based on the actions just listed. For each branch, use a declarative rule condition, selecting an existing condition that matches the associated action (`Start`, `Completed`, `MoreInfo`, `Wad`, and `Enhancement`).

The `ifAssignedStart` branch will simply have a `SetState` activity to move the workflow to the `Active` state. The partially completed sequence should look like Figure 15-28.

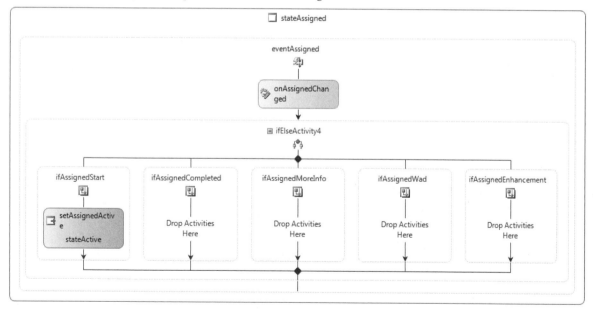

Figure 15-28. *The partial eventAssigned sequence*

Using the UpdateTask Activity

For the other four branches, the work task will be suspended. You won't close it, in case the issue is resubmitted by the requestor or the tester finds an issue with the resolution. Instead, the task status will be changed to "Waiting on someone else." Also, since you will reuse this task, you'll need to clear the selected action. If the developer edits this task, the action should be set back to the default value of None, which will make them select an appropriate action again.

To do this you'll use the UpdateTask activity. Drag an UpdateTask activity to the ifAssignedCompleted branch and rename it **updateAssignedResolved**. In the Properties window, select taskToken for the CorrelationToken property. You'll need to specify the task properties that are to be changed and the task that is to be updated. You'll do this by binding the TaskProperties and TaskId properties to a dependency property and then setting these values in code.

In the Properties window, select the TaskId property and then click the ellipses. In the dialog that appears, click the second tab. Enter the new member name as **updateWorkTask_TaskId**, as shown in Figure 15-29. Click the OK button to create the class member.

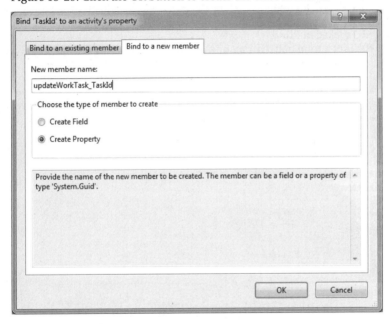

Figure 15-29. *Creating a dependency property*

In the same way, select the TaskProperties property, click the ellipses, click the second tab, and enter the name **updateWorkTask_TaskProperties**. The Properties window should look like Figure 15-30.

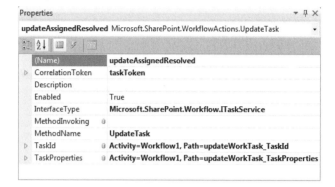

Figure 15-30. *The updateAssignedResolved Properties window*

This creates a class member, referred to as a dependency property that is bound to the UpdateTask activity. You can then update this class member in code before the UpdateTask activity is executed.

Go to the code-behind file, Workflow1.cs. Notice that code has been added to set up the dependency properties that you just created. Add the methods shown in Listing 15-6.

Listing 15-6. *Modifying the UpdateTask Properties*

```
/*----------------------------------------------------------*/
/* Set the UpdateTask properties                            */
/*----------------------------------------------------------*/
private void updateWorkWaiting_MethodInvoking(object sender, EventArgs e)
{
    updateWorkTask_TaskId = _workTaskId;
    updateWorkTask_TaskProperties = new SPWorkflowTaskProperties();
    updateWorkTask_TaskProperties.ExtendedProperties[
        workflowProperties.TaskList.Fields.GetField("Status")
            .Id] = "Waiting on someone else";
    updateWorkTask_TaskProperties.ExtendedProperties[
        workflowProperties.TaskList.Fields.GetField("Issue Assigned Action")
            .Id] = "None";
}

private void updateWorkAvailable_MethodInvoking(object sender, EventArgs e)
{
    updateWorkTask_TaskId = _workTaskId;
    updateWorkTask_TaskProperties = new SPWorkflowTaskProperties();
    updateWorkTask_TaskProperties.ExtendedProperties[
        workflowProperties.TaskList.Fields.GetField("Status")
            .Id] = "In Progress";
    updateWorkTask_TaskProperties.ExtendedProperties[
        workflowProperties.TaskList.Fields.GetField("Issue Assigned Action")
            .Id] = "None";
    updateWorkTask_TaskProperties.ExtendedProperties[
        workflowProperties.TaskList.Fields.GetField("Issue Started")
            .Id] = "False";
```

337

}

This first method puts the work task in the "Waiting on someone else" status. The second puts it in the "In Progress" status. Both methods clear the Issue Assigned Action property. Go back to the workflow diagram and select the updateAssignedResolved activity. In the Properties window, select the updateWorkWaiting_MethodInvoking method for the MethodInvoking property. This method will be called before the UpdateTask is executed, which allows you to specify the TaskID and the TaskProperties that should be changed.

Finishing the Assigned State

Copy this UpdateTask activity to the other three branches, giving them appropriate names (**updateAssignedMoreInfo**, **updateAssignedWad**, and **updateAssignedEnhancement**).

Drag a SetStateActivity to all four branches. The ifAssignedCompleted branch will move to the Resolved state. The other three branches will move to the Waiting state. The completed sequence should look like Figure 15-31.

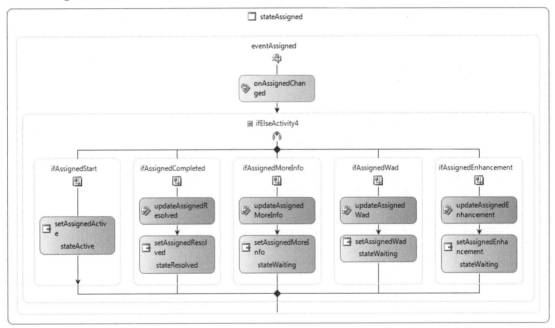

Figure 15-31. *The eventAssigned sequence*

Designing the Active State

The event handler for the Active state is identical to the Assigned state, except there is a Pause action instead of a Start action. The Start action moves the workflow to the Active state, while the Pause action moves it back to the Assigned state. If the developer starts working on an issue and then decides that they need to stop for a while, they can use the Pause action to indicate that it is no longer being actively worked on.

The easiest way to implement this is to select all the activities on the eventAssigned sequence (hold down the Ctrl button and click each of the activities) and then copy them (right-click any of the selected activities and click the *Copy* link) to the eventActive sequence (navigate to the eventActive activity, right-click it, and then click the *Paste* link). You will need to rename all of the activities.

Make sure you change the OnTaskChanged activity to call the onActiveChanged_Invoked method. Also, rename the ifAssignedStart branch to **ifActivePause**, use the Pause declarative rule condition, and change the SetStateActivity to move to the Assigned state. The completed sequence should look like Figure 15-32.

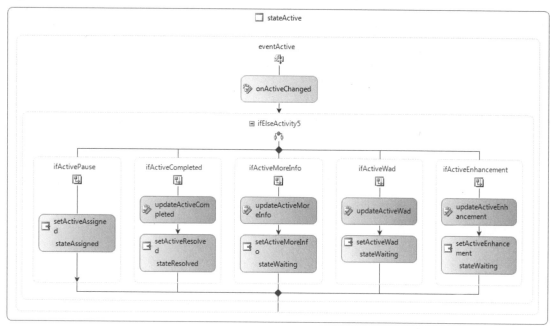

Figure 15-32. *The eventActive sequence*

Designing the Resolved State

The event handler for the Resolved state will start with an OnTaskChanged activity. It will then have two branches for the two possible actions, Resolved and Not Resolved.

Double-click the eventResolved activity from the main workflow diagram. Drag an OnTaskChanged activity to this sequence and rename it **onResolvedChanged**. In the Properties window, select the resolvedToken and the onResolvedChanged_Invoked method for the Invoked property.

Drag an IfElseActivity below the onResolvedChanged activity. Rename the branches **ifResolved** and **ifNotResolved**. Select the existing Resolved and notResolved declarative rule conditions.

■**Caution**   The first branch handles the case when the issue is marked as resolved and the second branch handles the scenario when it is marked as not resolved. It is possible that neither action was chosen. Since each branch specifies a different condition, if neither is satisfied, then neither branch will be executed. This is exactly how you want this to work. If the action is still None, then the tester has not finished the task.

If the issue is resolved, you will need to complete the current task (the tester's task) as well as the work task. You also need to update the issue to mark it as closed and move to the final state. Drag two CompleteTask activities to the ifResolved branch and rename them **completeResolved** and **completeResolvedWork**. For the first one, select the resolvedToken and the completeTask_MethodInvoking method. For the second activity, select the taskToken and the completeWorkTask_MethodInvoking method. Also, drag a CodeActivity and select the codeSetResolved_ExecuteCode method. Finally, add a SetStateActivity and select the Final state.

If the issue is not resolved, you'll still need to complete the current task and update the work task to change the status to In Progress. You'll also move the workflow to the Assigned state.

Copy the first CompleteTask activity from the first branch to the second branch and rename it **completeNotResolved**. Then drag an UpdateTask activity below this. Select the taskToken and bind the TaskId and TaskProperties to the dependency properties that you created earlier. You can do that by selecting the property, clicking the ellipses, and then selecting the appropriate class member from the dialog box. You will also need to select the updateWorkAvailable_MethodInvoking method for the Invoking property.

Finally, drag a SetStateActivity and set the TargetStateName to stateAssigned. The complete sequence should look like Figure 15-33.

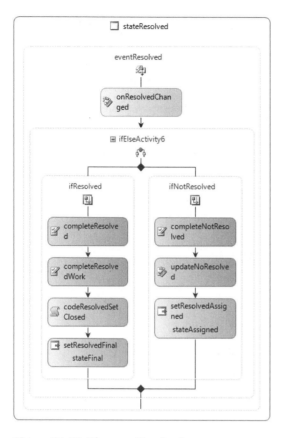

Figure 15-33. *The eventResolved sequence*

Designing the Waiting State

The event handler for the Waiting state is basically the same as the Resolved state. There are two possible actions, Close and Resubmit. If the Close action is taken, the current task is completed as well as the work task. The issue is closed and the workflow enters the Final state. If the Resubmit action is chosen, the current task is completed and the work task is updated.

However, there may not be a work task. If the workflow went to the Waiting state directly from the New state, then the task was never assigned to a developer and no work task was created. In this case, with the Close action, you need to skip the step that completes the work task. With the Resubmit action, you'll need to skip the UpdateTask activity and move to the New state instead of the Assigned state.

From the main workflow diagram, double-click the eventWaiting activity to display the empty sequence. Drag an OnTaskChanged activity to the sequence and rename it **onWaitingChanged**. In the Properties window, select the waitingToken and the onWaitingChanged_Invoked method. Drag an IfElseActivity below this and rename the branches **ifWaitingClose** and **ifWaitingResubmit**. For these two branches, use the Close and Resubmit declarative rule conditions, respectively.

Drag a `CompleteTask` activity onto the `ifWaitingClose` branch and rename it **completeWaiting**. In the Properties window, select the `waitingToken` and the `completeTask_MethodInvoking` method. Copy this activity to the `ifWaitingResubmit` branch and rename it **completeWaitingResubmit**.

Drag an `IfElseActivity` to both branches. Rename the left branch of each of these `IfElseActivity` objects **ifWorkTask** and **ifWorkTaskResubmit**, respectively. Choose the `WorkTask` declarative rule condition for both of these left branches.

Drag a `CompleteTask` activity to the `ifWorkTask` branch and rename it **completeWaitingWork**. In the Properties window, select the `taskToken` and the `completeWorkTask_MethodInvoking` method. Drag a `CodeActivity` below the `IfElseActivity` in the `ifWaitingClosed` branch. Rename it **codeWaitingClosed** and select the `codeSetClosed_ExecuteCode` method. Drag a `SetStateActivity` below this, rename it **setWaitingFinal**, and set the `TargetStateName` to `stateFinal`.

Drag an `UpdateTask` activity to the `ifWorkTaskResubmit` branch and rename it **updateWaiting**. In the Properties window, select the `taskToken` and the `updateWorkAvailable_MethodInvoking` method. Also, bind the `TaskID` and `TaskProperties` to the dependency properties that you set up earlier. Drag a `SetStateActivity` after this, rename it **setWaitingAssigned**, and set the `TargetStateName` to `stateAssigned`.

Finally, drag a `SetStateActivity` to the right branch, rename it **setWaitingNew**, and set its `TaregtStateName` to `stateNew`. The completed sequence should look like Figure 15-34.

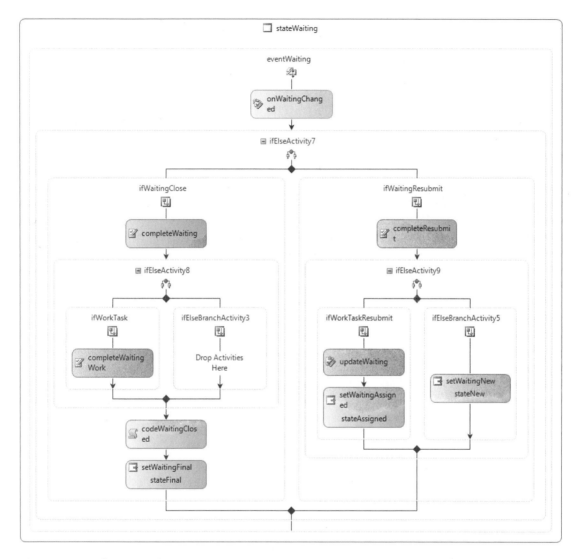

Figure 15-34. *The eventWaiting sequence*

The complete state diagram should look like Figure 15-35.

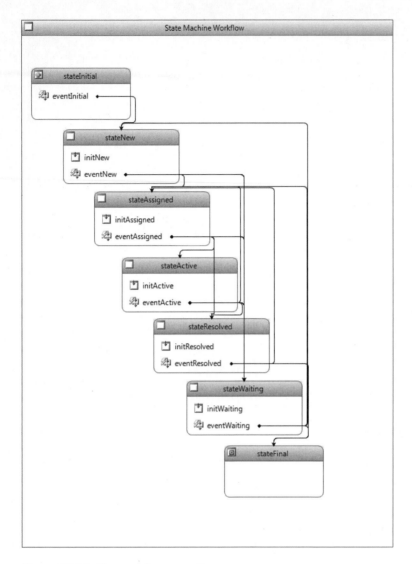

Figure 15-35. *The complete state diagram*

Configuring the Workflow

Now you'll add an association form that will allow the end users to configure the admin and test users. This workflow is configured to start automatically when an item is added to the Issues list. An initiation form is not helpful here because it is used only when starting a workflow manually. However, the association form will allow the users to configure the workflow when it is associated with a list—the Issues list in this case.

Adding an Association Form

From Solution Explorer, right-click the Workflow1 feature and select Add ➤ New Item. In the Add New Item dialog box, select the Workflow Association Form template, and enter the name as **Chapter15Association.aspx**, as shown in Figure 15-36.

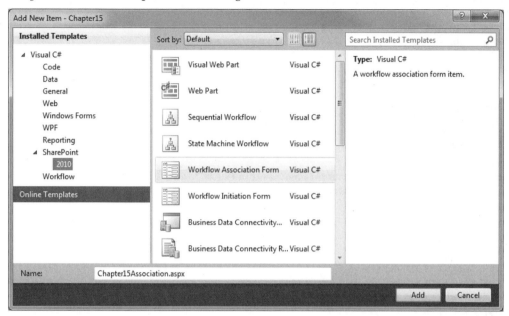

Figure 15-36. *Adding an association form*

Listing 15-7 shows the contents of the Chapter15Association.aspx file, with the lines that you'll need to add in bold.

Listing 15-7. *Implementation of Chapter15Association.aspx*

```
<%@ Assembly Name="$SharePoint.Project.AssemblyFullName$" %>
<%@ Assembly Name="Microsoft.Web.CommandUI, Version=14.0.0.0, Culture=neutral,
               PublicKeyToken=71e9bce111e9429c" %>
<%@ Import Namespace="Microsoft.SharePoint" %>
<%@ Import Namespace="Microsoft.SharePoint.ApplicationPages" %>
<%@ Register Tagprefix="SharePoint"
           Namespace="Microsoft.SharePoint.WebControls"
           Assembly="Microsoft.SharePoint, Version=14.0.0.0, Culture=neutral,
               PublicKeyToken=71e9bce111e9429c" %>
<%@ Register Tagprefix="Utilities"
           Namespace="Microsoft.SharePoint.Utilities"
           Assembly="Microsoft.SharePoint, Version=14.0.0.0, Culture=neutral,
               PublicKeyToken=71e9bce111e9429c" %>
<%@ Register Tagprefix="asp"
```

```
                Namespace="System.Web.UI"
                Assembly="System.Web.Extensions, Version=3.5.0.0, Culture=neutral,
                        PublicKeyToken=31bf3856ad364e35" %>

<%@ Page Language="C#"
    DynamicMasterPageFile="~masterurl/default.master"
    AutoEventWireup="true"
    Inherits="Chapter15.Workflow1.Chapter15Association"
    CodeBehind="Chapter15Association.aspx.cs" %>

<asp:Content ID="Main" ContentPlaceHolderID="PlaceHolderMain" runat="server">

    Admin User:  
    <SharePoint:PeopleEditor
        AllowEmpty="false"
        ValidatorEnabled="true"
        id="adminUser"
        runat="server"
        ShowCreateButtonInActiveDirectoryAccountCreationMode="true"
        SelectionSet="User" /> <br/><br/>

    Test User:  
    <SharePoint:PeopleEditor
        AllowEmpty="false"
        ValidatorEnabled="true"
        id="testUser"
        runat="server"
        ShowCreateButtonInActiveDirectoryAccountCreationMode="true"
        SelectionSet="User" /> <br/><br/>

    <asp:Button ID="AssociateWorkflow"
                runat="server"
                OnClick="AssociateWorkflow_Click"
                Text="Associate Workflow" />
          

    <asp:Button ID="Cancel"
                runat="server"
                Text="Cancel"
                OnClick="Cancel_Click" />
</asp:Content>

<asp:Content ID="PageTitle"
            ContentPlaceHolderID="PlaceHolderPageTitle"
            runat="server">
    Workflow Association Form
</asp:Content>

<asp:Content ID="PageTitleInTitleArea"
            runat="server"
            ContentPlaceHolderID="PlaceHolderPageTitleInTitleArea">
```

```
    Workflow Association Form
</asp:Content>
```

This code adds two PeoplePicker controls to the form: one to select the admin user and the other to select the test user. Now open the Chapter15Association.aspx.cs code-behind file, and add the following namespaces:

```
using System.Linq;
using System.Xml.Linq;
using System.Collections.Generic;
```

Then provide the following implementation for the GetAssociationData() method:

```
private string GetAssociationData()
{
    XElement data = new XElement("InitiationData",
        new XElement("AdminUsers",
                    from PickerEntity x in adminUser.Entities.ToArray()
                    select new XElement("Name", x.Description)),
        new XElement("TestUsers",
                    from PickerEntity x in testUser.Entities.ToArray()
                    select new XElement("Name", x.Description)));

    return data.ToString();
}
```

This code creates an XML string that contains the values from the PeoplePicker controls. It allows for multiple users to be selected for each.

Using the Association Data

Finally, open the Workflow1.cs code-behind file, and add the code from Listing 15-8 to the onWorkflowActivated1_Invoked method.

Listing 15-8. *Code to Add to the onWorkflowActivated Event Handler*

```
// Get the association data
if (workflowProperties.AssociationData != null)
{
    XElement data = XElement.Parse(workflowProperties.AssociationData);

    foreach (XElement x in data.Element("AdminUsers").Elements())
    {
        _admin = x.Value;
        break;  // just get the first one
    }
    foreach (XElement x in data.Element("TestUsers").Elements())
    {
        _test = x.Value;
```

```
            break;  // just get the first one
        }
    }
}
```

This code takes the first user from the AdminUser collection and stores it in the _admin class member. Likewise, the _test member is set using the first user from the TestUsers collection. If no association data is available, the workflow will use the hard-coded values.

Associating the Workflow

Now you're ready to deploy and test the workflow. Press F6 to build the solution and fix any compiler errors. Then, from Solution Explorer, right-click the Chapter15 project, and click the *Deploy* link. Visual Studio should have already associated the workflow with the Issues list. However, you'll now associate it manually so you can use the association form that you provided.

Go to the SharePoint site and select the Issues list. From the List ribbon, click the Workflow Settings button, as shown in Figure 15-37.

Figure 15-37. *Selecting the Workflow Settings page*

This will display the Workflow Settings page shown in Figure 15-38.

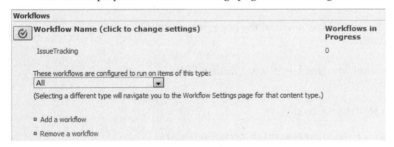

Figure 15-38. *The Workflow Settings page*

This page shows all the workflows associated with this list and the number of workflow instances currently in progress. Click the *IssueTracking* link to display the standard association page shown in Figure 15-39. Everything on this page should default correctly; these are the settings you specified when setting up the project in Visual Studio. Click the Next button to display the next page.

Content Type	
Select the type of items that you want this workflow to run on. Content type workflows can only be associated to a list content type, not directly to the list.	Run on items of this type: All ▼ (Selecting a different type will navigate you to the Add a Workflow page for that content type.)
Workflow	
Select a workflow to add to this list. If the workflow template you want does not appear, contact your administrator to get it added to your site collection or workspace.	Select a workflow template: Disposition Approval IssueTracking PM_Chapter12 - BuildTestCycle TestCycle Description: My SharePoint Workflow
Name	
Type a name for this workflow. The name will be used to identify this workflow to users of this list.	Type a unique name for this workflow: IssueTracking
Task List	
Select a task list to use with this workflow. You can select an existing task list or request that a new task list be created.	Select a task list: Tasks ▼ Description: Use the Tasks list to keep track of work that you or your team needs to complete.
History List	
Select a history list to use with this workflow. You can select an existing history list or request that a new history list be created.	Select a history list: Workflow History ▼ Description: History list for workflow.
Start Options	
Specify how this workflow can be started.	☐ Allow this workflow to be manually started by an authenticated user with Edit Item permissions. ☐ Require Manage Lists Permissions to start the workflow. ☐ Start this workflow to approve publishing a major version of an item. ☑ Start this workflow when a new item is created. ☐ Start this workflow when an item is changed.

Figure 15-39. *The standard workflow association page*

The next page, shown in Figure 15-40, will be the custom page that you created. It has two PeoplePicker controls on it. Enter a user for the Admin User and Test User fields, and click the Associate Workflow button.

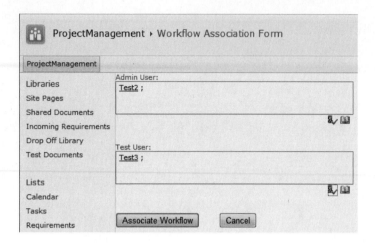

Figure 15-40. *The custom association page*

Testing the Workflow

Go to the Issues list and add a new item to the list. Just enter the title and description, and leave the other fields as they are, as shown in Figure 15-41. Then click the Save button.

Issues - New Item
Edit
Save
Cancel
Paste
Cut
Copy
Attach File
Spelling
Commit
Clipboard
Actions
Spelling
Title *
The login screen needs hints
Date Created
12 AM
00
The date on which this resource was created
PM Issue Status *
New
Description *
Please provide hints to help me remember my password
Priority
(2) Normal
Assigned To
Date Completed
Resolution Type
Resolution
Issue Feedback
Save
Cancel

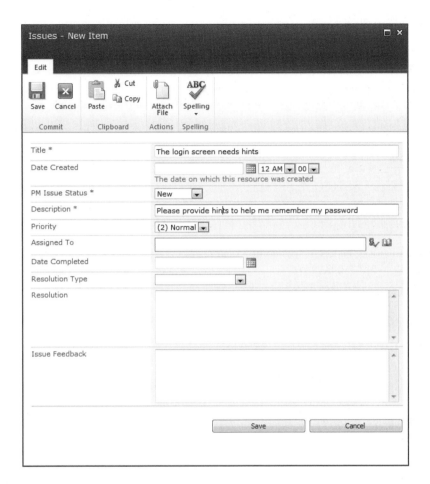

Figure 15-41. *Entering a new issue*

The item will be added to the `Issues` list and the workflow will be activated. The workflow will start by generating a task in the `Tasks` list. Go to the `Tasks` list and you should see a new task, as shown in Figure 15-42.

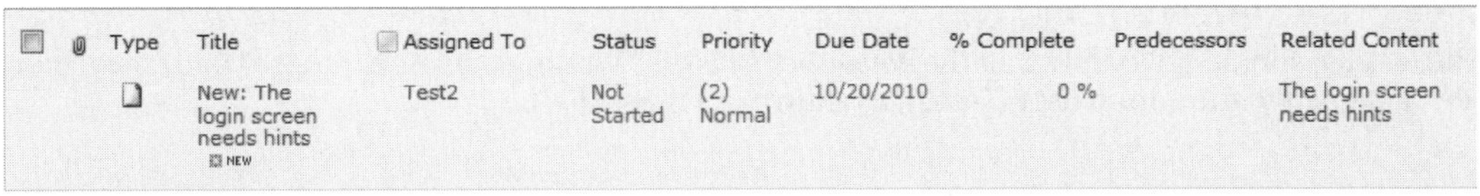

Type
Title
Assigned To
Status
Priority
Due Date
% Complete
Predecessors
Related Content
New: The login screen needs hints
NEW
Test2
Not Started
(2) Normal
10/20/2010
0 %
The login screen needs hints

Figure 15-42. *A new task added to the Tasks list*

■**Note**   The workflow runs in the background, and depending on other activity on the server, the workflow may be suspended for a while. If the task does not appear immediately, just a wait a few seconds and refresh the page.

Edit this task and select the Assign action. Enter a user on the PeoplePicker control and set the priority as shown in Figure 15-43. Click the Save button.

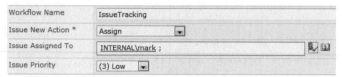

Figure 15-43. *Modifying the new task*

The Tasks list should now show that the first task is complete and a new task has been assigned to the developer, as demonstrated in Figure 15-44.

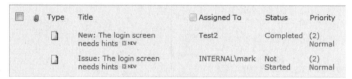

Figure 15-44. *A new task has been assigned to the developer.*

Edit this task, select the Enhancement action, enter a comment explaining that this is an enhancement as shown in Figure 15-45, and save the form.

Figure 15-45. *Modifying the developer's task*

The task list should now show that the developer's task is "Waiting on someone else" and a new task has been assigned to the admin user (Test2), as shown in Figure 15-46.

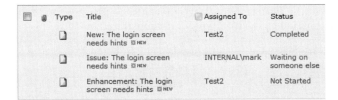

Figure 15-46. *An Enhancement task has been added to the list.*

Edit the Enhancement task and choose the Resubmit action. Enter a comment in the feedback field and click the Save button, as shown in Figure 15-47.

Workflow Name	IssueTracking
Issue Waiting Action *	Resubmit ▾
Issue Feedback	No, the requirements clearly indicate that this feature should be included.

Figure 15-47. *Modifying the Enhancement task*

The workflow will close the Enhancement task and change the developer's task to In Progress, as shown in Figure 15-48.

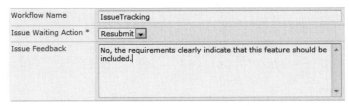

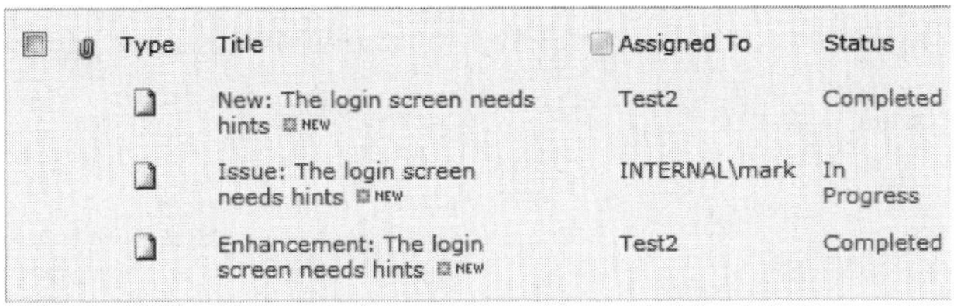

Figure 15-48. *The updated Tasks list*

Edit the developer's task and select the Issue Started check box. Leave the action set to None, as shown in Figure 15-49. This is simply indicating that you have started on this task.

Workflow Name	IssueTracking
Issue Assigned Action *	None ▾
Issue Started	☑
Resolution	OK, I'll add it...

Figure 15-49. *Selecting the Issue Started check box*

Now go to the Issues list. You should see that the status is currently Active. Also notice that the Priority and Assigned To columns have been updated by the workflow, as demonstrated in Figure 15-50.

☐	✉	Title	PM Issue Status	Priority	☐ Assigned To
		The login screen needs hints ⊞ NEW	Active	(3) Low	INTERNAL\mark

Figure 15-50. *The updated Issues list*

The requestor may not have access to the Tasks list, but they can view the Issues list to see the progress of their request. Go back to the Tasks list and edit the developer's task. Set the action to Completed, enter a resolution, and click the Save button, as shown in Figure 15-51.

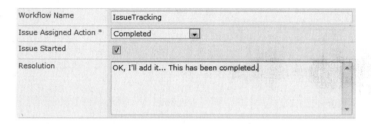

Figure 15-51. *Modifying the developer's task to show the work is completed*

The workflow will then generate a new task assigned to the tester (Test3), as shown in Figure 15-52.

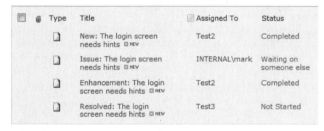

☐	✉	Type	Title	☐ Assigned To	Status
		🗋	New: The login screen needs hints ⊞ NEW	Test2	Completed
		🗋	Issue: The login screen needs hints ⊞ NEW	INTERNAL\mark	Waiting on someone else
		🗋	Enhancement: The login screen needs hints ⊞ NEW	Test2	Completed
		🗋	Resolved: The login screen needs hints ⊞ NEW	Test3	Not Started

Figure 15-52. *A new task for the tester has been added to the Tasks list*

Edit the new task, set the action to Resolved, and enter a feedback comment, as shown in Figure 15-53.

Figure 15-53. *Modifying the tester's task*

The Tasks list should now show that all tasks are complete, including the developer's task, as demonstrated in Figure 15-54.

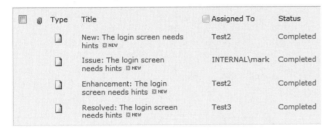

Figure 15-54. *The final Tasks list with tasks completed*

Go back to the Issues list and display the issue. The form should look like Figure 15-55.

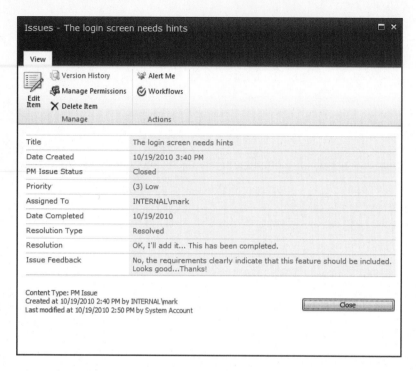

Figure 15-55. *Details of the completed issue*

The issue was initially created with only the `Title` and `Description` columns populated. As you work the tasks that are generated by the workflow, the details of this are automatically filled in. You can also see the tasks details by clicking the Workflow button on this form. The task details that are displayed are shown in Figure 15-56.

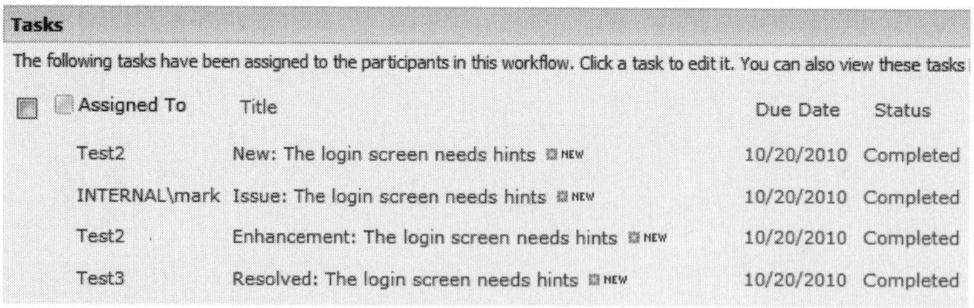

	Assigned To	Title	Due Date	Status
	Test2	New: The login screen needs hints 🗒 NEW	10/20/2010	Completed
	INTERNAL\mark	Issue: The login screen needs hints 🗒 NEW	10/20/2010	Completed
	Test2	Enhancement: The login screen needs hints 🗒 NEW	10/20/2010	Completed
	Test3	Resolved: The login screen needs hints 🗒 NEW	10/20/2010	Completed

Tasks

The following tasks have been assigned to the participants in this workflow. Click a task to edit it. You can also view these tasks

Figure 15-56. *Displaying the task details*

Summary

Congratulations! You just implemented a fairly complex state machine workflow. This is a very effective way to manage a multistep process involving several people. All of the participants—the admin, developer, and tester—simply work off of their tasks list. Imagine this process with dozens of issues being worked on simultaneously in various stages of the process.

In the chapter's example, I used a view of the Tasks list that showed all tasks so you could see what was happening as the workflow progressed. Normally, each person would only see the active tasks assigned to them. After they complete a task it is removed from their view and they can pick another task from the list.

The requester or a project manager can look at the Issues list to see which issues are still open, what state they are in, and who they are assigned to. This provides a good view into the process without needing all the task details. The details are available as well by looking at the workflow history.

As I'm sure you noticed, the task forms are somewhat awkward, with lots of fields that the users do not need to be concerned about. In the next chapter I'll show you how to use InfoPath 2010 to create custom task forms.

CHAPTER 16

Creating Custom Forms

In the previous chapter you implemented a task-based tracking system using a state machine workflow. When an item was added to the Issues list, the workflow took over, generating tasks according to the business rules. The participants performed the tasks assigned to them as the issue progressed through the workflow. The Tasks list and the individual task forms are the primary interface to this system.

Each task type (e.g., New, Assigned, Resolved) used a different content type, allowing each to define the specific columns that are needed. For example, the New task needs a place to assign a developer while the Resolved task needs a place to indicate whether the issue was resolved. These content types were derived from the Workflow Task content type. Because of this they inherited a large number of columns that, while important to the workflow process, are not needed on the task forms.

Creating a Custom Task Form

In this chapter you will use InfoPath 2010 to create custom task forms. Each form will only include the columns that the user needs to see or update, which will provide a much better user experience.

Connecting to SharePoint

To accomplish that, you'll create a custom form specifically for each new content type. Start the InfoPath 2010 Designer application. Select File ➤ New, and then select the SharePoint List template. Click the Design Form button, as shown in Figure 16-1.

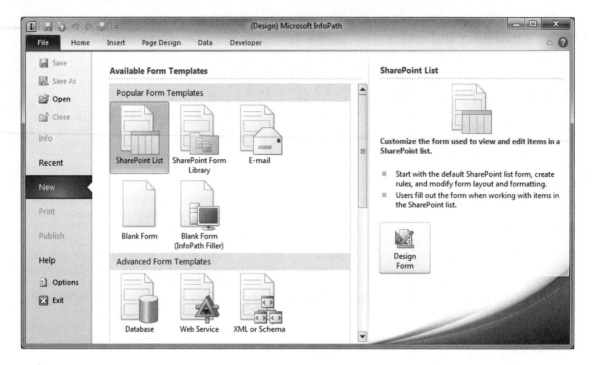

Figure 16-1. *Selecting the SharePoint List template*

■**Tip** If you get an error message indicating that Microsoft Office Forms Services 2010 is not available, you will need to activate this feature in the SharePoint server. Unfortunately, it is not listed as a configurable feature in SharePoint's Central Administration tool. Instead, you'll need to use the PowerShell utility. From the Windows Start menu, select the Microsoft SharePoint 2010 Products folder and run the SharePoint 2010 Management Shell application.

Then execute the following commands:

```
Install-SPFeature -path "IPFSSiteFeatures" - force
Install-SPFeature -path "IPFSWebFeatures" - force
```

Executing these commands will activate InfoPath Forms Services and should resolve this error.

This will display the Data Connection Wizard, as shown in Figure 16-2.

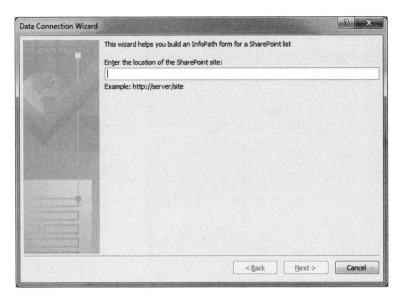

Figure 16-2. *The Data Connection Wizard*

Enter the URL for your site, such as **http://omega5/pm**, and click the Next button. In the next dialog box, choose the option to customize an existing list, and select the Tasks list, as shown in Figure 16-3.

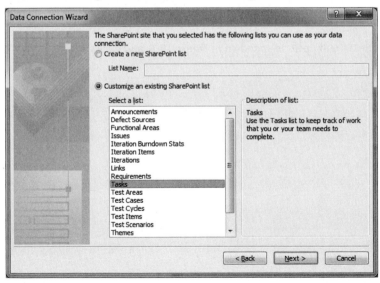

Figure 16-3. *Selecting the existing Tasks list*

The next dialog box, shown in Figure 16-4, lists the content types that are supported by the Tasks list. Select the custom Issue New content type, and click the Next button.

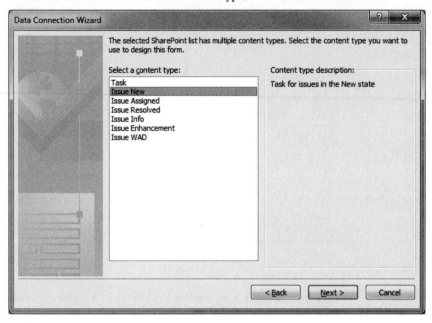

Figure 16-4. *Selecting the Issue New content type*

For the final dialog box, leave the default options as shown in Figure 16-5, and click the Finish button.

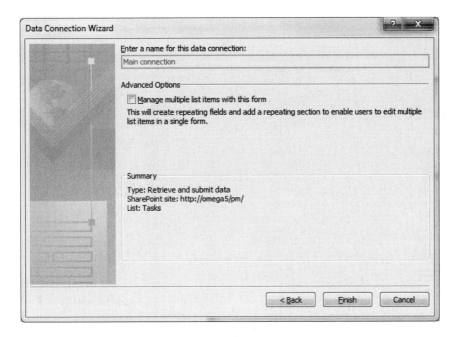

Figure 16-5. *Using the default options for the final dialog box*

Modifying the Form Layout

The InfoPath designer will then display the existing form that was retrieved from the SharePoint site, which should be similar to the one shown in Figure 16-6.

Figure 16-6. *The initial InfoPath form*

The list of fields in the Fields navigation window was obtained from the content type definition. The current form is roughly based on how the standard form is formatted. You'll need to delete most of the rows on this form. To delete a row, right-click the row label and choose Delete ➤ Rows in the context menu, as shown in Figure 16-7. You can also select several rows and delete them this way.

Figure 16-7. *Deleting rows from the form*

Delete all the rows except the Title, Description, Related Content, Issue New Action, Issue Assigned To, and Issue Priority. Change the labels for some of the columns as follows:

- Related Content: **Issue**

- Issue New Action: **Action**

- Issue Assigned To: **Assign To**

- Issue Priority: **Priority**

The form should look like Figure 16-8.

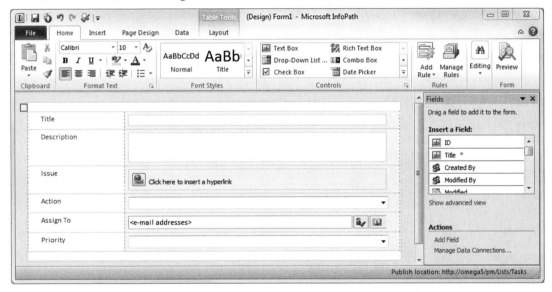

Figure 16-8. *Updated form definition*

Select the Control Tools ribbon. Click the Title field, and select the Read-Only check box, as shown in Figure 16-9.

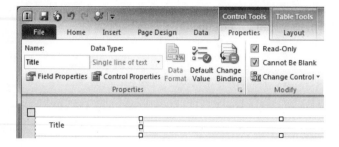

Figure 16-9. *Using the Control Tools ribbon to make the title read-only*

Select the Description and Issue fields, and make them read-only as well. The user should not be able to modify these fields from the task form.

Publishing the Form

Because you started with an existing list form, InfoPath knows exactly where to publish the new form. From the File menu, click the Quick Publish button, as shown in Figure 16-10.

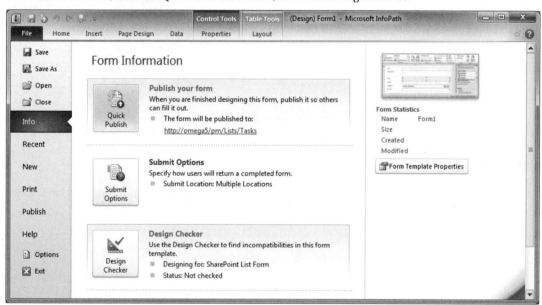

Figure 16-10. *Using the Quick Publish feature*

When the form has been published, you'll see a confirmation dialog box, as shown in Figure 16-11. Click the OK button and then close the InfoPath application.

Figure 16-11. *Publish confirmation dialog box*

Testing the Custom Form

Open the SharePoint site and select one of the generated New tasks. It should now display using the custom form, as shown in Figure 16-12.

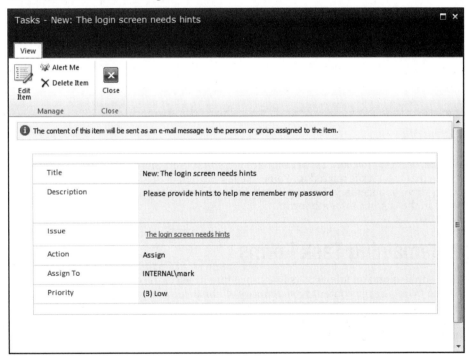

Figure 16-12. *The custom display form*

If you click the Edit Item button, the edit form should be displayed, as shown in Figure 16-13.

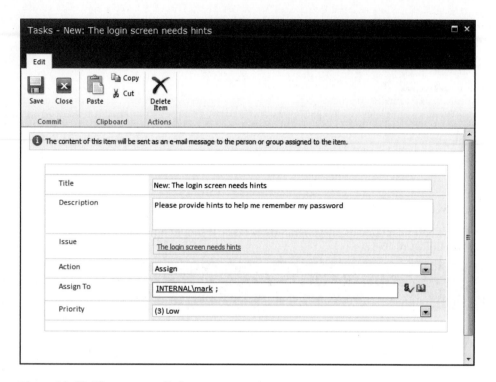

Figure 16-13. *The custom edit form*

Notice that the Title, Description, and Issue fields are not editable on this form. These are derived from the Issues list item that this task is related to. You can click the link in the Issue field to display the issue and make changes there, if necessary. Try displaying one of the other tasks; it should use the standard form rather than the custom InfoPath form.

Creating the Remaining Task Forms

Start the InfoPath 2010 application and follow the same procedure to select the existing Tasks list. This time, however, select the Issue Assign content type. Remove all the fields except Title, Description, Related Content, Issue Assigned Action, Issue Started, and Resolution. Then rename Related Content as **Issue**, Issue Assigned Action as **Action**, and Issue Started as **Started**. Also, set Title, Description, and Issue to be read-only. The form should look like Figure 16-14.

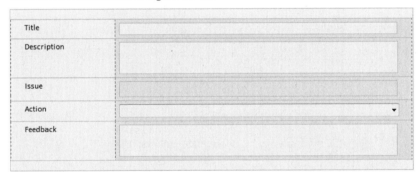

Figure 16-14. *The Issue Assigned custom task form*

From the File tab, click the Quick Publish button to update the form in the SharePoint server. From the File tab, select the New menu and then the SharePoint List template, and then click the Design Form button. Navigate to the Issue Resolved content type and edit the form just like the previous two. The form should look like Figure 16-15.

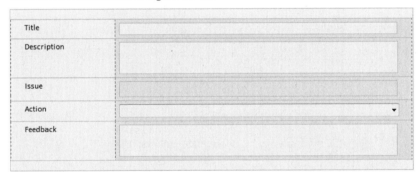

Figure 16-15. *The Issue Resolved custom task form*

■**Tip**   Because the admin may have tasks with different task types assigned to them, and most of these have the same fields, it would be helpful to indicate the reason they are in the Waiting state. You'll add some static text to each form to indicate that.

Follow the same procedure to create a custom task form for the Issue Info content type. Remove the unneeded rows, rename the labels, and set the read-only property as you have with the other forms. Then right-click the Title label and insert a new row, as shown in Figure 16-16.

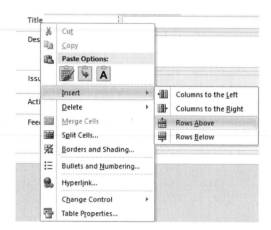

Figure 16-16. *Adding a new row*

In the new row, enter **More information is requested:** and change the font size to 14. The form should look like Figure 16-17.

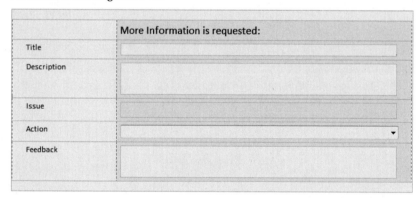

Figure 16-17. *The Issue Info custom task form*

Publish this form to the server. Follow the same steps to create custom task forms for the Issue Enhancement and Issue WAD content types. Enter **This is an enhancement:** and **Working as designed:** on each form, respectively. Make sure you publish the form after you finish making the changes.

Creating a Custom Issue Form

As I demonstrated in the previous chapter, most of the columns on the Issues list are populated by the workflow as the associated tasks are completed. While we need to display these fields, we don't want to allow anyone to modify them. To accomplish that, you'll implement a custom form.

Start the InfoPath 2010 Designer application and navigate to the Issues list. Because there is only one content type allowed for this list, the additional dialog to select the content type is skipped. The existing form is displayed in Figure 16-18.

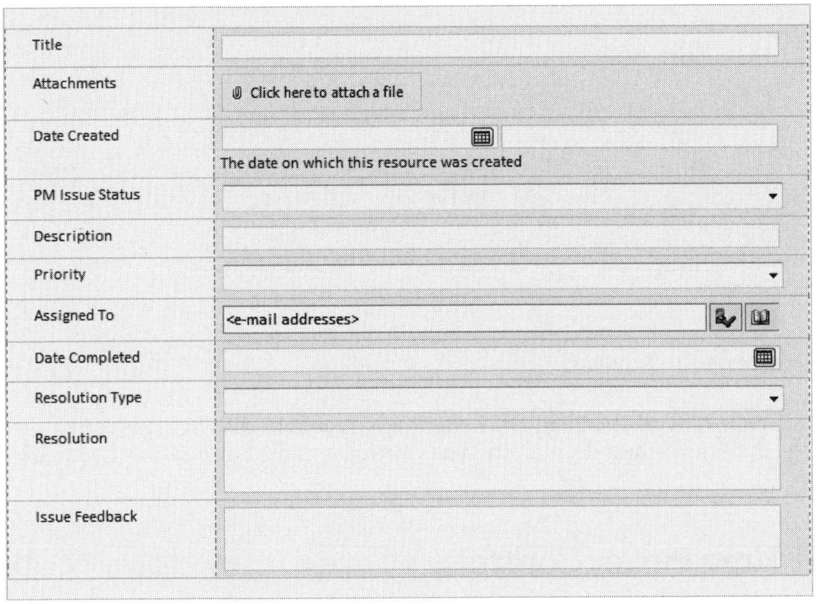

Figure 16-18. *The current Issue form*

All the fields except for Title, Attachments, and Description should be marked as read-only. Select the Resolution control and select the Read-Only check box in the Control Tools ribbon. Update the Issue Feedback control to also be read-only.

Changing the Control Type

InfoPath will only allow to you to make text fields read-only. Combo boxes and date fields, for example, cannot be made read-only. To resolve this, you'll need to first change the field to use the Text Box control. Select the PM Issue Status control (select the control in the second column, not the label). In the Control Tools ribbon, click the Change Control button and the click the *Text Box* link, as shown in Figure 16-19.

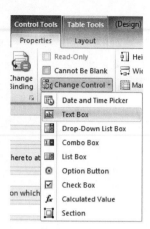

Figure 16-19. *Changing the control type to Text Box*

After you have changed the control type, the Read-Only check box should be available for you to select. In the same way, change the Priority and Resolution Type controls to Text Box controls and mark them as read-only.

Handling Date and Time Picker Controls

Select the Date Created control and change it to a Text Box like you did with the other fields. Then right-click the control and click the *Text Box Properties* link, as shown in Figure 16-20.

Figure 16-20. *Selecting the Text Box Properties link*

The Text Box Properties dialog box, shown in Figure 16-21, allows you to configure how the date field is converted to a text string. Click the Format button to select how you want the date formatted.

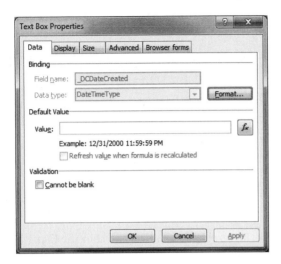

Figure 16-21. *The Text Box Properties dialog box*

Click the OK button to save the changes. Notice that there are two Text Box controls in the cell, along with some helper text, as shown in Figure 16-22.

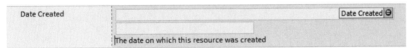

Figure 16-22. *The Date Picker control after being converted to a Text Box control*

This column supports both date and time, and is usually presented as a Date Picker followed by a Time control. The conversion to a text box converted both controls. Select the second control and delete it. The helper text is defined on the site column. You can also delete this from the form, as it is not needed.

Select the Date Completed control and change it to a Text Box control. Because this field only displayed the date portion, there is only one control. You should also go to the text box properties and select the appropriate format, like you did with the Date Created control.

Handling Person/Group Picker Controls

The Assigned To column is bound to a Person/Group Picker control, and InfoPath does not support converting these to any other type of control. Select the control and delete it.

■**Caution**   Delete the control from the cell; do not delete the row.

Select the empty cell, and from the Control Tools ribbon, select the Calculated Value control, as shown in Figure 16-23.

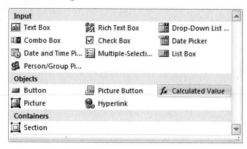

Figure 16-23. *Selecting the Calculated Value control*

This will insert a Calculated Column control in this cell. Right-click this control and click the *Change Binding* link, as shown in Figure 16-24.

Figure 16-24. *Changing the binding of an existing field*

Click the *Advanced* link, and then select the DisplayName property of the Assigned To column, as shown in Figure 16-25.

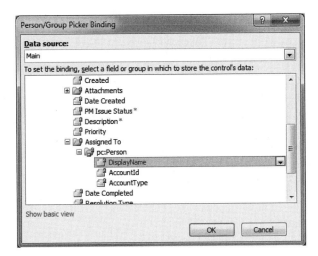

Figure 16-25. *Selecting the DisplayName property*

Changing the Labels

Before finishing this form, change a few of the labels. Change PM Issue Status to **Status** and Issue Feedback to **Feedback**. Also, enlarge the Description column to allow more lines for entering data. The completed form should look like Figure 16-26.

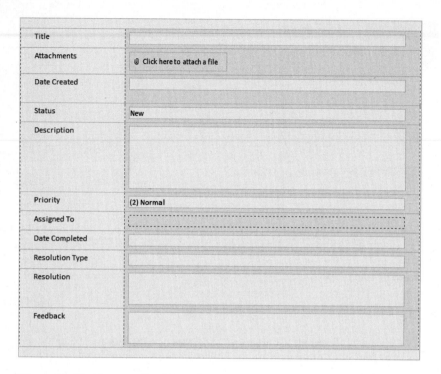

Figure 16-26. *The completed Issue form*

From the File tab, click the Quick Publish button to publish these changes to the SharePoint server.

Testing the Form

Display the existing issue in the list. The display form should look like Figure 16-27.

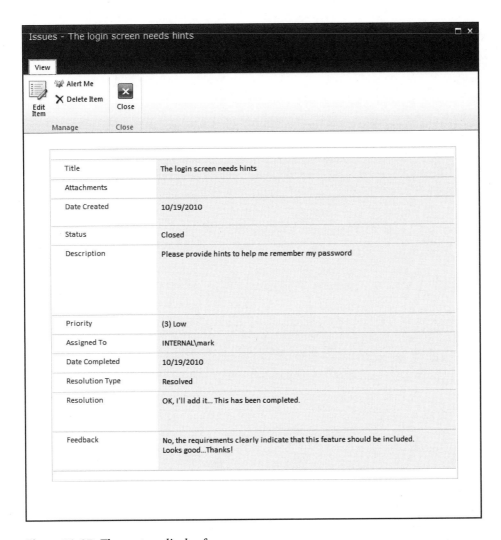

Figure 16-27. *The custom display form*

Close this form and then click the *Add new item* link to create a new issue. The new form is shown in Figure 16-28.

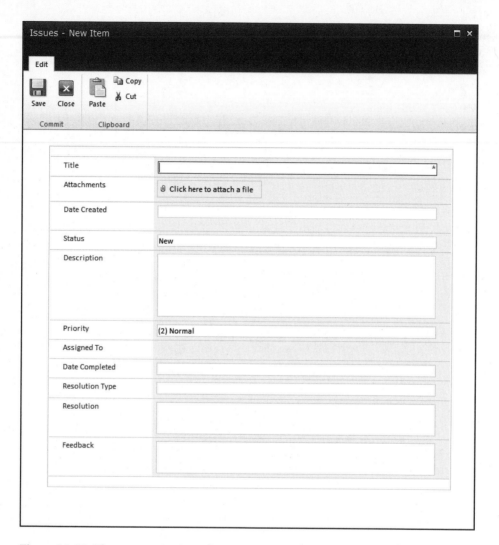

Figure 16-28. *The custom new issue form*

Notice that the only editable fields are the Title, Attachments, and Description columns.

Summary

In this chapter you used InfoPath 2010 to create a custom task form for each content type. You used the Quick Publish feature to publish the new form to the SharePoint server. You also created a custom form for creating and viewing items in the Issues list. This form converted may of the controls to Text Box controls that were then made read-only.

In the last three chapters, using a combination of tools including Visual Studio 2010, Windows Workflow, and InfoPath 2010, you created a custom SharePoint application with a rich user interface.

Epilogue

If you have worked through all the chapters in this book, then you should already have a powerful project management tool. Hopefully it will meet most of your needs. If so, great! More importantly, however, I hope I have planted a seed that you can grow by adding your own creativity and diligence to produce something really great.

I planned the activities in this book with the intention of imparting to you two necessary ingredients. The first is an understanding of how to employ the features of SharePoint. This is a very broad topic, and I tried to demonstrate a subset of features that I found to be particularly helpful; everything from document libraries to state machine workflows. The second ingredient includes some useful project management techniques, such as user stories, iteration backlogs, test cycles, and gathering quality metrics. Some of these may be new ideas to you. Undoubtedly, you'll find some of these useful for your scenario, and others less of a good fit.

In each chapter I paired up a management technique with a SharePoint feature in a logical fashion. Many of the technology solutions can be used in many applications, not just the one I paired it with. An automated process for gathering metrics, for example, can be used in many places besides testing.

The third ingredient, which you must supply, is imagination. Only you can envision the appropriate application of technology to produce a solution that is uniquely suited to your environment. The building blocks that I have given you, plus others that you will create yourself, are at your disposal.

Isaac Newton once wrote, "If I have seen a little further it is by standing on the shoulders of giants." My goal is to help you see a little further than I have. Enjoy!

Index

■A

Active states, 284–285, 329, 338–339

Add a Web Part link, 68, 114, 138, 152–154, 188, 208, 234

Add a workflow link, 38

Add as a new version to existing files check box, 178

Add button, 57

Add document link, 176

Add Existing Site Column button, 93, 128, 147, 197, 203, 216, 221, 289, 296

Add Features Wizard, Server Manager application, 26

Add from existing site columns link, 113, 118, 167, 183, 237, 252–253, 272

Add new discussion link, 62

Add New Item dialog box, Solution Explorer, 345

Add new item link, 13, 22, 96, 109, 155, 195, 199, 205, 267, 271

Add new link link, 186

Add Required Features button, 27

Add to all content types check box, 252, 254

Add to default view check box, 252–254

Add to formula link, 51

Additional Column Settings section, 48, 55, 61, 167, 236, 249, 272

Admin User field, 349

Administrative Tools menu, 29

AdminUser collection, 348

Advanced button, 77

Advanced link, 374

advanced mode, 25–26, 31–33

agile methodology, 103–105

agile testing, 213

All Items link, 96

All Items page, 13

All Items view, 21, 149, 152, 160, 219, 232

All Links view, 188

Allow, 17

Allow attachments check box, 148, 198, 217, 221

Allow blank values? check box, 16, 89, 106, 127, 146, 201, 215, 287–288, 291

Allow button, 77

Allow management of content types check box, 12, 21, 94, 109, 131, 148, 198, 204, 217, 290

Allow multiple values check box, 55, 117

■J

■K

■L

■M

■U

■XYZ

You Need the Companion eBook

Your purchase of this book entitles you to buy the companion PDF-version eBook for only $10. Take the weightless companion with you anywhere.

We believe this Apress title will prove so indispensable that you'll want to carry it with you everywhere, which is why we are offering the companion eBook (in PDF format) for $10 to customers who purchase this book now. Convenient and fully searchable, the PDF version of any content-rich, page-heavy Apress book makes a valuable addition to your programming library. You can easily find and copy code—or perform examples by quickly toggling between instructions and the application. Even simultaneously tackling a donut, diet soda, and complex code becomes simplified with hands-free eBooks!

Once you purchase your book, getting the $10 companion eBook is simple:

❶ Visit **www.apress.com/promo/tendollars/**.

❷ Complete a basic registration form to receive a randomly generated question about this title.

❸ Answer the question correctly in 60 seconds, and you will receive a promotional code to redeem for the $10.00 eBook.

233 Spring Street, New York, NY 10013

Offer valid through 5/11.